A COMPLETE GUIDE TO GUN LAW IN LOUISIANA

LOUISIANA GUN LAW

Armed And Educated

Written by James Reeves and published in the United States of America.

U.S. LawShield, LLP
ISBN 978-0-578-50942-6

To order additional books by phone or
for wholesale orders call (877) 448-6839.

TABLE OF CONTENTS

PREFACE

After traveling all over the Great State of Louisiana, speaking to folks about the laws of firearms and self-defense, interacting with police officers, and other experiences intimately intertwined with being a gun owner, it became obvious that a comprehensive firearms manual was needed to help people get a better grasp on the responsibilities that arise when you decide to become a gun owner. Over the last several years, we have advised thousands of good, hardworking Americans about their questions and concerns arising from their lawful exercise of gun ownership.

As lawyers, we have represented countless gun owners who have found themselves in the unfortunate situation of having been forced to use their gun to protect themselves, their loved ones, or even their property. We have seen at the ground level how traumatizing compulsory participation in the criminal justice system can be for law-abiding citizens.

We wanted to share what we have learned with all Louisianans and tell of our experiences in an effort to educate and spread awareness to all gun owners, so that if the unthinkable happens, you have a plan. This book aspires to be your one-stop shop to firearms issues and laws distilled from firsthand experience in representing and navigating gun owners through the criminal and civil justice systems. This book will take you through the procedure of purchasing a firearm and obtaining a Louisiana Concealed Handgun Permit, laws relating to firearms and other weapons, the law protecting a person's use of force and deadly force, and everyday tips for the law-abiding gun owner.

Keep in mind, the law is a dynamic beast and is ever-changing. We guarantee that the law will change. Some changes will be small, while others can be so monumental, they alter the legal landscape. Therefore, it is important that you consult with your attorney regarding any specific legal issues in which you become involved.

What makes this book different than other books covering similar topics? We go deeper than anyone else into firearms issues. We go the extra mile to make sure every issue is picked to pieces and analyzed to leave you with as little confusion as possible.

You hold in your hands the collective efforts of many people who care deeply about the rights of all Americans (especially Louisianans) and the safety of yourself and your family. Many people have had significant input in producing this book. There is no way this book would be possible without their contributions and expertise.

The people of U.S. LawShield have for many years been dedicated to the preservation of the rights of the people: the right to keep and bear arms, the right to freedom of speech, the right of due process, and the right to be secure against unreasonable searches and seizures. U.S. LawShield has always viewed education as an essential part of its mission in helping people protect their rights and live their lives as freely as the founders of this great nation intended.

➢ CHAPTER ONE ➣

BRIEF LEGAL HISTORY OF THE RIGHT TO BEAR ARMS And The Laws Regulating Firearms

I. INTRODUCTION AND OVERVIEW

To fully understand gun rights today in Louisiana or the United States, one should start first at the beginning: the formation document for our federal government, the United States Constitution. The Constitution was written without any enumerated guaranteed individual rights. The founding fathers thought it obvious that individuals had rights; therefore, there was no reason to elucidate them in a document that was supposed to control the government. James Madison also thought that by naming certain rights, it would imply that those were the only rights an individual possessed. After much discussion, and a complete change of opinion by Madison, the lack of enumerated rights was remedied in the first Congressional session and the state ratification process. When the dust settled, ten amendments were added to the Constitution; these ten amendments are the Bill of Rights. It is the Second Amendment that concerns firearms specifically, though throughout this book we will reference many others, including the Fourth and Fifth Amendments that both affect your rights to bear arms and the fundamental rights for us all.

II. DO I HAVE A CONSTITUTIONAL RIGHT AS AN INDIVIDUAL TO KEEP AND BEAR ARMS?

Yes; the United States Supreme Court has decided that an individual has a constitutionally given right to keep and bear arms that flows from the Second Amendment, which states simply:

> "A well-regulated Militia, being necessary to the security of a free State, the right of the people to keep and bear Arms, shall not be infringed."

From a plain reading, there are two important parts to this amendment: first, that a well-regulated militia is necessary to the security of a free state, and second, that there is a right of the people to keep and bear arms. For years, before the issue was decided, anti-gun activists have tried to argue that the Second Amendment only applied to "militias" and not to individuals. Luckily, this argument is not the law. Nevertheless, despite the Supreme Court rulings stating otherwise, this myth seems to persist. What do these parts of the Second Amendment mean? Are they the same, or are they different?

A. What is a "well-regulated militia?"

As we discussed earlier, the first part of the Second Amendment references a "well-regulated militia." What is a well-regulated militia? The U.S. Supreme Court has held what this phrase does and does not mean. In 1939, in the case of *United States v. Miller*, 307 U.S. 174, 179 (1939) (ironically, a ruling that upheld firearms regulation), the Court defined a militia as comprising "all males physically capable of acting in concert for the common defense." Based on how the amendment was drafted, the Court stated, it was clear that the Militia pre-dated Article I of the Constitution, because unlike armies and navies, it did not have to be created by Congress. What then is "well-regulated" per the Court? It is exactly what it sounds like: the imposition of discipline and training. So, is this just the National Guard? No.

In the case of *D.C. v. Heller*, 554 U.S. 570 (2008), the Supreme Court stated that the well-regulated militia is not the state's military forces, but a separate entity altogether. The Supreme Court stated that the word "militia" referred to the body of the people, and they—the people—were required to keep a centralized government in check. The Supreme Court considered and rejected the position that the National Guard is the current militia under the Second Amendment.

B. How has the phrase "right to keep and bear arms" been interpreted by the courts?

One of the first cases to directly deal with the Second Amendment was *United States v. Miller*. In *Miller*, the Supreme Court found that the National Firearms Act ("NFA"), which imposed registration requirements on machine guns, short-barreled weapons, destructive devices, and other similarly unique firearms, did not violate the Second Amendment. The Court used the reasoning that possession of weapons regulated by the NFA did not reasonably relate to the preservation or efficiency of a well-regulated militia, therefore, the NFA was held constitutional.

UNITED STATES V. MILLER, 307 U.S. 174 (1939)

THE FACTS

Defendants, Miller and Layton, transported a double barrel 12-gauge shotgun with a barrel length of less than 18 inches from Oklahoma to Arkansas, and were being prosecuted under the National Firearms Act (which required certain types of firearms to be registered and a tax to be paid). Defendants challenged the NFA as an unconstitutional violation of the Second Amendment.

THE LEGAL HOLDINGS

The Court upheld the National Firearms Act as Constitutional.

An interesting quirk of history in the *Miller* case (and not a shining moment for the legal system) is that Miller's attorney never appeared at the arguments before the U.S. Supreme Court because he was court-appointed and had not been paid. There was no written brief and no legal representation at oral arguments by the party arguing that the law was unconstitutional. The Court only heard the government's side. To make matters worse, Miller was shot to death before the decision was rendered.

C. 69 years later, the Supreme Court interprets the Second Amendment again: *D.C. v. Heller*

It would be 69 years after *Miller* until the U.S. Supreme Court addressed the Second Amendment directly again, except this time the Court would hear both the Government's and the Defendant's arguments. Fortunately, freedom and Second Amendment rights prevailed in court that day. The Court held that individuals have a right to keep and bear arms.

DISTRICT OF COLUMBIA V. HELLER, 554 U.S. 570 (2008)

THE FACTS

Heller had applied for a handgun ownership permit and was denied; without such a permit, D.C. required that all firearms (including rifles and shotguns) be kept unloaded and disassembled, or bound by a trigger lock, even in a person's own home.

THE LEGAL HOLDINGS

1. The Supreme Court found that the Second Amendment protects an individual right of firearms ownership for purposes of self-defense, not connected with any militia or military purposes; it further elaborated that individual self-defense is "the central component" of the Second Amendment. *D.C. v. Heller* at 599. Further, handguns are the primary defensive weapon of choice and are protected by the Second Amendment.
2. A well-regulated militia is not the state's military forces.
3. The Court also discussed what the phrase "bear arms" meant: "wear, bear, or carry… upon the person or in clothing or in a pocket, for the purpose… of being armed and ready for offensive or defensive action in a case of conflict with another person."
4. The D.C. regulation was held to be unconstitutional.
5. The Court concluded that like other rights, the right to bear arms is not completely absolute. Reasonable provisions and restrictions have been upheld.

Keep in mind *D.C. v. Heller* was a split 5-4 decision; only one justice away from a completely different outcome, where the Second Amendment (according to the dissent) had outlived its usefulness and should be ignored.

D. Can states ignore the Second Amendment? *McDonald v. City of Chicago*

Heller had a slight quirk: the District of Columbia is under the exclusive jurisdiction of Congress and is not part of any state. Therefore, the case shed no light on the question of what states can do when it comes to regulating or banning firearms. How do state constitutions interact with the Second Amendment and can states ban guns outright? *McDonald v. City of Chicago* sought to answer these questions.

***MCDONALD V. CITY OF CHICAGO*, 561 U.S. 742 (2010)**

THE FACTS

A Chicago ordinance banned handgun possession (among other gun regulations). McDonald was a 76-year-old retired maintenance engineer who wanted a handgun for self-defense. Chicago required that all handguns had to be registered, but refused all handgun registration after a 1982 citywide handgun ban.

THE LEGAL HOLDINGS

The Supreme Court held that the Second Amendment is fully applicable to the states and that individual self-defense is "the central component" of the Second Amendment. Therefore, the Second Amendment prohibits states from enacting bans on handguns for self-protection in the home.

E. Legal limitations of the right to keep and bear arms

The U.S. Supreme Court has stated: "Of course the right [to keep and bear arms] was not unlimited, just as the First Amendment's right of free speech was not[.]" *D.C. v. Heller*, 554 U.S. 570, 595 (2008). Courts may have struggled over the years with what the Second Amendment means, but they have been resolute that there is an element of self-defense. The *Heller* Court stated that, "The Second Amendment [does not] protect the right of citizens to carry arms for any sort of confrontation," focusing their decision on self-defense. Further, the *Miller* Court stated that the weapons protected were those "in common use at the time" of the decision. *United States v. Miller*, 307 U.S. 174, 179 (1939). This is supported by historical traditions of prohibiting the carry of "dangerous and unusual weapons" that are commonly used by criminals offensively, as opposed to being used by law-abiding citizens for defensive purposes.

The Second Amendment does not protect against prohibitions on firearm possession by felons and the mentally ill; *Heller* made this point in its decision, and many circuit court cases such as *U.S. v. Everist* follow the same reasoning. The Court of Appeals in *U.S. v. Everist* states that the Second Amendment is "subject to 'limited narrowly tailored specific exceptions or restrictions for particular cases that are reasonable . . . it is clear that felons, infants and those of unsound mind may be prohibited from possessing firearms." *U.S. v. Everist*, 368 F.3d 517, 519 (5th Cir. 2004). Along this same train of thought, the *Heller* Court did not want to eliminate laws that imposed conditions and qualifications on the commercial sales of firearms.

It also does not mean that the Second Amendment includes the right to carry anywhere a person wants. The *Heller* Court stated that their opinion was not meant to allow the "carrying of firearms in sensitive places such as schools and certain government buildings[.]" *D.C. v. Heller*, 554 U.S. 570, 626 (2008).

F. The Future of the Second Amendment

With the passing of Supreme Court Justice Antonin Scalia, one of the key supporters and author of the 5-4 decision that was *Heller*, the split-down-the-middle Supreme Court truly seemed poised to either continue protecting firearms rights, or backslide to the position that the Second Amendment only applied to militia activity. When the dust settled, the empty seat ended up going to Neil Gorsuch. How Justice Gorsuch has treated the Second Amendment in the past will be a central component of its future. Similarly, even though the Supreme Court seems to have gone out of its way to deny hearing a vast number of cases, a few Second Amendment petitions are awaiting conference.

PRACTICAL LEGAL TIP

Currently, the two most important court decisions fortifying our gun rights are *Heller* and *McDonald*. But, those cases were very, very close to going the other way! Both were decided by a 5-4 majority, meaning that if only one other Supreme Court Justice had decided differently, our individual right to possess and carry firearms could have been severely limited.

Although Justice Scalia's opinion in *Heller* established the right for individuals to bear arms, it includes the famous caveat: "Like most rights, the right secured by the Second Amendment is not unlimited." *D.C. v. Heller*, 554 U.S. at 595. That sentence left open the possibility that some gun regulations could pass muster, without spelling out the criteria for constitutionality. Overall, these regulations can be generalized into three major archetypes: those that impose registration requirements on firearms or their owners, those that ban certain types of firearms or firearm accessories, and those that prohibit the carrying of firearms in public (be it through impossible-to-obtain licensing schemes, or piecemeal prohibition). The sheer volume of such cases allowing the erosion of the Second Amendment is alarming, but not as alarming as how many are denied certiorari.

In the years since *McDonald*, there have been more than 70 U.S. Circuit Court opinions upholding state restrictions on the Second Amendment that the U.S. Supreme Court has refused to review. These restrictions include requiring the registration of firearms, prohibiting "large capacity" magazines, banning certain firearms as "assault rifles," and creating classes of individuals who are restricted from owning firearms.

A Ninth Circuit case that many observers thought the U.S. Supreme Court would review is *Peruta v. County of San Diego*, 742 F.3d 1144 (9th Cir. 2014). On June 26, 2017, the Supreme Court again denied certiorari. However, Justice Thomas along with newly appointed Justice Gorsuch issued an opinion decrying the Court's decision and stated therein:

> The Court's decision to deny certiorari in this case reflects a distressing trend: the treatment of the Second Amendment as a disfavored right. ... The Constitution does not rank certain rights above others, and I do not think this Court should impose such a hierarchy by selectively enforcing its preferred rights. ... For those of us who work in marbled halls, guarded constantly by a vigilant and dedicated police force, the guarantees of the Second

Amendment might seem antiquated and superfluous. But the Framers made a clear choice: They reserved to all Americans the right to bear arms for self-defense. I do not think we should stand by idly while a State denies its citizens that right, particularly when their very lives may depend on it. *Peruta v. County of San Diego*, 582 U.S. ___ (2017) (THOMAS, J., dissenting from denial of certiorari) (slip op., at 7-8).

III. MAJOR FIREARMS STATUTES EVERY GUN OWNER NEEDS TO KNOW

At the Federal level, there are plenty of laws and regulations that concern firearms, but this section will focus on some of the more major legislative actions that all gun owners need to know.

A. Gun Control Act of 1968

The Gun Control Act of 1968 ("GCA") was enacted by Congress to "provide for better control of the interstate traffic in firearms." This law is primarily focused on regulating interstate commerce in firearms by generally prohibiting interstate firearms transfers, except among licensed manufacturers, dealers, and importers, however, interstate commerce has been held by the courts to include nearly everything. It also contains classes of individuals to whom firearms should not be sold. For the specifics of who can and can't purchase a firearm, please refer to Chapter 3. Among other things, the GCA created the Federal Firearms License ("FFL") system, imposed importation restrictions on military surplus rifles (adding a "sporting purpose test" and a "points system" for handguns), and marking requirements.

B. The Brady Handgun Violence Prevention Act

The Brady Handgun Violence Prevention Act, commonly referred to as the Brady Law, instituted federal background checks (the National Instant Criminal Background Check System or NICS) for firearm purchasers in the United States. It also prohibited certain persons from purchasing firearms; for more information on who can or can't purchase a firearm, *see* Chapter 3.

C. The Firearm Owners' Protection Act

The Firearm Owners' Protection Act ("FOPA") revised many provisions of the original Gun Control Act, including "reforms" on the inspection of FFLs. This same Act updated the list of individuals prohibited from purchasing firearms that was introduced by the GCA. The FOPA also banned the ownership by civilians of any machine gun that was not registered under the NFA as of May 19, 1986. FOPA created what is called a "safe passage" provision of the law, which allows for traveling across states with a firearm. Finally, FOPA prohibited a registry for non-NFA items that directly linked firearms to their owners.

D. The Public Safety and Recreational Firearms Use Protection Act

The Public Safety and Recreational Firearms Use Protection Act, commonly referred to as the Federal Assault Weapons Ban, was a subsection of the Violent Crime Control and Law Enforcement Act of 1994. It banned outright the manufacture and transfer of certain semi-automatic firearms and magazines. This ban grandfathered-in previously legally owned weapons, but no prohibited firearm could be acquired or manufactured after September 13, 1994. With great foresight, the drafters of this law included a so-called "sunset provision," that stated the ban would expire ten years later, unless renewed. The ban expired in 2004, and all attempts to renew it have been unsuccessful.

E. The National Firearms Act

The National Firearms Act ("NFA") regulates and imposes a statutory excise tax on the manufacture and transfer of certain types of firearms and weapons: machine guns, short-barreled weapons, suppressors, explosive devices, and "any other weapons" (AOWs can range from everyday objects that are actually firearms, such as an umbrella that can fire a round, to other weapons the ATF decides to place in this category). The tax is $200 if you make or transfer an item (other than for the transfer of AOWs); the tax for transferring AOWs is $5. The NFA is also referred to as Title II of the federal firearms laws. For more information on how to navigate the NFA while remaining legal, please *see* Chapter 14.

IV. DO LOUISIANANS HAVE A RIGHT TO KEEP AND BEAR ARMS IN THE LOUISIANA CONSTITUTION?

Yes. The Louisiana Constitution acknowledges the right to keep and bear arms in Article I, Section 11. The provision reads:

> "The right of each citizen to keep and bear arms is fundamental and shall not be infringed. Any restriction on this right shall be subject to strict scrutiny."

The courts in Louisiana have acknowledged that Section 11 allows the legislature to create laws to prohibit certain types of carrying weapons and have upheld restrictive laws for certain carriers and license requirements. *State v. Draughter*, 2013-0914, (La. 12/10/13); 130 So. 3d; State ex rel. D.V., 2013-1283 (La.App. 4 Cir. 5/7/14); 144 So. 3d 1097.

A. Can Louisiana prohibit local municipalities from making certain gun laws?

Yes. The Louisiana Legislature can, and does, prohibit local municipalities from making certain gun laws by the legal doctrine known as "preemption." A preemption statute is a mechanism by which the Louisiana Legislature sets certain areas off-limits to local governments, which helps ensure the uniformity of law across the state, in this case, firearms law.

B. What local governments may not regulate

The Louisiana preemption statute can be found in Louisiana Revised Statutes Annotated § 40:1796. It states what areas of law municipalities are not allowed to regulate. Local municipalities cannot regulate the:

- Sale,
- Purchase,
- Possession,
- Ownership,
- Transfer,
- Transportation,
- License, or
- Registration

of firearms, ammunition, or components of firearms or ammunition. *See* La. Rev. Stat. Ann. § 40:1796(a).

C. What local governments may regulate

Local municipalities under state law are empowered to, and may, regulate the following:

- The levy and collection of sales and use taxes,

- License fees, taxes, and permit fees, and
- The possession of a "firearm in certain commercial establishments and public buildings." *See* La. Rev. Stat. Ann. § 40:1796(a).

➢ CHAPTER TWO ◂

LEGAL DEFINITIONS AND CLASSIFICATIONS OF FIREARMS: What is Legal?

I. INTRODUCTION AND OVERVIEW

Before discussing the law of firearms and all its different facets, it is important first to understand what the law defines as a "firearm." Firearms laws are governed on both the federal and state levels; therefore, throughout this Chapter we will explore the interactions federal and state law have on the purchase and possession of firearms.

A. What is a firearm?

FEDERAL DEFINITION

Under the federal law, a firearm is defined as "any weapon (including a starter gun) which will or is designed to or may readily be converted to expel a projectile by the action of an explosive[.]" 18 U.S.C. § 921(a)(3). The federal definition of a firearm also includes "the frame or receiver of any such weapon[,] any firearm muffler or firearm silencer, or [] any destructive device." 18 U.S.C. § 921(a)(3).

LOUISIANA DEFINITION

Louisiana defines the term "firearm" differently depending on the set of laws that apply to the particular circumstance where a definition is needed.

For example, Louisiana Revised Statutes Section 95, "Illegal carrying of weapons," defines the term one way. Note that Section 95 concerns most owners and concealed weapons carriers in Louisiana. Section 14:95.1 defines "firearm" as "any pistol, revolver, rifle, shotgun, machine gun, submachine gun, black powder weapon, or assault rifle which is designed to fire or is capable of firing fixed cartridge ammunition or from which a shot or projectile is discharged by an explosive." However, this definition is limited to just this section.

Compare Louisiana Revised Statutes Section 40:1781. For purposes of Title 40, "Public health and safety," Section 40:1781 defines a firearm (excluding black powder weapons) as shotguns with a barrel of less than 18 inches in length, rifles with a barrel of less than 16 inches in length, weapons made from either a rifle or a shotgun if said weapon has been modified to have an overall length of less than 26 inches from which a shot is discharged by an explosive (if that weapon is capable of being concealed on the person), or a machine gun, grenade launcher, flame thrower, bazooka, rocket launcher, or gas grenade. Firearm includes mufflers and silencers for any firearm, regardless of whether that firearm is included in the definition contained in § 40:1781.

Strangely, Title 40 of the Louisiana law excludes from the definition of firearm most guns we would assume to be firearms: "Pistols and revolvers and those rifles and shotguns which have not previously been defined in this Paragraph as firearms from which serial numbers or marks of identification have not been obliterated are specifically exempt from this definition." Thus, Louisiana's definition of firearm tends to encompass only those firearms that are regulated by the National Firearms Act, ("NFA") such as "sawed off shotguns" (*i.e*., shotguns with barrels shorter than 18 inches); short barreled rifles ("SBRs"), which are rifles with barrels under 16 inches; and silencers. Thus, conventional, non-NFA firearms are not defined as firearms. This is likely because Title 40 imposes a requirement that all firearms (NFA items) be registered with the state police. Perhaps a term other than firearm would have been more suitable for this Title.

Conventional, non-NFA firearms are also considered "dangerous weapons," under Louisiana law. To determine if a device is a dangerous weapon, the test is not whether the weapon is inherently dangerous but whether it is dangerous "in the manner used." This test was distinctly enunciated by the Louisiana Supreme Court in *State v. Washington*, 104 La. 443, 29 So. 55 (1900), where the Court declared, "Whether the weapon used by defendant was dangerous within the meaning of the statute was a question for the jury to determine upon considering not only the character of such weapon, but by whom, upon whom, and in what manner it was used."

In another case defining firearms, the Fourth Circuit Court of Appeals turned to the dictionary to define firearm and weapon in the case of *Schmit v. Guidry*, 204 So.2d 646, 648 (La. Ct. App. 1967):

> "A firearm is something from which a shot is propelled. The word is usually applied only to small arms and, by definition, is any weapon from which a shot is discharged by an explosive as gunpowder (Webster's New International Dictionary, Second Edition, Unabridged, page 951). A weapon is defined as 'An instrument of offensive or defensive or defensive combat; something to fight with; anything used, or designed to be used, in destroying, defeating, or injuring, an enemy, as a gun, a sword, a shield, *etc*.' (Webster's New International Dictionary, Second Edition, Unabridged, page 2892)."

Accordingly, while it might seem tricky to understand what exactly a firearm is in Louisiana, at the end of the day, law-abiding citizens and gun owners will probably not be faced with a circumstance where there is a misunderstanding over whether or not a production firearm is a firearm or deadly weapon under the law.

Why might it be important to know the different ways the term firearm is defined under federal and state law? It is because if a person finds themselves charged with a crime by federal authorities, the federal definition of a firearm will apply. Likewise, if the charge is under a violation of state law, then the Louisiana definition will apply. Thus, the primary difference in the definitions and their impact on a defendant charged with a crime involving a firearm lies with how a person may be in trouble with the law. As we will see in the next section, the definitions of what does and does not constitute a firearm, although similar in many aspects, contain an array of differences that make violating the law unwittingly easy.

1. What is a handgun?

Louisiana law does not specifically define handguns, nor does it specify laws regarding them. Federal law, however, does define and separate laws regarding handguns. Ultimately, the term handgun is defined in a common manner: it simply refers to any firearm that is designed to be fired by using only one hand. While it is true that most individuals will use two hands when firing a handgun for safety and accuracy purposes, the emphasis in the legal definition of a handgun rests purely in its design to be held or fired with a single hand.

FEDERAL DEFINITION

The United States Code of Federal Regulations defines a handgun as "(a) [a]ny firearm which has a short stock and is designed to be held and fired by the use of a single hand; and (b) any combination of parts from which a firearm described in paragraph (a) can be assembled." 27 C.F.R. § 478.11.

2. What is a rifle?

Federal law defines a rifle as "[a] weapon designed or redesigned, made or remade, and intended to be fired from the shoulder, and designed or redesigned and made or remade to use the energy of the explosive in a fixed metallic cartridge to fire only a single projectile through a rifled bore for each single pull of the trigger." 27 C.F.R. § 478.11. In addition, a non-NFA rifle must have a barrel length of

16 inches or greater, and includes any weapon made from a rifle which is at least 26 inches overall in length. Louisiana law does not provide a definition for a rifle.

Minimum lengths

In order for a rifle to not be subject to the National Firearms Act, it must have a barrel of at least 16 inches in length. The ATF procedure for measuring barrel length is accomplished by "measur[ing] from the closed bolt (or breech-face) to the furthermost end of the barrel or permanently attached muzzle device." *See* www.atf.gov/firearms. Below is an example of a rifle that does not meet the minimum barrel length requirement after measurement:

The barrel is "measured by inserting a dowel rod into the barrel until the rod stops against the bolt or breech-face. The rod is then marked at the furthermost end of the barrel or permanently attached muzzle device, withdrawn from the barrel, and then measured." *See* www.atf.gov/firearms. Any measurement of less than 16 inches will classify the rifle as being short-barreled under federal law and subject the firearm to the NFA. For short-barreled rifles and other non-compliant firearms, *see* Chapter 14, which discusses the NFA.

Note: for overall length, rifles with collapsible/folding-stocks are measured from the "extreme ends," unless the stock is "easily detachable," in which case it is measured without the stock.

3. What is a shotgun?

The federal definition of a shotgun is "[a] weapon designed or redesigned, made or remade, and intended to be fired from the shoulder, and designed or redesigned and made or remade to use the energy of the explosive in a fixed shotgun shell to fire through a smooth bore either a number of ball shot or a single projectile for each single pull of the trigger." 27 C.F.R. § 478.11. Like rifles, legal shotguns have requirements for minimum barrel and overall lengths. Shotgun barrels must be at least 18 inches long and must also comply with the same 26 inch overall length requirement. Louisiana law does not specifically define "shotgun."

Minimum lengths

In order for a shotgun to not be subject to the National Firearms Act, it must have a barrel of at least 18 inches in length. The ATF procedure for measuring the barrel length of a shotgun is the same as it is for a rifle. *See* www.atf.gov/firearms. Below is an example of a shotgun that does not meet the minimum barrel length requirement after measurement:

Any measurement of less than 18 inches will classify the shotgun as a short-barreled weapon and illegal under federal law, unless the requirements of the NFA are satisfied. For short-barreled shotguns and other non-compliant firearms, *see* Chapter 14. Note: the collapsible/folding-stock rule that applies to rifles applies to shotguns as well.

B. Antique firearms and replica firearms

When is a firearm not legally a "firearm?" It is when the law defines it as not being one, such as with "antique" firearms.

1. Federal definition of "antique firearm"

1898 or prior

The federal definition of firearm under Title 18, Section 921 of the United States Code excludes "antique firearms." Even though an antique firearm still functions ballistically similar to a "modern" firearm, under federal law, antique firearms are regulated differently, if at all. An antique firearm under federal law includes any firearm with a matchlock, flintlock, or percussion cap, or similar type of ignition system manufactured in or before 1898 or any replica of a firearm just described so long as the replica "is not designed or redesigned for using rimfire or conventional centerfire fixed ammunition, or uses rimfire or conventional centerfire fixed ammunition which is no longer manufactured in the United States and which is not readily available in the ordinary channels of commercial trade[.]" 18 U.S.C. §§ 921(a)(16)(A) and (B). So, an "antique firearm" is not a "firearm" for purposes of federal regulation; it is an "antique firearm."

Muzzle loading

In addition, federal law does not consider "any muzzle loading rifle, muzzle loading shotgun, or muzzle loading pistol, which is designed to use black powder, or a black powder substitute, and which cannot use fixed ammunition" as a firearm. Be aware, however, that the term "antique firearm" does "not include any weapon which incorporates a firearm frame or receiver, any firearm which is converted into a muzzle loading weapon, or any muzzle loading weapon which can be readily converted to fire fixed ammunition by replacing the barrel, bolt, breechblock, or any combination" of these parts. 18 U.S.C. § 921(a)(16)(C).

2. Louisiana definition of "antique firearm"

Louisiana law does not define "antique firearm," but instead references the federal definition in the 18 U.S.C. § 921. Thus, Louisiana law treats antique firearms the same way as does federal law.

C. What firearms are illegal?

Under Louisiana law, the following firearms are prohibited and illegal:

- machine guns (*see* La. Rev. Stat. Ann. § 40:1752);
- unregistered firearms (*see* La. Rev. Stat. Ann. § 40:1785); and
- firearms with an obliterated, destroyed, altered, removed, or concealed serial number or identifying mark (*see* La. Rev. Stat. Ann. § 40:1792(A)).

However, note that in spite of the fact that machine guns are technically illegal to possess in Louisiana, Louisiana residents apparently possess these weapons successfully through a number of exceptions. Perhaps the only exception applying to an individual owner who wants to have a machine gun for collector or recreational purposes would be through Louisiana Revised Statutes Section

40:1752(3) which allows "persons possessing war relics may purchase and possess machine guns which are relics of any war in which the United States was involved, may exhibit and carry the machine guns in the parades of any military organization, and may sell, offer to sell, loan, or give the machine guns to other persons possessing war relics."

Accordingly, if the machine gun purchased or possessed qualifies as a "war relic," it may be legal to possess so long as all other state and federal laws are complied with. The exception to the prohibition against possession of machine guns as war relics extends to the Korean and Vietnam conflicts, notwithstanding that those were not wars declared by formal act of Congress. Op. Atty. Gen., No. 87-389, Oct. 1, 1987.

Under federal law, the following firearms are regulated by the National Firearms Act:

- short-barreled shotguns;
- short-barreled rifles;
- machine guns;
- firearm silencers or suppressors;
- weapons or devices capable of being concealed on the person from which a shot can be fired;
- pistols or revolvers having a smooth bore (as opposed to rifled bore) barrel designed to fire a fixed shotgun shell;
- pistols or revolvers with a vertical handgrip;
- destructive devices; and
- weapons classified as "Any Other Weapon," or AOWs.

See 26 U.S.C. § 5845. For more information on these weapons, *see* Chapter 14 discussing the National Firearms Act.

Although these firearms and/or weapons are prohibited by statute, it does not mean a person absolutely cannot possess one. Many of these weapons may be legally possessed with proper documentation under the National Firearms Act. For more information on these prohibited weapons and the NFA, *see* Chapter 14.

D. How big of a gun can a person possess?

Federal law dictates that any firearm which has any barrel with a bore of more than one-half inch in diameter is a "destructive device" and is subject to the National Firearms Act. *See* 26 U.S.C. § 5845(f). Possession of any such firearm without the proper paperwork associated with NFA firearms is illegal. Note, however, that some shotguns are regulated differently. For more information on destructive devices and the NFA, *see* Chapter 14.

II. AMMUNITION AND THE LAW

No discussion concerning firearms laws would be complete without examining laws concerning the ammunition that goes into a firearm. Just like firearms, the law regulates the possession, sale, and even composition of "legal" ammunition. This section addresses the essential aspects of the law concerning ammunition and what gun owners need to know, both under federal and Louisiana law.

A. How does the law define ammunition?

Under federal law, the term ammunition is defined under 18 U.S.C. § 921(a)(17)(A) and "means ammunition or cartridge cases, primers, bullets, or propellant powder designed for use in any firearm." Thus, the federal definition of ammunition includes the finished product and all of the components in making a round of ammunition. However, the federal definition of ammunition does not include: "(a) any shotgun shot or pellet not designed for use as the single, complete projectile load for one shotgun hull or casing, nor (b) any unloaded, non-metallic shotgun hull or casing not having a primer." *See* 27 C.F.R. § 478.11. In other words, individual ammunition components are legally defined as ammunition themselves, even if they are simply parts, except that shotgun ammunition components, if not completely assembled, are not ammunition.

Under Louisiana law, there is no statutory definition for mere "ammunition." Louisiana law only provides a definition for armor-piercing bullets, which we will discuss later in this chapter.

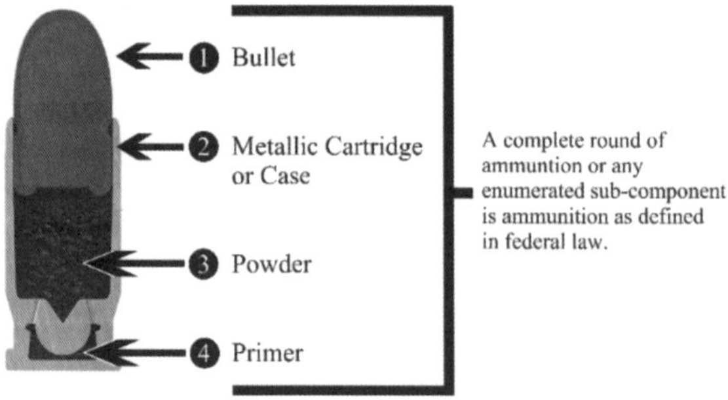

B. Is there a difference in ammunition that is used in different types of firearms?

Yes. Ammunition can be divided into two classifications: ammunition for handguns and ammunition for long guns. Long gun ammunition can be further divided into ammunition for rifles and ammunition for shotguns.

Handgun ammunition means ammunition that is meant to be fired from a handgun, and it comes in many different calibers. Rifle ammunition is meant to be fired from a rifle and is similar to handgun ammunition in that it comes in many different calibers.

Shotgun ammunition, on the other hand, comes in self-contained cartridges loaded with some form of shot or a shotgun slug, which is designed to be fired from a shotgun.

PRACTICAL LEGAL TIP

Even with firearms, having the right tool for the job is important. Practically speaking, you should choose the firearm and ammo that you feel most comfortable using. At the end of the day, why you started shooting is always more important than what you chose to shoot with.

C. What ammunition is illegal?

Armor-piercing bullets are the only ammunition which has explicit prohibitions under both federal and Louisiana law. *See* La. Rev. Stat. Ann. § 40:1811. The federal definition of armor-piercing ammunition is found in 18 U.S.C. § 921(a)(17)(B) and means "(i) a projectile or projectile core which may be used in a handgun and which is constructed entirely (excluding the presence of traces of other substances) from one or a combination of tungsten alloys, steel, iron, brass, bronze, beryllium copper, or depleted uranium; or (ii) a full jacketed projectile larger than .22 caliber designed and intended for use in a handgun and whose jacket has a weight of more than 25 percent of the total weight of the projectile."

FEDERAL LAW

Under federal law, while there is no blanket prohibition on the mere possession of armor-piercing ammunition, it is prohibited under four conditions:

1. Prohibition one: it is illegal to make or import armor-piercing ammunition.

Under 18 U.S.C. § 922(a)(7) it is unlawful "for any person to manufacture or import armor-piercing ammunition, unless: (A) the manufacture of such ammunition is for the use of the United States, any department or agency of the United States, any State, or any department, agency, or political subdivision of a State; (B) the manufacture of such ammunition is for the purpose of exportation; or (C) the manufacture or importation of such ammunition is for the purpose of testing or experimentation and has been authorized by the [United States] Attorney General[.]"

2. Prohibition two: it is illegal for manufacturers and importers to sell or deliver armor-piercing ammunition.

Federal law states that it is unlawful "for any manufacturer or importer to sell or deliver armor-piercing ammunition, unless such sale or delivery: (A) is for the use of the United States, any department or agency of the United States, any State, or any department, agency, or political subdivision of a State; (B) is for the purpose of exportation; or (C) is for the purpose of testing or experimentation and has been authorized by the [United States] Attorney General[.]" See 18 U.S.C. § 922(a)(8).

3. Prohibition three: an FFL or other license-holder cannot sell or deliver armor-piercing ammunition without the proper documentation.

Under 18 U.S.C. § 922(b)(5), it is "unlawful for any licensed importer, licensed manufacturer, licensed dealer, or licensed collector to sell or deliver . . . armor-piercing ammunition to any person unless the licensee notes in his records, [as required under 18 U.S.C. § 923,] the name, age, and place of residence of such person if the person is an individual, or the identity and principal and local places of business of such person if the person is a corporation or other business entity."

4. Prohibition four: it is illegal to possess armor-piercing ammunition if a person is involved in a crime of violence or a drug-trafficking crime.
Pursuant to 18 U.S.C. § 924(c)(5), it is unlawful for "any person who, during and in relation to any crime of violence or drug trafficking crime (including a crime of violence or drug trafficking crime that provides for an enhanced punishment if committed by the use of a deadly or dangerous weapon or device) for which the person may be prosecuted in a court of the United States, use or carries armor piercing ammunition[.]" Individuals who use or carry armor-piercing ammunition in the commission of a crime of violence or during a drug-trafficking crime are subject to heightened sentencing standards should they be found guilty.

As you can see, while possession of armor-piercing ammunition itself is not illegal, obtaining armor-piercing ammunition without violating one of the foregoing prohibitions is almost impossible.

LOUISIANA LAW

Louisiana Revised Statute Annotated § 40:1810 defines armor-piercing bullets as those that have "a steel inner core or core of equivalent density and hardness, truncated cone," and are "designed for use in a pistol or revolver as a body armor or metal piercing bullet" or have been "primarily manufactured or designed, by virtue of its shape, cross-sectional density, or any coating applied thereto, to breach or penetrate body armor when fired from a handgun."

Louisiana Revised Statute Annotated § 40:1811 prohibits the importation, manufacture, sale, purchase, possession, and transfer of armor-piercing bullets. Violation of the statute results in a misdemeanor charge with a possible fine of $1,000 and a maximum jail sentence of one year.

A couple of notable exceptions to this law are available, however. The prohibition does not apply to:

- Law enforcement officers and employees acting in the lawful performance of their duties;
- Law enforcement or other authorized agencies conducting a firearms training course, operating a forensic ballistics laboratory, or specializing in the development of ammunition or explosive ordinance;
- Department of Corrections officials and employees authorized to carry firearms while engaged in the performance of their official duties;
- Members of the armed services or reserve forces of the United States or Louisiana National Guard while engaged in the performance of their official duties;
- Federal officials authorized to carry firearms while engaged in the performance of their official duties;
- The lawful manufacture, importation, sale, purchase, possession, or transfer of armor-piercing bullets exclusively to or for persons authorized by law to possess such bullets; or
- A bona fide collector licensed by the Department of Public Safety.

See La. Rev. Stat. Ann. § 40:1812.

By definition, it should be noted that not all ammunition that can pierce armor is actually armor-piercing. Both the federal and

Louisiana definitions contain specific requirements for a particular round of ammunition's composition in order to make it armor-piercing. Federal law requires that the ammunition be comprised of certain alloys, while Louisiana law requires that the ammunition be designed primarily for the purpose of penetrating armor. *See* 18 U.S.C. § 921(a)(17)(B) and La. Rev. Stat. Ann. § 40:1810(b). For instance, 5.7 millimeter ammunition for an FN57 handgun or a PS90 rifle, while capable of piercing armor based on its size and velocity, is not ammunition that is armor-piercing as defined under the law because such ammunition, sold commercially, is primarily for sporting purposes, according to the ATF. *See* www.atf.gov/news/pr/armor-piercing-ammunition-exemption-framework.

PS90

D. Does modifying traditional ammunition make it illegal?

No, outside of armor-piercing ammunition, there is no handgun or long gun ammunition that is prohibited under the federal or Louisiana law. In fact, there are many examples of hollow-point rounds, which are modified in a way to become more lethal, such as the R.I.P. ammunition, Black Talons, *etc.*, which expand outward upon impact in order to do more internal damage. Such ammunition, though it looks different from traditional ammunition rounds, is perfectly legal.

Factory and Expanded Hollow Point Rounds

E. Is it legal to use ammunition that works in both handguns and rifles?

Yes, except for armor-piercing ammunition that is used principally in handguns. This is because the federal and Louisiana definitions of armor-piercing ammunition contemplate handguns only. Armor-piercing ammunition for a rifle is perfectly legal, though it may complicate matters at trial in trying to demonstrate to the jury any differentiation. Beyond armor-piercing ammunition, it is legal to use ammunition that is available in common calibers and that functions in both handguns and rifles.

With a solid understanding of what is and is not a firearm and ammunition, as well as what firearms and ammunition a person may legally possess without the necessity of obtaining additional documentation, we are now ready to move to the next chapter discussing the purchase and possession of firearms.

F. The future of the Second Amendment

How will the Second Amendment be treated going forward? With the passing of Supreme Court Justice Antonin Scalia, one of the key supporters and author of the 5-4 decision that was *Heller*, the split-down-the-middle Supreme Court truly seemed poised to either continue protecting firearms rights, or backslide to the position that the Second Amendment only applied to militia activity. When the dust settled, the empty seat ended up going to Neil Gorsuch. How Justice Gorsuch has treated the Second Amendment in the past will be a central component of its future. Similarly, even though the Supreme Court seems to have gone out of its way to deny hearing a vast number of cases, a few Second Amendment petitions are awaiting conference.

Although Justice Scalia's opinion in *Heller* established the right for individuals to bear arms, it includes the famous caveat: "Like most rights, the right secured by the Second Amendment is not unlimited." *D.C. v. Heller*, 554 U.S. at 595. That sentence left open the possibility that some gun regulations could pass muster, without spelling out the criteria for constitutionality. Overall, these regulations can be generalized into three major archetypes: those that impose registration requirements on firearms or their owners, those that ban certain types of firearms or firearm accessories, and those that prohibit the carrying of firearms in public (be it through impossible-to-obtain licensing schemes, or piecemeal prohibition).

The sheer volume of such cases allowing the erosion of the Second Amendment is alarming, but not as alarming as how many are denied certiorari.

In the years since *McDonald*, there have been more than 70 U.S. Circuit Court opinions upholding state restrictions on the Second Amendment that the U.S. Supreme Court has refused to review. These restrictions include requiring the registration of firearms, prohibiting "large capacity" magazines, banning certain firearms as "assault rifles," and creating classes of individuals who are restricted from owning firearms.

A Ninth Circuit case that many observers thought the U.S. Supreme Court would review is *Peruta v. County of San Diego*, 742 F.3d 1144 (9th Cir. 2014). On June 26, 2017, the Supreme Court again denied certiorari. However, Justice Thomas along with newly appointed Justice Gorsuch issued an opinion decrying the Court's decision and stated therein:

> The Court's decision to deny certiorari in this case reflects a distressing trend: the treatment of the Second Amendment as a disfavored right. … The Constitution does not rank certain rights above others, and I do not think this Court should impose such a hierarchy by selectively enforcing its preferred rights. … For those of us who work in marbled halls, guarded constantly by a vigilant and dedicated police force, the guarantees of the Second Amendment might seem antiquated and superfluous. But the Framers made a clear choice: They reserved to all Americans the right to bear arms for self-defense. I do not think we should stand by idly while a State denies its citizens that right, particularly when their very lives may depend on it. *Peruta v. County of San Diego*, 582 U.S. ___ (2017) (THOMAS, J., dissenting from denial of certiorari) (slip op., at 7-8).

➤ CHAPTER THREE ➤

KNOW YOUR RIGHTS: PURCHASING, TRANSFERRING, AND POSSESSING FIREARMS

I. LAWS OF PURCHASING AND POSSESSING: THE BASICS

The laws of purchasing, selling, gifting, or otherwise transferring a firearm are distinct and different from the laws of possessing a firearm. It may be legal for someone to possess a firearm, and it still be illegal for them to "purchase" the firearm. Further, each of these sets of laws for "purchasing" or "possessing" has a federal and a state component; both of which must be satisfied in order to stay on the right side of the law.

On the federal level, the Bureau of Alcohol, Tobacco, Firearms, and Explosives ("ATF") is charged with regulating firearms, including sales, purchases, and transfers through Federal Firearms Licensees ("FFLs" or "dealers"). However, a multitude of federal agencies can be involved in any given firearms law investigation or police function, most currently falling under a branch of the U.S. Department of Homeland Security. Louisiana has no direct state-level counterpart to the ATF.

A. What is an FFL?

FFL or Federal Firearms License is a license required by federal law for those persons or entities that are engaged in the business of buying and selling firearms. A federal firearms licensee is often called an "FFL" or "dealer." When an individual purchases, sells, or transfers a firearm through a dealer, the FFL and the individual must both comply with specific federal law requirements, paperwork, and procedures concerning the buying, selling, or transferring of those firearms. These requirements will be addressed throughout this Chapter.

B. Who must obtain an FFL?

Federal law requires a federal firearms license if a person is engaged in business as a firearms dealer, manufacturer, or importer. For the purposes of our discussion in this Chapter, a person is engaged in business when the person "devotes time, attention, and labor to dealing in firearms as a regular course of trade or business with the principal objective of livelihood and profit through the repetitive purchase and resale of firearms, but such term shall not include a person who makes occasional sales, exchanges, or purchases of firearms for the enhancement of a personal collection or for a hobby, or who sells all or part of his personal collection of firearms[.]" 18 U.S.C. § 921(a)(21)(C).

C. What is a private sale?

A private sale is just what it sounds like: a sale, purchase, or transfer of a firearm by parties that are not licensed dealers. A private sale is perfectly legal for both handguns and long guns in Louisiana, as long as all other legal requirements are met. We will discuss the ins-and-outs of private sales in greater detail in this Chapter under Section IV.

D. What is the legal age to purchase and possess a firearm?

Federal law controls all FFL firearms transactions and requires that a person be 21 years of age or older before they may purchase a handgun or 18 years of age for the purchase of a long gun. *See* 18 U.S.C. § 922(b)(1). However, under Louisiana law, a handgun or long gun may be purchased in a private sale by a person who is age 18. Louisiana Revised Statute Annotated § 14:91 makes the "selling or otherwise delivering for value of any firearm or other instrumentality customarily used as a dangerous weapon to any person under the age of eighteen" a misdemeanor crime. It is important to note that lack of knowledge of the minor's age is not a defense.

REQUIRED AGE TO PURCHASE FIREARMS	FEDERAL LAW: FROM DEALER	LOUISIANA LAW: PRIVATE SALE
Handgun	21	18
Long gun	18	18

Under federal law, a person must be at least 18 years of age in order to possess a handgun or ammunition for a handgun. *See* 18 U.S.C. § 922(x)(2). Unlike the law on purchasing a long gun, there is no federal age requirement for the possession of a rifle or shotgun. Louisiana law prohibits anyone under the age of 17 from possessing a handgun. *See* La. Rev. Stat. Ann. § 14:95.8. There is no minimum age requirement for the possession of long guns in Louisiana.

E. Criminal liability for allowing a minor access to firearms

In Louisiana, there is no crime for allowing a minor access to firearms. It is only a crime to sell or "otherwise deliver" a firearm to a minor. *See* La. Rev. Stat. § 14:91(A).

F. When may children legally possess firearms?

Louisiana law allows for the legal possession of firearms under specific exceptions included in the law. These exceptions include the following:

1. Minors who are "[a]ttending a hunter's safety course or a firearms safety course."

This exception includes traveling to or from these activities. *See* La. Rev. Stat. Ann. § 14:95.8(C)(1).

2. "Engaging in practice in the use of a firearm or target shooting at an established range."

This exception includes traveling to or from these activities. *See* La. Rev. Stat. Ann. § 14:95.8(C)(2).

3. "Hunting or trapping pursuant to a valid license issued to [the minor] pursuant to [Louisiana law]."

An adult is legally permitted to take a child hunting, or to the shooting range and permit the child to have access to a firearm, so long as that adult supervises the child. This exception also includes traveling to or from these activities. *See* La. Rev. Stat. Ann. § 14:95.8(C)(3).

4. "On real property with the permission of [the minor's] parent or legal guardian and with the permission of the owner or lessee of the property."
See La. Rev. Stat. Ann. § 14:95.8(C)(5).

5. A minor with the written permission of his parent or legal guardian; provided that he carries a copy of the written permission on his person.
See La. Rev. Stat. Ann. § 14:95.8(C)(7).

G. Youth handgun signage and notice requirements

Federal law requires that FFLs who deliver handguns to non-licensees display at their licensed premises (including temporary business locations at gun shows) a sign that customers can readily see. These signs are provided by the ATF and contain the following language:

(1) "The misuse of handguns is a leading contributor to juvenile violence and fatalities.

(2) Safely storing and securing firearms away from children will help prevent the unlawful possession of handguns by juveniles, stop accidents, and save lives.

(3) Federal law prohibits, except in certain limited circumstances, anyone under 18 years of age from knowingly possessing a handgun, or any person from transferring a handgun to a person under 18.

(4) A knowing violation of the prohibition against selling, delivering, or otherwise transferring a handgun to a person under the age

> of 18 is, under certain circumstances, punishable by up to 10 years in prison."

See 27 C.F.R. § 478.103(b).

In addition to the displayed sign, federal law requires FFLs to provide non-licensee customers with a written notification containing the same four points as listed above (*see* 27 C.F.R. § 478.103(a)), as well as sections 922(x) and 924(a)(6) of Title 18, Chapter 44 of the United States Code. This written notification is available as a pamphlet published by the ATF entitled "Youth Handgun Safety Act Notice" and is sometimes referred to as ATF information 5300.2. Alternatively, this written notification may be delivered to customers on another type of written notification, such as a manufacturer's brochure accompanying the handgun or a sales receipt or invoice applied to the handgun package. Any written notification delivered to a customer other than the one provided by the ATF must include the language described here, and must be "legible, clear, and conspicuous, and the required language shall appear in type size no smaller than 10-point type." 27 C.F.R. § 478.103(c).

II. FEDERAL LAW DISQUALIFICATIONS FOR PURCHASING AND POSSESSING FIREARMS

Federal law lists categories of persons disqualified from legally purchasing and possessing a firearm. This list comprises disqualifications that come from several different pieces of federal legislation including the Gun Control Act of 1968, the Brady Handgun Violence Protection Act, and the Violence Against Women Act. If a person buys or attempts to buy a firearm from an FFL, they must not be disqualified under any of the laws. Before an FFL may sell or otherwise transfer a firearm, the purchaser must fill out an ATF Form 4473. This form has questions concerning each of the criteria that disqualify a person to purchase a firearm under federal law. These disqualifications include:

(1) if the person is not the actual purchaser of the firearm—also known as a "straw man purchaser;"
(2) if the person is under indictment or information in any court for a felony or any other crime for which the judge could imprison the person for more than one year;
(3) if the person has ever been convicted in any court for a felony or other crime for which the judge could imprison the person for more than one year;
(4) if the person is a fugitive from justice;
(5) if the person is an unlawful user of, or addicted to marijuana, or any depressant, stimulant, narcotic drug, or controlled substance;
(6) if the person has ever been adjudicated as mentally defective or has been committed to a mental institution;
(7) if the person has been dishonorably discharged from the Armed Forces;
(8) if the person is subject to an active protective order restraining the person from harassing, stalking, or threatening the person's child, or an intimate partner or child of such partner;
(9) if the person has been convicted in any court for a misdemeanor crime of domestic violence;
(10) if the person has ever renounced their United States citizenship;
(11) if the person is an alien illegally in the United States; and
(12) if the person is admitted under a non-immigrant visa and does not qualify for an exception.

The purchaser must legally affirm that they are not subject to any of the criteria listed above before they may purchase a firearm. If a prospective purchaser answers any question on the form in a manner that indicates they are legally disqualified, it is illegal for the FFL to sell that person the firearm, and it is illegal for the purchaser to complete the transaction or possess the firearm.

A. Understanding who is disqualified

1. Can I buy a firearm for another person?

No. This would be a "straw man" purchase. In order to legally purchase a firearm from a dealer, you must be the "actual purchaser or transferee." If you are not the actual purchaser or transferee, it is illegal for you to complete the transfer or sale under federal law. Purchases for third persons are often called "straw man" purchases and are illegal. If you are not the actual purchaser, beware!

In fact, the ATF has a campaign called "Don't Lie for the Other Guy" that is targeted at (as they term it on their website) detection and deterrence of "straw man" purchases. The ATF website lists numerous examples of prosecutions for "straw man" purchases, and a United States Supreme Court case examined and upheld federal law on this matter. *Abramski v. United States*, 134 S.Ct. 2259 (2014).

So, who is the "actual" buyer or transferee so as not to be a "straw man?" The ATF states that you are the "actual transferee/buyer if [you are] purchasing the firearm for [yourself] or otherwise acquiring the firearm for [yourself] (*e.g.*, redeeming the firearm from pawn, retrieving it from consignment, firearm raffle winner)." The ATF goes on to state you are "also the actual transferee/buyer if [you are] legitimately purchasing the firearm as a bona fide gift for a third party." *See* ATF Form 4473.

EXAMPLE:

Mr. Smith asks Mr. Jones to purchase a firearm for Mr. Smith. Mr. Smith gives Mr. Jones the money for the firearm. Mr. Jones then buys the firearm with Mr. Smith's money and gives Mr. Smith the firearm.

Mr. Jones is not the "actual buyer" (he is legally a "straw man") of the firearm and if Mr. Jones indicates that he is the "actual buyer" of the firearm on ATF Form 4473, he has committed a federal crime. The Supreme Court ruling in *Abramski*, however, did not make "gifts" of firearms illegal. *Abramski v. United States*, 134 S.Ct. 2259, 2271 (2014).

When completing ATF Form 4473, if a person checks "yes" to the box asking if the person is the "actual purchaser," then that person cannot have engaged in a separate transaction to sell or transfer the firearm privately. Please note: the Supreme Court's ruling held that a person cannot legally purchase a firearm on behalf of another even if the person receiving the firearm would not otherwise be prohibited from making the purchase themselves. So don't buy a firearm for another person no matter how good a friend, relative, or person they are—it is likely a crime!

FREQUENTLY ASKED QUESTION FROM ATF WEBSITE

Q: MAY I BUY A FIREARM FROM AN FFL AS A "GIFT" FOR ANOTHER PERSON?

A: Yes.

Editor's note: Instead of the previous example where Mr. Smith paid Mr. Jones to purchase a firearm for him, if Mr. Jones decides to buy a firearm with his own money and then give the firearm to Mr. Smith as a present, then Mr. Jones is the actual buyer/transferee of the firearm. Since Mr. Jones is the actual buyer, there exists no sham or "strawman," and the purchase is legal.

Q: MAY A PARENT OR GUARDIAN PURCHASE A FIREARM AS A GIFT FOR A JUVENILE?

A: Yes, however, possession of handguns by juveniles is generally unlawful under federal law. Juveniles may only receive and possess handguns with the written permission of a parent or guardian for limited purposes, *e.g.*, employment, ranching, farming, target practice, or hunting.

See www.atf.gov/firearms/firearms-frequently-asked-questions-unlicensed-persons.

2. A person cannot purchase a firearm if they have been convicted or are under "indictment or information" for a felony or certain misdemeanors

If a person has been convicted of a felony or other crime for which a judge may sentence, or could have sentenced, the person to more than one year imprisonment, that person may not legally purchase a firearm (unless the crime was a state misdemeanor punishable by imprisonment of two years or less). *See* 18 U.S.C. § 921(a)(20)

(B). Likewise, if a person is under "indictment" or "information" for a felony, or any other crime for which a judge may sentence the person to more than one year imprisonment, that person is disqualified from purchasing a firearm. *See* 18 U.S.C. § 922(g)(1). An "indictment" or "information" is a formal accusation of a crime punishable by imprisonment for a term exceeding one year. *See* 18 U.S.C. § 921(a)(14). It is important to point out that the actual sentence received is not the determining factor for disqualification, rather, it is the possible maximum sentence. A person may have only been sentenced to 30 days imprisonment, but if the crime for which they were charged allowed a maximum penalty of five years, then that person is disqualified. *See Schrader v. Holder*, 831 F. Supp. 2d 304 (D.D.C. 2011, aff'd, 704 F.3d 980 (D.C. Cir. 2013)).

3. What does it mean to be a "fugitive from justice" so as to be disqualified from purchasing a firearm?

A "fugitive from justice" is a person who, after having committed a crime, flees from the jurisdiction of the court where the crime was committed. A fugitive from justice may also be a person who goes into hiding to avoid facing charges for the crime of which he or she is accused. *See* 18 U.S.C. § 921(a)(15). Such individuals are not eligible to purchase or possess firearms. *See* 18 U.S.C. § 922(g)(2).

4. Unlawful users of or persons addicted to drugs are disqualified from purchasing firearms

Federal law is very broad in that it disqualifies persons from the purchase of firearms if they are either users of or addicted to marijuana or any depressant, stimulant, narcotic drug, or any controlled substance. *See* 18 U.S.C. § 922(g)(3). Under federal law, an "addict" is defined as a person that "habitually uses any narcotic drug so as to endanger the public morals, health, safety, or welfare, or who is so far addicted to the use of narcotic drugs as to have lost the power of self-control with reference to his addiction." 21 U.S.C. § 802(1). However, in using the terms "users of," no such frequency or dependence seems contemplated in the words, nor did Congress give further guidance. Illegal users and addicts are prohibited from purchasing firearms from any person under federal law, and are likewise prohibited from possessing firearms. *See* 18 U.S.C. §§ 922(d) and (g).

5. A person can't legally buy or possess firearms if they are "mentally defective"

What does "mentally defective" mean? A person is considered to have been adjudicated as "mentally defective" if there has been a "determination by a court, board, commission, or other lawful authority that a person, as a result of marked subnormal intelligence, or mental illness, incompetency, condition, or disease: (1) [i]s a danger to himself or to others; or (2) [l]acks the mental capacity to contract or manage his own affairs." 27 C.F.R. § 478.11(a). The term "mentally defective" includes "(1) [a] finding of insanity by a court in a criminal case; and (2) [t]hose persons found incompetent to stand trial or found not guilty by reason of lack of mental responsibility[.]" 27 C.F.R. § 478.11(b).

"Mentally defective" also includes a person who has been committed to a mental institution by a court, board, commission, or other lawful authority, or who has been involuntarily committed to a mental institution. The term includes commitment for mental defectiveness or mental illness, and also includes commitment for other reasons, such as drug use. However, it does not include a person in a mental institution for observation or a voluntary admission to a mental institution. Individuals who have been adjudicated as mentally defective are also prohibited from possessing firearms under federal law. *See* 18 U.S.C. § 922(g)(4).

6. A person subject to a restraining order may not purchase or possess a firearm

Under 18 U.S.C. § 922(g)(8), firearms may not be sold to or received by a person "subject to a court order that—(A) was issued after a hearing of which such person received actual notice, and at which such person had an opportunity to participate; (B) restrains such person from harassing, stalking, or threatening an intimate partner . . . or child of such intimate partner or person, or engaging in other conduct that would place an intimate partner in reasonable fear of bodily injury to the partner or child; and (C) (i) includes a finding that such person represents a credible threat to the physical safety of such intimate partner or child; or (ii) by its terms explicitly prohibits the use, attempted use, or threatened use of physical force against such intimate partner or child that would reasonably be expected to cause bodily injury[.]" An "intimate partner" of a person is the spouse or former spouse of the person, the parent of a child of the person, or an individual who cohabitates with the person. *See* 18 U.S.C. § 921(a)(32).

7. Domestic violence issues and disqualifications

A person who has ever been convicted of the crime of domestic violence may not purchase or possess firearms under federal law. *See* 18 U.S.C. § 922(g)(9). These restrictions were passed in what is known as the Violence Against Women Act in 1994 and amended in 1996. This is an often misunderstood law, and, in fact, the ATF has numerous "Frequently Asked Questions" concerning this disqualification on its website: www.atf.gov. The ATF does a good job of explaining the scope of this subject in their FAQs. Due to the complexity of this issue, the ATF examples are included here:

FREQUENTLY ASKED QUESTION FROM ATF WEBSITE

Q: WHAT IS A "MISDEMEANOR CRIME OF DOMESTIC VIOLENCE"?

A: A "misdemeanor crime of domestic violence" is an offense that:
(1) is a misdemeanor under Federal, State, or Tribal law;
(2) has, as an element, the use or attempted use of physical force, or the threatened use of a deadly weapon; and
(3) was committed by a current or former spouse, parent, or guardian of the victim, by a person with whom the victim shares a child in common, by a person who is cohabiting with or has cohabited with the victim as a spouse, parent, or guardian, or by a person similarly situated to a spouse, parent, or guardian of the victim.

However, a person is not considered to have been convicted of a misdemeanor crime of domestic violence unless:
(1) the person was represented by counsel in the case, or knowingly and intelligently waived the right of counsel in the case; and
(2) in the case of a prosecution for which a person was entitled to a jurycase was tried, either –
  (a) the case was tried by a jury, or
  (b) the person knowingly and intelligently waived the right to have the case tried by a jury, by guilty plea or otherwise.

In addition, a conviction would not be disabling if it has been expunged or set aside, or is an offense for which the person has been pardoned or has had civil rights restored (if the law of the jurisdiction in which the proceedings were held provides for the loss of civil rights upon conviction for such an offense) unless the pardon, expunction, or restoration of civil rights expressly provides

that the person may not ship, transport, possess, or receive firearms, and the person is not otherwise prohibited by the law of the jurisdiction in which the proceedings were held from receiving or possessing firearms.
[18 U.S.C. 921(a)(33); 27 CFR 478.11]

Editor's note: A significant number of people make the mistake of overlooking or forgetting about a court issue or family law judicial proceeding. However, if you meet the above criteria, you are federally disqualified from possessing a firearm. The fact that it may have happened a long time ago, or that you did not understand the ramifications, is legally irrelevant.

Q: MUST A MISDEMEANOR CRIME OF DOMESTIC VIOLENCE (MCDV) BE DESIGNATED AS A "DOMESTIC VIOLENCE" OFFENSE?

A: No. A qualifying offense need not be designated as a domestic violence offense. For example, a conviction for assault may qualify as an MCDV even if the offense is not designated as a domestic violence assault.
[18 U.S.C. 921(a)(33) and 922(g)(9); 27 CFR 478.11 and 478.32(a)(9)]

Q: DOES THE PROHIBITION ON RECEIPT OR POSSESSION OF FIREARMS AND AMMUNITION APPLY IF THE PERSON WAS CONVICTED OF AN MCDV PRIOR TO THE ENACTMENT OF 18 U.S.C. 922(G)(9) ON SEPTEMBER 30, 1996?

A: Yes.

Editor's note: For those wondering why this is not an unconstitutional ex-post facto law, multiple federal appeals courts have ruled against that argument and the Supreme Court has consistently declined to review any of those cases, effectively accepting the ruling of the courts of appeals and upholding the law.

Q: IS AN INDIVIDUAL WHO HAS BEEN PARDONED, OR WHOSE CONVICTION WAS EXPUNGED OR SET ASIDE, OR WHOSE CIVIL RIGHTS HAVE BEEN RESTORED, CONSIDERED CONVICTED OF A MISDEMEANOR CRIME OF DOMESTIC VIOLENCE?

A: No, as long as the pardon, expungement, or restoration does not expressly provide that the person may not ship, transport, possess, or receive firearms. A restoration of civil rights, however, is only effective to remove the Federal firearms disability if the law of the jurisdiction provides for the loss of civil rights for a conviction of such a misdemeanor.
[18 U.S.C. 921(a)(33); 27 CFR 478.11]

Q: IS THE RELATIONSHIP BETWEEN THE PARTIES AN ELEMENT OF AN MCDV?

A: No. The "as an element" language in the definition of "misdemeanor crime of domestic violence" only applies to the use of force provision of the statute and not the relationship provision. However, to be disabling, the offense must have been committed by someone whose relationship to the victim meets the definition in the Gun Control Act (GCA).
[18 U.S.C. 921(a)(33); 27 CFR 478.11]

Editor's note: This basically means that if illegal force was used against another person, regardless of the language in the underlying statute, if the illegal force was used against a member of the protected class under the statute, federal law will deem this as satisfying the requirements and disqualify the individual from purchasing and possessing firearms.

Q: IN DETERMINING WHETHER A CONVICTION IN A STATE COURT IS A "CONVICTION" OF A MISDEMEANOR CRIME OF DOMESTIC VIOLENCE, DOES FEDERAL, STATE OR TRIBAL LAW APPLY?

A: The law of the jurisdiction determines whether a conviction has occurred. Therefore, if the law of the jurisdiction does not consider the person to be convicted, the person would not have the Federal disability.
[18 U.S.C. 921(a)(33); 27 CFR 478.11]

Q: DOES THE DISABILITY APPLY TO LAW ENFORCEMENT OFFICERS?

A: Yes. The Gun Control Act was amended so that employees of government agencies convicted of misdemeanor crimes of domestic violence would not be exempt from disabilities with respect to their receipt or possession of firearms or ammunition. Thus, law enforcement officers and other government officials who have been convicted of a disqualifying misdemeanor may not lawfully possess or receive firearms or ammunition for any purpose, including performance of their official duties. The disability applies to firearms and ammunition issued by government agencies, purchased by government employees for use in performing their official duties, and personal firearms and ammunition possessed by such employees.
[18 U.S.C. 922(g)(9) and 925(a)(1); 27 CFR 478.32(a)(9) and 478.141]

Q: ARE LOCAL CRIMINAL ORDINANCES "MISDEMEANORS UNDER STATE LAW" FOR PURPOSES OF 18 U.S.C. 922(D)(9) AND (G)(9)?

A: Yes, assuming a violation of the ordinance meets the definition of "misdemeanor crime of domestic violence" in all other respects.

Q: WHAT STATE AND LOCAL OFFENSES ARE "MISDEMEANORS" FOR PURPOSES OF 18 U.S.C. 922(D)(9) AND (G)(9)?

A: The definition of misdemeanor crime of domestic violence in the Gun Control Act (GCA) includes any offense classified as a "misdemeanor" under Federal, State or Tribal law. In States that do not classify offenses as misdemeanors, the definition includes any State or local offense punishable by imprisonment for a term of 1 year or less or punishable by a fine.
[18 U.S.C. 921(a)(33); 27 CFR 478.11]

Q: WHAT SHOULD AN INDIVIDUAL DO IF HE OR SHE HAS BEEN CONVICTED OF A MISDEMEANOR CRIME OF DOMESTIC VIOLENCE?

A: Individuals subject to this disability should immediately dispose of their firearms and ammunition, such as by abandonment to a law enforcement agency.
[18 U.S.C. 922(g)(9); 27 CFR 478.32]

See www.atf.gov/qa-category/misdemeanor-crime-domestic-violence

PRACTICAL LEGAL TIP

If you or a loved one are going through court proceedings involving family issues and a restraining or protective order is entered in your case, it can suspend your ability to purchase or possess firearms. Language in the court order prohibiting any acts of family violence whether or not family violence actually occurred, make it so the person against whom the order is entered is legally barred from the purchase or possession of any firearm. Believe it or not, the Family Courts have the ability to suspend your Second Amendment rights.

8. Illegal aliens or aliens admitted under a non-immigrant visa

Persons who are illegally in the United States may not legally purchase, possess, or transport firearms. Generally, non-immigrant aliens are also prohibited from legally purchasing, possessing, or transporting firearms. *See* 18 U.S.C. § 922(g)(5).

Exceptions for nonimmigrant aliens

However, a nonimmigrant alien who has been admitted under a non-immigrant visa is not prohibited from purchasing, receiving, or possessing a firearm if the person falls within one of the following exceptions:

1. if the person was "admitted to the United States for lawful hunting or sporting purposes or is in possession of a hunting license or permit lawfully issued in the United States;"

2. if the person is "an official representative of a foreign government who is—accredited to the United States Government or the Government's mission to an international organization having its headquarters in the United States;"
3. if the person is "an official representative of a foreign government who is—. . . en route to or from another country to which that alien is accredited;"
4. if the person is "an official of a foreign government or a distinguished foreign visitor who has been so designated by the Department of State;"
5. if the person is "a foreign law enforcement officer of a friendly foreign government entering the United States on official law enforcement business[;]"
6. if the person has received a waiver from the prohibition from the Attorney General of the United States.

See 18 U.S.C. §§ 922(y)(2) and (3).

III. LOUISIANA LAW DISQUALIFICATIONS: WHO CANNOT BUY A FIREARM UNDER LOUISIANA LAW?

As mentioned earlier, Louisiana has restrictions on the sale, transfer, and possession of firearms that are separate and distinct from the federal restrictions. If a person runs afoul of the law, they could potentially face prosecution in both state and federal court.

A. Louisiana law disqualifications for "purchasing" a firearm

The disqualifications for purchasing firearms under Louisiana law are contained in Title 14, Section 95.1.3 of the Louisiana Revised Statutes Annotated and apply to all transactions in Louisiana. This section makes it a crime for a person to:

1. "[K]nowingly solicit, persuade, encourage, or entice a licensed dealer or private seller of firearms or ammunition to

sell a firearm or ammunition under circumstances which the person knows would violate [Louisiana law] or [the laws] of the United States.

2. [P]rovide to a licensed dealer or private seller of firearms or ammunition what the person knows to be materially false information with intent to deceive the dealer or seller about the legality of a sale of a firearm or ammunition."

See La. Rev. Stat. Ann. § 14.95.1.3(A).

B. Louisiana law disqualifications for "possessing" firearms

Similar to the disqualifications for purchasing firearms under Louisiana law, Title 14, Section 95 also includes prohibitions on the possession of firearms. These prohibitions include:

1. The intentional concealment without a CHL (*see* La. Rev. Stat. Ann. § 14:95(A)(1));
2. The ownership, possession, custody, or use of any firearm at any time by an enemy alien (*see* La. Rev. Stat. § 14:95(A)(2));
3. The possession of a firearm by someone convicted of any of the following crimes:
   - A felony listed in Louisiana Revised Statute 14:2(B);
   - Simple burglary;
   - Burglary of a pharmacy;
   - Burglary of an inhabited dwelling;
   - Felony illegal use of weapons or dangerous instrumentalities;
   - Manufacture or possession of a delayed action incendiary device;
   - Manufacture or possession of a bomb;
   - The possession of a firearm while in the possession of or during the sale or distribution of a controlled dangerous substance;
   - A sex offense defined in Louisiana Revised Statute 15:541;

- Any crime defined as an attempt to commit one of the above-enumerated offenses; and
- Any crime of another state of the United States or any foreign government or country that, if committed in Louisiana, would be one of the above-enumerated crimes. (*See* La. Rev. Stat. § 14:95.1(A)).

4. Intentionally receiving, possessing, carrying, concealing, buying, selling, or transporting "any firearm from which the serial number or mark of identification has been obliterated" (*see* La. Rev. Stat. § 14:95.7(A));
5. The knowing and intentional possession of a handgun upon his person by a juvenile (one who has not attained the age of 17) (*see* La. Rev. Stat. § 14:95.8(A)); or
6. Possession of a firearm by one convicted of domestic abuse battery (*see* La. Rev. Stat. § 14:95.10(A)).

Note: Even though a person may not be disqualified from possession of a firearm under state law, that person may nevertheless still be disqualified to possess a firearm under federal law.

EXAMPLE:

Scott was convicted of a class A misdemeanor of family violence in 1992. He has a Smith & Wesson .357 Magnum in his nightstand for self-defense.

Under Louisiana law, Scott may be in legal possession of his firearm because more than 10 years have lapsed following either his conviction or release from supervision. *See* La. Rev. Stat. Ann. § 14:95.1(C). However, if push-comes-to-shove and if federal law enforcement pursued the issue, Scott is in unlawful possession of a firearm under 18 U.S.C. § 922(g)(9) and 27 C.F.R. § 478.32(a)(9), regardless of how legal he might be under state law.

C. Understanding who is disqualified under Louisiana law

1. What does Louisiana law define as a "minor" for the purpose of selling a firearm?

A "minor" refers to any person who is under 18 years of age. *See* La. Rev. Stat. § 14:91(A). See also age discussion under Section I(D) of this Chapter.

2. Differences in federal and Louisiana law concerning convicted felons possessing firearms

Under federal law, a person convicted of a felony is prohibited from possessing firearms. Louisiana law, however, relaxes such restrictions. Under Louisiana law, a convicted felon is permitted to possess firearms in the person's home after 10 years from the date of the person's release from confinement, supervision under community supervision, parole, or mandatory supervision—whichever is later. *See* La. Rev. Stat. Ann. § 14:95.1(C).

A convicted felon is not, however, able to purchase firearms because federal law precludes it. *See* 18 U.S.C. § 922(g)(1).

3. Will my juvenile record prevent me from purchasing and possessing a firearm?

Juvenile records will not be released to the public, and, therefore, to firearms dealers for the purpose of prohibiting one from purchasing a firearm, unless the individual was over the age of 14 when the crime was committed and the offense committed was a crime of violence defined by Louisiana Revised Statute Annotated § 14:2(B). *See* La. Child. Code Ann. § Art.412. Additionally, under Article 897 of the Louisiana Children's Code, a court may prohibit a child from possessing a firearm or carrying a concealed weapon if he has been adjudicated for any of the following offenses and probation is not otherwise prohibited:

- First or second degree murder;
- Manslaughter;
- Aggravated battery;
- Aggravated or first degree rape;
- Forcible or second degree rape;
- Simple or third degree rape;
- Aggravated crime against nature;
- Aggravated kidnapping;
- Aggravated arson;
- Aggravated or simple burglary;
- Armed or simple robbery;
- Burglary of a pharmacy;
- Burglary of an inhabited dwelling;
- Unauthorized entry of an inhabited dwelling;
- Any violation of the Uniform Controlled Dangerous Substances Law which is a felony; or
- Any crime defined as an attempt to commit one of these enumerated offenses.

See La. Child. Code Ann. § Art.897(B)(1)(c).

IV. UNDERSTANDING "PRIVATE SALES" LAWS

A. What are the legal restrictions on "private sales" of firearms?

Private individuals may legally buy, sell, gift, or otherwise transfer firearms to another private individual in Louisiana. However, when doing so, careful attention needs to be paid to not violate the laws regulating these transactions. So, what are the legal restrictions? First, the ATF website has an informative pamphlet entitled "Best Practices: Transfers of Firearms by Private Sellers" located on its website http://www.atf.gov/files/publications/download/p/atf-p-5300-21.pdf. This pamphlet should be a must-read before entering into a "private sale" transaction involving a firearm. So, what are the rules in Louisiana regarding private sales?

1. Residency requirements

In order for the private sale of a firearm to be legal in Louisiana, both parties must reside in the same state. This means, for our purposes, that both the buyer and seller of the firearm must be Louisiana residents. Similarly, under federal law, an unlicensed (non-dealer) may only "transfer" a firearm to another unlicensed person in the same state. This means that if a person is a resident of Louisiana, federal law prohibits the person from directly (not through a dealer) selling or transferring the firearm to a resident of another state. Federal law makes these transactions illegal from both the buyer/transferee and seller/transferor perspective. It is illegal for a private individual to transport into or receive within his own state a firearm which was purchased in another state from a private seller. *See* 18 U.S.C. § 922(a)(3). Likewise, it is illegal for a private seller to sell or deliver a firearm to an individual whom the private seller knows, or has reason to believe, is not a resident of the seller's state. *See* 18 U.S.C. § 922(a)(5).

EXAMPLE:

Bob is visiting his best friend from high school, Jim. Ten years ago, after high school was over, Bob moved to Nebraska from Louisiana. One night, Bob and Jim decide to go to the shooting range during Bob's trip, and Bob borrows one of Jim's handguns. After shooting at the range, impressed with both the feel and action of Jim's handgun, Bob asks Jim if he could buy it from him. Since they've been friends for so many years, Jim says yes, and even offers him a good price for the transaction. Before leaving to go home to Nebraska, Bob pays Jim and packs his new handgun.

Has Bob committed a crime in selling the handgun to Jim? Has Jim committed a crime in purchasing the handgun from Bob? The answer to both questions is yes! Under federal law, Bob is not allowed to privately purchase a handgun in another state and transport it back to his home state. Likewise, Jim is not allowed to sell a firearm legally to a person he knows lives in another state. In this example, both Bob and Jim know that Jim is not a Louisiana resident—the place where Bob has sold his firearm. Bob has committed the crime of willful receipt of a firearm from out-of-state by an unlicensed person, while Jim has committed the federal crime of willful sale of a firearm to an out-of-state resident. *See* 18 U.S.C. §§ 922(a)(3) and (5). The penalties for these crimes include jail time up to 5 years and/or a fine of $250,000.00. *See* 18 U.S.C. § 924(a)(1)(D).

What if the situation is less obvious? Let's take a look at an example where "reasonable cause to believe" comes into play.

EXAMPLE:

Frank, a Louisiana resident, recently posted his Glock 19 for sale on an internet message board in Louisiana. Frank receives an email from a person named Ted who would like to buy the handgun. Frank and Ted agree, via email, on a purchase price and arrange to meet at a place in Louisiana one week later to facilitate the transfer. When Ted pulls up in his 1978 Ford LTD Wagon, Frank notices the car's Tennessee license plates. Nevertheless, Frank shrugs and sells Ted the gun anyway without going through any of the formalities of a bill of sale, or asking for identification. Two weeks later, Frank finds himself at an FBI field office in New Orleans answering questions about a shooting that took place with his (former) Glock 19.

Is Frank in trouble? It is highly likely. Although Frank is not the center of the shooting investigation, Frank is probably the center of an investigation for illegally selling the firearm to an out-of-state resident under federal law.

2. Private sales: don't knowingly sell to the "wrong" people

A private individual may sell a firearm to a private buyer in the same state so long as the seller does not know or have reasonable cause to believe that the person purchasing the firearm is prohibited from possessing or receiving a firearm under federal or state law. *See* 18 U.S.C. § 922(d). Also, see discussion in the previous sections on "disqualifications."

EXAMPLE:

Gordon and Josh are friends and Josh tells Gordon that he has just attempted to buy a gun from a local FFL, but he was denied because he was disqualified for some reason under federal law (something about a conviction or restraining order or drug use or psychiatric problems–Josh was too mad to remember). Gordon says, "no problem, I'll just sell you one of mine," and he does.

Gordon has almost certainly committed a federal and state crime, because he knew (or at least had reasonable cause to believe) that Josh was prohibited from purchasing a firearm under the law. See our earlier discussion concerning disqualifications.

B. How does the law determine a person's residence when buying or selling a firearm?

1. Individuals with one residence

For the purpose of firearms purchases, the person's state of residence is the state in which the person is present and where the individual has an intention of making a home. 27 C.F.R. § 478.11.

2. What if a person maintains a home in two states?

If a person maintains a home in two (or more) states and resides in those states for periods of the year, he or she may, during the period of time the person actually resides in a particular state, purchase a firearm in that state. However, simply owning property in another state does not qualify a person as a resident of that state so as to purchase a firearm in that state. To meet the residency requirements, a person must actually maintain a home in a state, which includes an intention to make a particular state a residence. *See* 27 C.F.R. § 478.11. This issue may ultimately be a fact question with evidence of residency being things like a driver's license, insurance records, recurring expenses in the state, as well as other things related to making a particular state a person's residence.

3. Members of the Armed Forces

A member of the Armed Forces on active duty is a resident of the state in which his or her permanent duty station is located. If a member of the Armed Forces maintains a home in one state and the member's permanent duty station is in a nearby state to which he or she commutes each day, then the member has two states of residence and may purchase a firearm in either the state where the duty station is located or the state where the home is maintained. *See* 18 U.S.C. § 921(b). *See also* ATF FAQs on residency at www.atf.gov.

4. Nonimmigrant aliens

Persons who are legally present in the United States are residents of the state in which they reside and where they intend to make a home. Such persons, provided they meet all other requirements and are not otherwise prohibited from purchasing a firearm are lawfully permitted to purchase a firearm. *See* 18 U.S.C. § 922(y).

C. Suggestion on how to document a private firearms sale

Protect yourself! This is practical advice that should not be ignored. If you engage in the private sale of a firearm, here are some practical tips:

- Ask for identification whether you are the buyer/transferee or seller/transferor to establish residency;
- Get and/or give a "bill of sale" for the transfer and keep a copy—identify the firearm including make, model, and serial number, as well as the date and place of transfer;
- Put the residency information on the "bill of sale" including names, addresses, and phone numbers;
- Do not sell or transfer a firearm or ammunition if you think the person may not be permitted or is prohibited from receiving the firearm.

Why do this? Not only will it help establish residency, but if you unfortunately happen to buy or sell a firearm that was previously used in a crime, or if you sell or transfer a gun that is later used in a crime, you want to be able to establish when you did and did not own or possess the firearm.

Further, as a matter of good course, if you are a seller or transferor in a private sale, you might ask whether there is any reason the buyer/transferee cannot own a firearm. Why? So that if there is an issue later, you can at a minimum say that you had no reason to know the buyer could not legally possess firearms. However, do not overlook behavior that may indicate the buyer is not telling you the truth, because law enforcement will not overlook facts that show you did know, or should have had reasonable cause to believe that the buyer/transferee could not own a firearm at the time of the transfer if a legal issue arises later. Protect yourself!

V. BUYING, SELLING, AND TRANSFERRING THROUGH AN FFL

A. Basic procedures

Persons purchasing firearms through dealers must comply with all legal requirements imposed by federal law. These include both paperwork and appropriate background checks or screenings to ensure that the purchaser is not prohibited from the purchase or possession of a firearm under federal law.

When purchasing through a dealer, the first thing a prospective buyer will do is select a firearm. Once a selection has been made, the prospective purchaser is required to show proper identification and complete ATF Form 4473. This form requires the applicant, under penalty of law, to provide accurate identifying information, as well as answer certain questions in order to establish whether a person may legally purchase a firearm. The information provided on Form 4473 is then provided to the National Instant Criminal Background Check System (NICS) for processing and approval in order to proceed with the transfer (however, no NICS background may be required if the transferee is legally exempt for reasons such as possessing a state-issued firearms license, like a Louisiana CHP). An FFL dealer can submit the check to NICS either by telephone or through the online website and only after the FFL completes all of these steps successfully is a purchaser/transferee allowed to take possession of the firearm.

B. What is Form 4473?

ATF Form 4473 is the ATF's form known as a Firearms Transaction Record, which must be completed when a person purchases a firearm from an FFL. *See* 27 C.F.R. § 478.124. Form 4473 requires the applicant to provide their name, address, birth date, state of residence, and other information including government issued photo identification. The form also contains information blanks to be filled-in including the NICS background check transaction number, the make, model, and serial number of the firearm to be purchased, and a series of questions that a person must answer. *See* 27 C.F.R. § 478.124(c). This series of questions and the corresponding answers help determine a purchaser's eligibility under federal law to purchase a firearm. Once the form is completed, the prospective purchaser will sign the form and attest that the information provided thereon is truthful and accurate under penalty of federal law. This means that if you lie or make false statements on this form, you can and will be prosecuted for a crime.

Likewise, the dealer must also sign Form 4473 and retain it for at least 20 years. *See* 27 C.F.R. § 478.129(b). The ATF is permitted to inspect, as well as receive a copy of Form 4473 from the dealer both during audits and during the course of a criminal investigation. *See* 27 C.F.R. § 478.121 and 18 U.S.C. § 923(g)(1)(B)(iii). The 4473 records must be surrendered to the Bureau of Alcohol, Tobacco, Firearms and Explosives in the event the FFL dealer retires or ceases business.

C. How are background checks administered when purchasing a firearm?

1. NICS: National Instant Criminal Background Check System

Background checks performed by dealers when transferring firearms are completed through the National Instant Criminal Background Check System or NICS, if required, prior to the transfer of a firearm from an FFL dealer to a non-dealer. *See* 18 U.S.C. § 922(t) and 27 C.F.R. § 478.102. When the prospective purchaser/transferee's information is given to NICS, the system will check the applicant against at least three different databases containing various types of records. Applicants are checked against the records maintained by the Interstate Identification Index (III), which contains criminal history records, the National Crime Information Center (NCIC), which contains records including warrants and protective orders, as well as the NICS Index, which contains records of individuals who are prohibited from purchasing or possessing firearms under either federal or state law. In addition, if the applicant is not a United States Citizen, the application is processed for an Immigration Alien Query (IAQ) through the Department of Homeland Security's Immigration and Customs Enforcement Division. *See* www.fbi.gov/services/cjis/nics/nics-process-for-ffls.

2. Responses from NICS

NICS responses to background checks come in three basic forms: proceed, delay, or deny. The "proceed" response allows for the transfer to be completed. The "delay" response means that the transfer may not legally proceed. If the dealer receives a response of "delay," NICS has three business days to research the applicant further. If the dealer has not received a notice that the transfer is denied after the three business days, then the transfer may proceed. "Deny" means the transfer does not take place; a transferee's options after a "deny" are discussed below. *See* www.fbi.gov/services/cjis/nics/nics-process-for-ffls.

PRACTICAL LEGAL TIP

Thinking about buying a gun on behalf of your buddy? Not a good idea! One of the purposes of ATF Form 4473 is to conduct a background check on individuals who want to purchase firearms in order to make sure they are legally allowed to do so. Acting as a "straw man" by purchasing it for your buddy circumvents this process and is a crime.

3. What transactions require background checks?

A background check is required before each and every sale or other transfer of a firearm from an FFL to a non-licensee, unless an exception is provided under the law. For every transaction that requires a background check, the purchaser/transferee must also complete ATF Form 4473. This includes:

- The sale or trade of a firearm;
- The return of a consigned firearm;
- The redemption of a pawned firearm;
- The loan or rental of a firearm for use off of an FFL's licensed premises; and
- Any other non-exempt transfer of a firearm.

4. What transactions do not require a background check?

A background check is not required under the following circumstances:

- The sale or transfer of a firearm where the transferee presents a valid state permit/license that allows the transferee to carry a firearm (for example, a Louisiana CHP) from the state where the FFL is located and the state permit/license is recognized by the ATF as a qualifying alternative to the background check requirement (*see* 27 C.F.R. § 478.102(d)(1));
- The transfer of a firearm from one FFL to another FFL (*see* 18 U.S.C. § 922(t));
- The return of a repaired firearm to the person from whom it was received (*see* 27 C.F.R. § 478.124(a));
- The sale of a firearm to a law enforcement agency or a law enforcement officer for official duties if the transaction meets the specific requirements of 27 C.F.R. § 478.134 including providing a signed certification from a person in authority on agency letterhead stating that the officer will use the firearm in official duties and where a records check reveals the officer does not have any misdemeanor convictions for domestic violence (*see* 27 C.F.R. § 478.134(a));
- The transfer of a replacement firearm of the same kind and type to the person from whom a firearm was received (*see* 18 U.S.C. § 922(a)(2)(A));
- The transfer of a firearm that is subject to the National Firearms Act if the transfer was pre-approved by the ATF (*see* 27 C.F.R. § 478.102(d)(2)).

5. If a person buys multiple handguns, a dealer must report that person to the ATF

Under federal law, FFLs are required to report to the ATF any sale or transfer of two or more pistols, revolvers, or any combination of pistols and revolvers totaling two or more to an unlicensed (non-FFL) individual that takes place at one time or during any five consecutive business days. This report is made to the ATF on Form 3310.4 and is completed in triplicate with the original copy sent to the ATF, one sent to the designated State police or local law enforcement agency in the jurisdiction where the sale took place, and one retained by the dealer and held for no less than five years. *See* 18 U.S.C. § 923(g)(3).

VI. WHAT IF I'M DENIED THE RIGHT TO PURCHASE A FIREARM?

A. If I am denied the right to purchase, how do I appeal?

Persons who believe they have been erroneously denied or delayed a firearm transfer based on a match to a record returned by the NICS may request an appeal of their "deny" or "delay" decision. All appeal inquiries must be submitted to the NICS Section's Appeal Service Team (AST) in writing, either online or via mail on the FBI's website at www.fbi.gov. An appellant must provide their complete name, complete mailing address, and NICS Transaction Number. For persons appealing a delayed transaction, a fingerprint card is required and must be submitted with the appeal, although the fingerprint card is merely recommended on appeals for denied applications. This may seem counter-intuitive, but it is required per the FBI's website.

B. What if I keep getting erroneously delayed or denied when I am attempting to buy a firearm?

Apply for a Unique Personal Identification Number ("UPIN") that is designed to solve this issue. Some individuals may have a name that is common enough (or happens to be flagged for other reasons) that it causes undue delays or denials in the background check verification process through NICS. For that reason, NICS maintains the Voluntary Appeal File database (VAF), which allows any applicant to apply by submitting an appeal request and then obtain a UPIN. A person who has been cleared through the VAF and receives a UPIN will then be able to use their UPIN when completing Form 4473 in order to help avoid further erroneous denials or extended delays. A person can obtain a UPIN by following the procedures outlined on the FBI's website at www.fbi.gov/services/cjis/nics/national-instant-background-check-system-nics-appeals.

VII. ADDITIONAL CONSIDERATIONS IN FIREARMS PURCHASING AND POSSESSION LAWS

A. How can I legally purchase a firearm from someone in another state?

Any individual who wishes to purchase a firearm from a person that lives in a different state than the purchaser must complete the transaction through an FFL. Sellers or transferors are legally authorized to facilitate a private transaction or transfer by shipping the firearm to the purchaser's FFL in the recipient/buyer's state, where the FFL will complete the transfer process. Without an FFL, it is a federal crime to sell or transfer a firearm between persons who are residents of different states, or where a transfer takes place in a state other than the transferee/transferor's singular state of residence. *See* 18 U.S.C. § 922(a).

B. Can I purchase firearms on the Internet?

Yes. However, all legal requirements for a transfer must be followed. If the buyer and seller are both residents of Louisiana, then the two may lawfully conduct a private sale so long as all other legal issues are satisfied (see our earlier discussion on disqualifications to purchasing and possessing firearms in this chapter). However, if buyer and seller are not residents of the same state, the transaction can only be legally facilitated through the intervention of an FFL.

C. Shipping firearms

1. Can I ship my firearm through the postal service?

Long guns: yes. Handguns: no. However, under federal law, a non-licensed individual may not transfer (and this would include shipping to someone) a firearm to a non-licensed resident (non-FFL) of another state. However, a non-licensed individual may mail a long gun to a resident of his or her own state, and may also mail a long gun to an FFL of another state. To that end, the USPS recommends that long guns be mailed via registered mail and that the packaging used to mail the long gun be ambiguous so as to not identify the contents. Handguns are not allowed to be mailed. *See* 18 U.S.C. §§ 1715, 922(a)(2)(A), (a)(3), and (a)(5). Rather, handguns must be shipped using a common or contract carrier (*e.g.*, UPS or FedEx).

2. Shipping handguns and other firearms through a common or contract carrier

Under federal law, a non-licensed individual may ship a firearm (including a handgun) by a common or contract carrier (*i.e.*, UPS or FedEx) to a resident of his or her own state, or to a licensed individual (FFL) in another state. However, it is illegal to ship any firearm to a non-FFL in another state. It is a requirement that the carrier be notified that the shipment contains a firearm, however, carriers are prohibited from requiring any identifying marks on the package that may be used to identify the contents as containing a firearm. *See* 18 U.S.C. §§ 922(a)(2)(A), (a)(3), (a)(5), and (e), 27 C.F.R. §§ 478.30 and 478.31.

D. Can I ship my firearm to myself for use in another state?

Yes. In accordance with the law as described in the preceding section, a person may ship a firearm to himself or herself in care of another person in another state where he or she intends to hunt or engage in other lawful activity. The package should be addressed to the owner and persons other than the owner should not open the package and take possession of the firearm.

E. If I am moving out of Louisiana, may I have movers move my firearms?

Yes, a person who lawfully possesses firearms may transport or ship the firearms interstate when changing the person's state of residence so long as the person complies with the requirements for shipping and transporting firearms as outlined earlier. *See* 18 U.S.C. § 922(e) and 27 C.F.R. § 478.31. However, certain NFA items such as destructive devices, machine guns, short-barreled shotguns or rifles, and so forth require approval from the ATF before they can be moved interstate. *See* 18 U.S.C. § 922(a)(4) and 27 C.F.R. § 478.28. It is important that the person seeking to move the firearms also check state and local laws where the firearms will be relocated to ensure that the movement of the firearms into the new state does not violate any state law or local ordinance.

F. May I loan my firearm to another person?

There is no prohibition on loaning a firearm to another person, so long as the person receiving the firearm may lawfully possess one. However, under Louisiana law, it is a crime to sell or otherwise deliver for value any firearm to a person under the age of 18 years of age. *See* La. Rev. Stat. Ann. § 14:91. Although this statute does not specifically use the word "loan," the term "deliver" is not defined and, thus, Louisiana firearms owners should be aware of this statute anytime the loan of a firearm to a minor takes place.

G. What happens to my firearms when I die?

Depending on the manner in which a person leaves his or her estate behind, firearms may be bequeathed in a customary manner like other personal property. However, firearms held in an estate are still subject to the laws of transfer and possession. Thus, careful consideration needs to be given in estate planning with respect for firearms laws of both the jurisdiction in which the estate is located, as well as the jurisdiction in which the person to receive the firearms is located.

VIII. AMMUNITION: THE LAW OF PURCHASING AND POSSESSION

A. Who is legally prohibited from purchasing ammunition under federal law?

Under federal law, there are six primary situations where a person is prohibited from buying, selling, or possessing ammunition (beyond armor-piercing ammunition, which was discussed in Chapter 2):

1. Under 18 U.S.C. § 922(b)(1), it is unlawful for a person to sell long gun ammunition to a person under the age of 18;
2. Under 18 U.S.C. § 922(b)(1), it is unlawful for a person to sell handgun ammunition to a person under the age of 21;
3. Under 18 U.S.C. § 922(x)(2)(B), it is unlawful for a juvenile to possess handgun ammunition;
4. Under 18 U.S.C. § 922(d), it is unlawful to sell ammunition to a person who is prohibited from purchasing firearms;
5. Under 18 U.S.C. § 922(g), it is unlawful for a person who is disqualified from purchasing or possessing firearms to possess firearm ammunition if such ammunition has moved in interstate commerce (which is nearly all ammunition); and
6. Under 18 U.S.C. § 922(h), it is unlawful for a person who is employed by a person who is disqualified from purchasing or possessing ammunition to possess or transport ammunition for the disqualified individual.

For the statutes that involve juveniles, there are a couple of notable exceptions to the law: first, the law against selling handgun ammunition to a juvenile and possession of handgun ammunition by a juvenile does not apply to "a temporary transfer of . . . ammunition to a juvenile or to the possession or use of . . . ammunition by a juvenile if the handgun and ammunition are possessed and used by the juvenile—(i) in the course of employment, in the course of ranching or farming related activities at the residence of the juvenile (or on property used for ranching or farming at which the juvenile, with the permission of the property owner or lessee, is performing activities related to the operation of the farm or ranch), target practice, hunting, or a course of instruction in the safe and lawful use of a handgun[.]" The law also does not apply to the temporary transfer to or use of ammunition by a juvenile if the juvenile has been provided "with the prior written consent of the juvenile's parent or guardian who is not prohibited by federal, state, or local law from possessing a firearm." *See* 18 U.S.C. § 922(x)(3).

Second, the law against selling ammunition to juveniles does not apply to juveniles who:

1) are members of the Armed Forces of the United States or the National Guard who possess or are armed with a handgun in the line of duty;
2) receive ammunition by inheritance; or
3) possess ammunition in the course of self-defense or defense of others and are permitted to possess ammunition.

B. When is a person prohibited from purchasing or possessing ammunition under Louisiana law?

Louisiana Revised Statutes Annotated 14:95.1.3(A) makes it a crime:

(1) "To knowingly solicit, persuade, encourage, or entice a licensed dealer or private seller of firearms or ammunition to sell . . . ammunition under circumstances which the person knows would violate the laws of this state or of the United States.
(2) To provide to a licensed dealer or private seller of firearms or ammunition what the person knows to be materially false information with intent to deceive the dealer or seller about the legality of a sale of . . . ammunition."

Aside from fraudulent purchase, there are no other restrictions regarding the purchase or possession of ammunition under Louisiana law, with the exception of armor-piercing handgun ammunition (*see* Chapter 2).

C. Can a person be disqualified from purchasing ammunition if they are disqualified from purchasing firearms?

Yes, under federal law. Under 18 U.S.C. § 922(g) it is unlawful for a person who is disqualified from purchasing or possessing firearms to possess ammunition if the ammunition has moved in interstate commerce. Since nearly all ammunition or ammunition components move through interstate commerce in one form or another, this disqualification includes essentially all ammunition. There is no disqualification under Louisiana law.

D. Can a person purchase ammunition that is labeled "law enforcement use only"?

Yes. Although some handgun ammunition is sold with a label "law enforcement use," such label has no legal meaning and is only reflective of a company policy or marketing strategy.

➤ CHAPTER FOUR ⮜

WHEN CAN I LEGALLY USE MY GUN: PART I
UNDERSTANDING THE LAW OF JUSTIFICATION
Some Basic Legal Concepts

I. IGNORANCE OF THE LAW IS NO EXCUSE!

When is it legal to use a gun as a weapon? The purpose of this chapter is to look at the essential, basic legal concepts of the law of when, and under what circumstances, a person is legally justified in using force or deadly force against other persons or animals. Know when you may legally shoot, because ignorance of the law holds no weight in a courtroom. That is why it is critical you know the law so that you are in the best possible situation to preserve your legal rights if you ever need them.

II. GUN OWNERS NEED TO KNOW SUBPART C OF THE LOUISIANA CRIMINAL CODE

In Louisiana, legal justifications appear in numerous places and areas of the law. Of particular importance to gun owners are the defenses found in Chapter 1, Subpart C of the Louisiana Criminal Code entitled "Culpability," which we cover in detail throughout this book. The full text of relevant provisions of that chapter of the Louisiana Criminal Code are found in the Appendix.

III. TO LEGALLY USE FORCE OR DEADLY FORCE, YOU MUST BE "JUSTIFIED." WHAT IS LEGAL JUSTIFICATION?

A. Basic definition of justification: an acceptable excuse

So, when is it legal to use force or deadly force against another person? When is it legal to even threaten to use force or deadly force against another? The answer is when there is a legal "justification," or defense. A legal justification is an acceptable reason or excuse under the law for taking an action that would otherwise be a crime.

EXAMPLE:

Rick is in his suburban back yard with his faithful dog, when out of nowhere, a coyote appears and is about to attack. Rick draws his handgun and shoots the coyote.

Rick has discharged his firearm in the city limits, which is ordinarily a crime. But Rick may not be guilty of the crime of "illegal discharge of a weapon" if he was legally justified in shooting the coyote. That is, the law will likely say the excuse for discharging the firearm in the city limits—protecting himself and his dog from a coyote—makes Rick's action of discharging a firearm in the city limits reasonable and, therefore, legally justified.

PRACTICAL LEGAL TIP

A defense to prosecution is not the same as a bar to prosecution. A "bar to prosecution" is where a person can't be prosecuted for engaging in certain conduct, whereas a "defense to prosecution" allows prosecution for the conduct, but offers defendants a justification that must be demonstrated with evidence in court.

B. Basic requirement: you must admit your action

If a person wants the potential protection of legal justification in Louisiana, in order to raise the defense of justification in court, a person is required to admit all of the elements of the crime for which they are charged. Then, the person must present "some evidence" of justification before a jury will be given an instruction that "a person is legally justified to use force if…" In plain English, a person will not be allowed to say "I didn't do it, but if I did do it, I was justified." You must admit the underlying elements of the charge.

EXAMPLE:

Jane is walking home one night, when a man jumps out of the bushes and demands her purse. Jane pulls out her handgun and points it at the man, who then runs away. Unfortunately, Jane does not call the police, but the criminal immediately does, reporting a crazy woman threatening him with a gun. Jane ends up charged with aggravated assault, even though Jane was the victim.

Because justification is a legal defense in Louisiana, if Jane's case goes all the way to trial, in order to offer a legal justification for committing "aggravated assault," she must admit in court that she did pull her handgun and point it at the would-be robber. Then, in order for the jury to consider a legal justification defense (*i.e.*, receive a jury instruction from the judge), she must offer some evidence of why she is legally justified under the law for having pulled her weapon (in this example, Jane believed she was being robbed). The result is that Jane is entitled to have the judge instruct the jury that they may find Jane not guilty because she was justified in her action. The jury will then decide whether they believe Jane and whether she is guilty or not guilty of the crime of aggravated assault.

On the other hand, if Jane does not admit to the elements of the criminal offense she is charged with, she will not be allowed to offer a legal justification defense under Subpart C of the Louisiana Criminal Code. Legal justification is, therefore, literally the law of "Yes, I did it, BUT…"

PRACTICAL LEGAL TIP

A jury instruction is a statement made by the judge to the jury informing them of the law applicable to the case in general, or some aspect of it.

IV. CATEGORIES OF FORCE FOR JUSTIFICATION UNDER SUBPART C

Anytime a person takes a physical action against another person, they have used force. Subpart C of the Louisiana Criminal Code divides uses of force into different levels. Whether or not a use of force was justified under the law often depends on how that force is categorized. These categories, which we will address throughout this book, are: 1) force and 2) deadly force.

A. What if a person uses greater force than the law allows?

The use of a legally appropriate level of force is important because if a person uses more force than is "reasonable and apparently necessary" (*see* La. Rev. Stat. Ann. § 14:19), that person may not be legally justified in using that level of force. Therefore, it is important to understand the differences in the levels of force and the circumstances under which the law allows the use of each.

For example, if a person uses deadly force, and the law allows only for the use of force, that person will not be legally justified. Likewise, if a person uses force when no force is legally allowed, that use of force will not be legally justified.

EXAMPLE:

Harry Homeowner looks out his window and sees a person standing on his front lawn. Harry yells at the fellow to get off his land. The fellow on the lawn does not respond. Harry rushes out to confront the fellow and demands that he leave Harry's lawn.

This fellow is now clearly a trespasser. What degree of force may Harry use to remove the trespasser? The law, as discussed later, will show that Harry is only allowed to use force in response to a mere trespasser. If Harry uses deadly force against the trespasser, he will not be legally justified and would be guilty of using unlawful force against the trespasser. Ultimately, using the correct degree of force is critical in determining whether a person has committed a crime or a legally justified action.

B. What is the legal definition of "force?"

Surprisingly, neither "force" nor "deadly force" is defined in the Louisiana Criminal Code. However, under federal law "deadly force" is defined as "force which a reasonable person would consider likely to cause death or serious bodily harm." *See* 10 C.F.R. § 1047.7.

EXAMPLE:

Timmy is being harassed and insulted by a bully, when the bully suddenly clenches his first and takes a swing at Timmy, but misses. Timmy reacts to the swing by punching the bully in the face.

The bully's action was a use of force. Even though he missed Timmy, the bully placed Timmy in fear of harm. Timmy's action of striking the bully was likewise a use of force, and as will be discussed later, legally justified because Timmy engaged in conduct which caused harm or a fear of harm to the bully.

C. Deadly force

1. Deadly force does not have to cause death

Deadly force is defined under federal law as "force which a reasonable person would consider likely to cause death or serious bodily harm." *See* 10 C.F.R. § 1047.7. On the surface, the legal definition of deadly force seems simple. However, the meaning of what is and is not deadly force can be legally tricky. A particular action does not necessarily have to result in death to be legally defined as deadly force—it just needs to be capable of causing death or serious bodily injury. Note: serious bodily injury is defined as "bodily injury which involves unconsciousness, extreme physical pain or protracted and obvious disfigurement, or protracted loss or impairment of the function of a bodily member, organ, or mental faculty, or a substantial risk of death." *See* La. Rev. Stat. Ann. § 14:102.12.

EXAMPLE:

Jim is being robbed and beaten by a group of individuals when he manages to draw his handgun and fire it at one of the most aggressive assailants. His shot misses his intended target, but breaks the group up, causing the would-be robbers to flee.

In our example, even though the bullet did not kill or even strike any of his assailants, Jim legally used deadly force because his conduct fit the legal definition of "capable of causing death or serious bodily injury." Thus, death is not a prerequisite for the existence of deadly force. Likewise, almost any object can be used as a weapon in a particular circumstance. Therefore, in this section of the law, the focus is on the object's intended use and not just on the object itself.

2. "Reasonable belief" requirement for deadly force

Deadly force can be used when one has a "reasonable belief" that it is necessary. A prosecutor must prove beyond a reasonable doubt that a person possessed a particular mental state applicable to a crime in order to meet the state's burden of proof and convict someone of a crime.

D. Warning shots

Warning shots are commonly portrayed in movies and television as a good idea. Leaving aside completely all practical issues of whether under a particular set of circumstances a warning shot is a good idea (and experience has taught us that very rarely are they a good idea), what does Louisiana law say about warning shots?

1. Are warning shots a use of deadly force?

First, the term "warning shot" does not appear in the Louisiana Criminal Code. Without clear guidance from statutory law, courts are left to determine if the action of firing a warning shot is to be considered under either the use of force standard or the use of deadly force standard.

Although the firing of a warning shot is not per se legally forbidden, you should be aware that if you fire a warning shot, it is highly likely that your conduct will be judged under the legal standard that you have used deadly force and not just mere force. This means that a person may only be allowed the legal argument of justification if a warning shot is fired in situations in which deadly force is justified under the law. Every gun owner should be aware that one likely argument a prosecutor may put forth against a defendant at trial is that the simple discharge of a firearm is an action that is capable of causing death or serious bodily injury. Such an argument, if successful, will shift the analysis of warning shots into the use of deadly force arena of whether a person intended that action or not.

Why is it important whether the law classifies a warning shot as a use of force or a use of deadly force, even if no one is injured? Let's take a look at an example:

EXAMPLE:

Harry Homeowner looks outside during broad daylight and sees a trespasser on his property. Not knowing what the trespasser is doing, Harry grabs his firearm to investigate. Harry confronts the trespasser and demands that he leave the property, but the trespasser ignores Harry. Being both scared and agitated, Harry fires a "warning shot" to get the trespasser's attention and compliance.

Does Harry's discharging his gun fit the definition of the use of deadly force? Likely, yes. Harry very likely may be guilty of a crime and not have a justification available as a defense, because he used a higher degree of force than the law allows.

V. WHAT DOES IT MEAN TO "REASONABLY" BELIEVE THAT THE USE OF FORCE OR VIOLENCE IS NECESSARY?

Under Louisiana law, the legal standard for a justified use of force is generally requires that a person must "reasonably" believe that the use of force is "necessary" to protect against the unlawful use of force. *See* generally La. Rev. Stat. Ann. §§ 14:18 and 14:19.

But, what does "reasonable" mean? Further, when is something necessary—and who decides whether it is or not? The answers to these questions are how the legal process decides guilt or justification. For all gun owners, these concepts are critical.

A. How does the law determine "reasonable?"

In determining what is reasonable, the law often uses what is known as the "reasonable person" standard to evaluate a person's conduct. It uses a hypothetical "reasonable person." Who is a reasonable person, and how does he or she act? Ultimately, a reasonable person is whatever a jury says it is.

The legal analysis behind the reasonable person goes like this: if a person used force or even deadly force, they must act like a reasonable person would have acted under the same or similar circumstances in order to be legally justified. However, if a person fails to act like a reasonable person, their conduct will fall below the acceptable legal standard and will not be justified. The reasonable person standard is the law's attempt to make the concept of reasonableness an objective and measurable test.

Under this standard, the law does not focus on whether you subjectively (or personally) believed force was reasonable, but whether a "reasonable person" would have considered it reasonable: an objective standard. If the legal system (and ultimately, again, this could be a jury) determines that a reasonable person would have believed that force was immediately necessary in response to another person unlawfully using force against you, then you will be found legally justified in using force.

Keep in mind, however, that judges, juries, and prosecutors are simply human beings, and people can have vastly different ideas of how a reasonable person should act under any given circumstances. This is particularly true if asked to decide whether force or deadly force was necessary or not.

B. What does "necessary" mean under the law?

When does someone have a reasonable belief that force is necessary? In Louisiana, it ultimately may be a jury that is tasked with determining whether someone had a reasonable belief that an action was necessary. The specific facts of each case will determine what is "reasonable" force. "Apparent," rather than actual necessity, is the test. La. Rev. Stat. Ann.§ 14:19.

Courts have held that "factors to consider in determining whether a [person] had a reasonable belief that [a] killing was necessary are the excitement and confusion of the situation, the possibility of using force or violence short of killing, and the [person]'s knowledge of the assailant's bad character." *State v. Mincey*, 2008-1315 (La. App. 3 Cir. 6/3/09).

EXAMPLE:

Where neither Harry Homeowner nor his family is present in their home when an intruder enters, the use of deadly force against the intruder is unreasonable and unnecessary. Should Harry employ a mechanical device or "trap" to use force against the intruder, his actions will not be justified because the elements of justifiable homicide cannot be satisfied as there will be no evidence that the action was "necessary." *See State v. Britt*, 510 So. 2d 670 (La. Ct. App. 1987).

EXAMPLE:

If Harry Homeowner was punched by his victim after the two had argued, it would be unreasonable for Harry to believe deadly force was necessary to protect himself from a punch. *See State v. Dozier*, 553 So. 2d 911 (La. Ct. App. 1989).

C. Legal presumptions: stop legal second-guessing

Under certain circumstances, a person's belief in the necessity of force or deadly force will be presumed "reasonable" under Louisiana law. This legal presumption can be a very powerful legal tool to stop legal second-guessing or "Monday morning quarterbacking" of the amount or time of the force used. A jury will be told that if a given set of circumstances exists (*e.g.*, if the intruder was in the process of forcibly entering one's dwelling and that person knew or had reason to believe that a forcible entry was occurring or had occurred), the law will presume "reasonable" a person's belief in the necessity of using force or deadly force, and that use of force or deadly force would, therefore, be legally justified.

PRACTICAL LEGAL TIP

Note: a presumption is not an absolute ticket to victory. A prosecutor may attempt to overcome the presumption with other evidence that shows you did not act in self-defense.

EXAMPLE:

Harry Homeowner is asleep in his house when he hears a noise in his kitchen. Harry enters his kitchen with his .45 drawn and confronts an armed burglar. Harry fires his weapon.

In this situation, was Harry's use of deadly force in firing his gun necessary, or, more precisely, was Harry's belief that deadly force was necessary reasonable? Did Harry, legally, have to take additional actions before firing in order to have acted reasonably? In Harry's current situation, the law will give Harry a powerful legal presumption that his belief that the use of deadly force was apparently necessary and "reasonable." In Harry's example, La. Rev. Stat. Ann. § 14:20 of the Louisiana Criminal Code will provide him with this presumption of "reasonableness" (as a victim of a home invasion in his occupied habitation). This presumption will prevent second-guessing by prosecutors that deadly force was not necessary. This has a practical effect of preventing arguments like a person should have used less force, no force, or retreated first. The legal presumption of reasonableness is a powerful tool for anyone facing a criminal charge and claiming legal justification.

Louisiana courts have warned against this presumption, however, stating that the statutory presumption is not mandatory. The statute does not state that the presumption is irrebuttable, nor does it create a license to kill. *See State v. Ingram*, 45546 (La. App. 2 Cir. 6/2/11); 71 So.3d 437.

D. No presumption of reasonableness: prosecutors are allowed to second-guess

As we discussed above, under certain circumstances, the law will presume the reasonableness of a person's belief that force or deadly force is apparently necessary. However, if a person uses force or deadly force under circumstances that do not qualify for this presumption, the issue of whether a belief of the apparent necessity to use force or deadly force was or was not reasonable is left to the jury, and prosecutors are allowed to second-guess the reasonableness of the timing and/or degree of force used by a defendant.

Accordingly, when a defendant does not qualify for a legal presumption, a prosecutor has the opportunity to argue that a person's use of force or deadly force was not apparently necessary. This allows for arguments in court like "should have retreated," "should have used lesser force," and so forth. In many circumstances, no legal presumption of reasonable belief is afforded for uses of force or deadly force at all. In those cases, a jury will decide the issue of the reasonableness of a person's belief and, ultimately, whether or not a person is guilty of a crime.

VI. THE BURDEN OF PROOF IN CRIMINAL CASES

In criminal cases, the state attorneys or prosecutors have the burden of proof. This means that it is the State's responsibility to present enough evidence to prove the defendant committed a crime. This burden of proof that the prosecutor bears is a standard called "beyond a reasonable doubt." It is the highest level of proof used in the American justice system. The state's job at trial in attempting to prove the defendant's guilt includes eliminating any reasonable doubt that the defendant's conduct was justified.

We are now ready to look at under what circumstances Louisiana law allows a person to use deadly force to protect themselves and others in the next chapter.

PRACTICAL LEGAL TIP

A word about juries. Juries are not "picked" in Louisiana. Rather, they are the first twelve people that are not "struck" from the pool of folks called a jury pool. Most of the time, in my opinion, juries get it "right," but after years of practice, some juries' decisions leave you scratching your head… That is why these legal presumptions can be critical.

➢ CHAPTER FIVE ➣

WHEN CAN I LEGALLY USE MY GUN: PART II

SELF-DEFENSE AND DEFENSE OF OTHERS

Understanding When Force And Deadly Force Can Be Legally Used Against Another Person

I. INTRODUCTION AND OVERVIEW

The question of "when can a person legally use deadly force against another person" is of critical importance if you are a legal Louisiana firearms owner. Although a firearm is nothing more than a tool, it is a tool that by its very nature has the ability to deliver deadly force. Thus, all responsible firearms owners should understand when they are justified in using force and deadly force under the law. Failure to understand the law gets lots of good folks in serious trouble!

The primary Louisiana statutes dealing with self-defense and defense of other people are contained in three Louisiana Criminal Code Sections in Title 14 of the Louisiana Revised Statutes:

14:19 Use of Force or Violence in Defense
14:20 Justifiable Homicide
14:22 Defense of Others

The law of justified self-defense is split between justification for the use of force in Section 19 and justification for the use of deadly force in Section 20. Each of these sections also contain legal presumptions of reasonableness that are available under certain circumstances and are extremely powerful when deciding if a use of force or deadly force was legally justified. Likewise, the language of both sections contains Louisiana's versions of the "Castle Doctrine" and "Stand Your Ground" laws, even though those specific terms are not mentioned in the statutes. Section 22 combines force and deadly force in providing justification for "Defense of Others."

In the previous chapter, several legal concepts, such as reasonableness, apparent necessity, and the categorization of force and deadly force were discussed. Those concepts have practical applications in this chapter. In this chapter, we will expand upon those topics to include when a person may be justified in using force or deadly force in self-defense, as well as those circumstances when the law specifically prohibits the use of force or deadly force.

II. DEFENDING PEOPLE WITH FORCE OR DEADLY FORCE

A. General self-defense justification: no presumption of reasonableness

The primary self-defense statutes in Louisiana are Sections 19 and

20 of Title 14 of the Louisiana Criminal Code. Section 19 lays out the legal requirements for the justified use of force, but not deadly force, for self-defense. This section establishes that a person is legally justified in using force against another when committed to prevent a forcible offense against the person or trespass against property in a person's lawful possession, "provided that the force or violence used [is] reasonable and apparently necessary to prevent such offense." La. Rev. Stat. Ann. § 14:19(A)(1)(a).

Likewise, Section 20 establishes the general standard for the justified use of deadly force. A person is legally justified in using deadly force for self-defense when he "reasonably believes that he is in imminent danger of losing his life or receiving great bodily harm and that the [deadly force] is necessary to save himself from that danger." La. Rev. Stat. Ann. § 14:20(A)(1). As discussed in the previous chapter, what a person believes is necessary and whether that belief is reasonable is the difference between justification (not guilty) and conviction (guilty).

Who decides whether an actor's belief is or is not reasonable that force or deadly force is necessary? Who decides if the degree of force used by someone was reasonable under a particular set of circumstances? The answer to both of these questions is the jury.

Therefore, if a person finds himself or herself facing a criminal charge and is claiming self-defense under the general self-defense provisions of Sections 19 and 20, the jury will decide if that person's belief was or was not reasonable regarding the necessity of the use of force or deadly force by that person. As can be imagined, this leaves a lot of room for juries to interpret what actions are reasonable or not. It also leaves the door open for legal second-guessing by prosecutors as to when and how much force was used, including arguments that there was no imminent threat and as such, the force or deadly force was not really necessary. If the prosecutor convinces a jury that a person used force or deadly force when or to a degree that was not "reasonably" believed to be necessary, a person's use of force or deadly force will not be legally justified, and that person will be guilty of using unlawful force or deadly force. However, under certain circumstances, Sections 19 and 20 allow persons a powerful additional protection in the form of a legal presumption of reasonableness in their belief that the use of force or deadly force was immediately necessary. *See* La. Rev. Stat. Ann. §§ 14:19 and 14:20.

PRACTICAL LEGAL TIP

In law school, they taught us that "reasonable minds can differ." Yet, reasonableness is a standard that we are held to whenever we face a legal issue. Thankfully, Louisiana provides us with presumptions of reasonableness so that even when reasonable minds do differ, you know where you stand with the law.

B. Presumption of reasonableness under Sections 19 and 20

Sections 19 and 20 contain several circumstances when the law gives far more protection than is available under the general self-defense standard. Under these statutes, a person's belief that it was necessary to use force or deadly force will be legally presumed reasonable. This legal presumption, if available to an accused, is a potentially powerful legal argument and limits prosecutors in court from second-guessing either when or the amount of force used by the accused in defending himself or herself (*e.g.*, should have used non-deadly force, dispute resolution methods, or should have retreated, and so forth). These legal presumptions take the form of the "Castle Doctrine" law (discussed in detail in Section C, below). If a defendant meets the conditions enabling him or her to be afforded the protection of this presumption, the law will deem "reasonable" a belief that the force that was used was necessary, limiting any argument that the force used by the accused was unreasonable. *See* La. Rev. Stat. Ann. §§ 14:19 and 14:20.

PRACTICAL LEGAL TIP

My experience in over 20 years as a trial lawyer is that many people serving on juries tend to ignore the rule of "innocent until proven guilty." Even though every person has a Constitutional right to not testify against themselves, by not doing so, it can cloud a juror's mind so as to make the notion of innocent until proven guilty be viewed with skepticism. -Edwin

C. The "Castle Doctrine" and "Stand Your Ground" laws

1. The "Castle Doctrine"

The term "Castle Doctrine" does not appear in Louisiana statutory law, however, the legal concept comes from the philosophy that every person is a king or queen of his or her "castle." As such, no king or queen is required to retreat before using force or deadly force against an intruder in their castle. In Louisiana, the "Castle Doctrine" type laws are implemented under Sections 19 and 20 of the Criminal Code and take the form of powerful presumptions of reasonableness. Louisiana "Castle Doctrine" laws extend to a person's occupied dwelling, motor vehicle, or place of business. *See* La. Rev. Stat. Ann. §§ 14:19 and 14:20.

As we discussed earlier, the general rule is that a person is legally justified in using force or deadly force:

> "When he reasonably believes that he is in imminent danger of losing his life or receiving great bodily harm and that the killing is necessary to save himself from that danger" (La. Rev. Stat. § 14:20(A)(1)); or
>
> "When committed for the purpose of preventing a forcible offense against the person . . . or trespass against property in a person's lawful possession, provided that the force or violence used must be reasonable and apparently necessary to prevent such offense." (La. Rev. Stat. Ann. § 14:19(A)(1)(a)).

If you are a victim of unlawful force or deadly force when you are in your occupied dwelling, motor vehicle, or place of business, the law will provide you protection beyond the general rule. In these "Castle Doctrine" circumstances, the law will presume "reasonable" a person's belief that force or deadly force was necessary. This presumption applies to you when:

(a) A person against whom force or violence was used was in the process of entering or had entered unlawfully and forcibly entered the dwelling, place of business, or motor vehicle; or

(b) The person who used force or violence knew or had reason to believe that an unlawful and forcible entry was occurring or had occurred.

See La. Rev. Stat. Ann. §§ 14:20(B)(1) and (2).

Section (a) covers the actions of the person unlawfully and forcibly entering one's "castle" and section (b) covers the reasonable belief of the person who used the force to protect his or her "castle." *See* La. Rev. Stat. Ann. §§ 14:20(B)(1) and (2). The "Castle Doctrine" presumption of "reasonableness" is a powerful legal tool for any person who is accused of a crime and claiming justification. The presumption will be further enhanced by having no duty to retreat (*see* No Duty to Retreat later in this chapter) and will prevent prosecutors in court from second-guessing when or the amount of force that was used. These presumptions are available only for occupied dwellings, motor vehicles, or places of business.

2. What is a dwelling under the "Castle Doctrine?"

Louisiana law, in defining "Castle Doctrine" rights, does not use the term home, house, or property; it uses the term "dwelling." The presumptions under Sections 19 and 20 are specific, limited, and do not cover an entire piece of real property—just a dwelling. The term "dwelling" is defined by Louisiana Revised Statute § 14:62.2 as a:

> "dwelling, house, apartment, or other structure used in whole or in part as a home or place of abode[.]"

This means, generally speaking, that structures which are detached from the building where you sleep at night are not considered to be your dwelling. However, recent Louisiana case law has expanded this definition to include garages and carports. The Louisiana Court of Appeals found that a garage, utility shed, and carport are part of an inhabited dwelling. Thus, if a structure is used as a home, a person may not enter any part of that structure, including a garage, utility shed, or carport, without authorization. *State v. Mitchell*, 50188, (La. App. 2 Cir. 11/18/15); 181 So. 3d 800.

3. What is a motor vehicle under the "Castle Doctrine?"

Louisiana "Castle Doctrine" legal presumptions and protections are applicable to occupied motor vehicles. If a person is attempting to "car-jack" you, which is to unlawfully, and with force, enter your vehicle while you are in it, or unlawfully, and with force, remove you from your vehicle, you will fall under the "Castle Doctrine." What does Louisiana define as a motor vehicle? Under Louisiana Revised Statute § 32.1(40), a "motor vehicle" is defined as:

> "every vehicle which is self-propelled, and every vehicle which is propelled by electric power obtained from overhead trolley wires, but not operated upon rails," and "a 'low-speed vehicle' which is a four-wheeled, electric-powered vehicle with a maximum speed of [20-25 miles per hour] and is equipped with the minimum motor vehicle equipment appropriate for vehicle safety[.]"

This is a very broad definition and appears to include anything that carries people or property from one place to another, including cars, trucks, boats, airplanes, golf carts, and so forth, but excludes motorized bicycles.

4. In Louisiana, "Stand Your Ground" means no duty to retreat!

"Stand Your Ground" is a common term for laws that provide that a person has no legal duty to retreat before using force or deadly force against a person that is a threat. The words "stand his or her ground" are actually used in the Louisiana Criminal Code. Louisiana Criminal Code § 20 provides that a "person who is not engaged in unlawful activity and who is in a place where he or she has a right to be shall have no duty to retreat before using deadly force . . . and may stand his or her ground and meet force with force." La. Rev. Stat. Ann. § 14:20(C). The provisions establishing no duty to retreat are located in the self-defense statutes of Sections 19(C) and (D) and Sections 20(C) and (D) of Subpart C of the Louisiana Criminal Code. These provisions will act to limit a prosecutor from arguing in court that a person's use of force or deadly force was not really "necessary" because the person could have or should have first retreated.

In order to receive the "No Duty to Retreat" protection under these statutes, first, a person must satisfy all the conditions in the Criminal Code (*see* La. Rev. Stat. Ann. §§ 14:19 and 14:20):

(1) he or she must have a legal right to be at the location where force or deadly force is used; and

(2) he or she cannot be engaged in criminal activity at the time force or deadly force was used.

PRACTICAL LEGAL TIP

Numerous jurisdictions like Louisiana have "No Duty to Retreat" laws that do not require fleeing before the legal use of deadly force. However, several states impose a duty on a person to retreat if reasonably available as a prerequisite to using deadly force. So when traveling, make sure you know the law of the state you are visiting.

Both of these conditions must be satisfied in order for the "No Duty to Retreat" provisions to apply. Further, if a person does not qualify for "No Duty to Retreat" provisions, it does not mean that the person's use of force or deadly force was not legally justified. It simply means that a jury will evaluate whether the person's belief was "reasonable" that the use of force or deadly force was necessary. If a person cannot satisfy both requirements, the prosecutor will be free to argue that because the accused could have but did not retreat, the accused's belief that the use of force or deadly force was necessary was not reasonable.

EXAMPLE:

One day, looking for a shortcut through the neighborhood, Tom hops a fence (a trespass) and is walking across open property to reach the street on the other side of the property. Tom is confronted by the property owner and tries to explain that he meant no harm and was just taking a shortcut. However, the property owner becomes irate and cocks his gun, aims it at Tom, and says "I'm going to kill you!"

Under this example, Tom is a trespasser, and since this is considered being "engaged in unlawful activity" under the statute, Tom is disqualified for any legal presumptions under Sections 19 and 20 of Subpart C of the Louisiana Criminal Code (see discussion later in this chapter regarding not being engaged in criminal activity). As such, any presumption of reasonableness to a belief in the necessity of force or deadly force will not be given to Tom, even though the property owner made his intention to kill Tom very clear. Further, because he is a trespasser and has no legal right to be at his location, Tom will not be entitled to the "No Duty to Retreat" protections of the law. Thus, a prosecutor could argue that before the use of force or deadly force by Tom was necessary, Tom should have retreated. It does not mean Tom may not be ultimately legally justified in defending himself, it just makes it more difficult to convince a jury of his justification.

Now let us take the example one step further:

EXAMPLE:

Tom is scared out of his mind as he looks down the barrel of the property owner's shotgun. The two are about 20 feet apart. Tom, hearing the property owner's threat to kill him, draws his own firearm and fires two shots, killing the property owner.

In this example, because Tom is not eligible for the presumptions under Sections 19 and 20 of Subpart C of the Louisiana Criminal Code, a prosecutor would be allowed to question and second-guess when and the degree of deadly force that was used. The prosecutor may argue that Tom did not really need to use deadly force because a "reasonable" person would have retreated under the circumstances. Tom does not lose his legal right to self-defense under this example, just the presumptions of reasonableness, and the protection that the "No Duty to Retreat" provisions offer.

D. A person who provokes an attack is not entitled to a presumption of reasonableness

According to Section 21 of Subpart C of the Louisiana Criminal Code, "[a] person who is the aggressor or who brings on a difficulty cannot claim the right of self-defense unless he withdraws from the conflict in good faith and in such a manner that [the other person] knows or should know that he desires to withdraw and discontinue the conflict." La. Rev. Stat. Ann. § 14:21.

E. Is a person legally entitled to a presumption of reasonableness if they were involved in criminal activity?

Under Louisiana law, there is a requirement that one not be engaged in unlawful activity in order to use force or deadly force against another. Louisiana Revised Statute § 14:20(A)(4)(b) creates a "drug activity exception." Thus, in Louisiana, a drug dealer who commits a homicide can still claim self-defense if he believes his life is in danger, but he is not entitled to the lessened "shoot-the-burglar" standard set out in La. Rev. Stat. Ann. § 14:20(A)(4)(a). *See State v. Revish*, 2015-0470 (La. App. 1 Cir. 11/09/15); 185 So. 3d 8.

F. When is the use of deadly force explicitly not legally justified under Louisiana Criminal Code §§ 19 and 20?

Louisiana statutory law does not lay out specific circumstances under which deadly force cannot be used (other than when one is himself the aggressor), but case law sheds some light on the type of situations wherein deadly force will not be justified:

EXAMPLE:

Harry Homeowner hears the doorbell ring around 8:15 pm. It is dark, so he doesn't want to answer the door. The callers, looking for a Halloween party down the street, leave, realizing they have the wrong house. Harry Homeowner opens the carport door with his firearm in hand. One of the callers, unmasked, raises his hands and exclaims that he was looking for the Halloween party. Although he sees the caller has no firearm, knife, or other weapon, Harry Homeowner shoots the caller once in the chest, killing him. *Hattori v. Peairs*, 95-0144 (La. App. 1 Cir. 10/6/95); 662 So. 2d 509.

Harry's actions are not justified. He did not have a reasonable belief that the caller who inadvertently trespassed on his property posed an imminent danger to his life or posed a threat of great bodily harm such that deadly force was necessary to save himself and his family.

G. When is force not legally justified under Louisiana law?

1. Resisting an officer

RESISTING AN OFFICER: LOUISIANA CRIMINAL CODE § 108

Resisting an officer is the intentional interference with, opposition or resistance to, or obstruction of an individual acting in his official capacity and authorized by law to make a lawful arrest, lawful detention, or seizure of property or to serve any lawful process or court order when the offender knows or has reason to know that the person arresting, detaining, seizing property, or serving process is acting in his official capacity.

Louisiana case law provides that a person does have the right to resist an unlawful arrest, detention, or deprivation of his or her liberty. *State v. Manuel*, 2006-0486 (La. App. 4 Cir. 11/21/06); 946 So. 2d 245. Note that even though an arrest or detention may feel "unlawful" in the moment, a prosecutor, judge, or jury may disagree. If you use force to resist what you believe to be an unlawful arrest, the cards may be stacked against you. Instead, this is a fight best left to your attorney in a courtroom.

2. Provocation/abandoning an encounter

What does it mean to provoke an attack so as to lose your right to self-defense presumptions? According to Louisiana case law, in order for an aggressor to claim a homicide was justified, he must withdraw from the conflict in such a way that the other person knows or should know of his desire to withdraw. If his withdrawal is not made sufficiently known to the other person, he is not eligible to claim self-defense for the homicide. *State v. Edwards*, 49635, (La. App. 2 Cir. 02/26/15); 162 So. 3d 512. Thus, if an aggressor loses his eligibility to claim the justification of self-defense, he certainly loses the presumption of reasonableness.

What if a person who started a fight soon realizes they bit off more than they can chew? Under the law, that person can abandon or clearly communicate his or her desire to abandon the encounter.

ABANDONMENT OF PROVOCATION MAY ALLOW JUSTIFICATION: LOUISIANA CASE LAW

"[A] person who has brought on the difficulty not only must withdraw from the conflict but the withdrawal must be in such a way that the other person 'knows or should know' of the desire to withdraw. If the aggressor's withdrawal is not made sufficiently known to his adversary, he is not eligible to claim the justification of self-defense for the homicide." *State v. Bowens*, 2014-0416 (La. App. 4 Cir. 12/10/14); 156 So. 3d 770, 775.

If, after a person abandons or attempts to abandon the encounter, the person who was provoked pursues and uses unlawful force against the provocateur, the provocateur may then be legally justified to fight back.

EXAMPLE:

Dave is at a bar when he notices another man checking-out his girlfriend. Dave tells the other man, "take a hike or you'll regret it" and slightly shoves the admirer. The other man responds by punching Dave in the face. Dave, who didn't really want a confrontation, holds both his hands up in surrender and says, "I don't want any more trouble!" However, the other man pulls out a knife and lunges at Dave.

In this scenario, Dave is legally justified to fight back: he attempted to abandon the incident and made his intention known to the other person. When the other man continued to attack, Dave is now legally justified to defend himself, even though he made the initial provocation.

III. DO I HAVE A LEGAL RESPONSIBILITY TO DEFEND ANOTHER PERSON?

Under Louisiana law, the average person has no duty to come to the defense of another, so long as that actor was not the cause of the situation or occurrence. This is true even if a crime is in progress (but note: this lack of a legal duty does not include police officers and other professionals that may have affirmative legal duties to assist). If you see a third person that is the victim of what you believe to be the unlawful use of force or deadly force, you have no legal duty to aid that person—it is your decision. This is equally true if you are legally carrying a gun pursuant to a CHP. But, what if you decide to help the third person?

A. When does Louisiana law allow for the justifiable use of force or deadly force to protect someone else?

In the last sections, we addressed the law of legal justification for the use of force or deadly force for self-defense. We now turn to when the law allows the justified use of force or deadly force to protect another person or persons.

JUSTIFIED USE OF DEADLY FORCE TO PROTECT ANOTHER PERSON: LA. REV. STAT. ANN. § 14:22
It is justifiable to use force or violence or to kill in the defense of another person when it is reasonably apparent that the person attacked could have justifiably used such means himself, and when it is reasonably believed that such intervention is necessary to protect the other person.

In general, if you place yourself in the "shoes" of the third person, and the law would allow the third person to use force or deadly force to protect themselves, then you are legally justified to use the same level of force to protect a third person. Louisiana Criminal Code § 22 allows a person to protect a third person from the unlawful use of force or deadly force by another in the same circumstances in which a person could justifiably use force under Section 19 or deadly force under Section 20 to protect themselves, so long as the person reasonably believes that the intervention is "necessary." By referencing back to the self-defense statutes in Sections 19 and 20, the law makes the legal analysis for defending third persons the same as for self-defense.

Therefore, the same legal justifications and presumptions of "reasonableness" for self-defense are also available for the defense of third persons. If a person decides to aid a third person, the law of justifiable use of force will allow a person to defend a third person to the extent they may defend themselves. As long as the person defending another reasonably believes that the third person would be justified in using force or deadly force to protect him or herself, the person defending may step in and use force or deadly force on that person's behalf. However, please note that the law still imposes a requirement that a person's belief in the necessity of the use of force or deadly force be reasonable. If a person decides to defend a third person, prudence dictates that the person defending must be sure they know what is truly happening in a situation before using force or deadly force. If a belief in the necessity of the use of force or deadly force turns out to be unreasonable, the use of force or deadly force will not be legally justified, no matter how well-intentioned a person may be.

B. What if the situation is not as I thought it appeared to be?

A third person and a "Good Samaritan" may not potentially see things as they really are. When a person elects to use force or deadly force to defend a third person, it can all go terribly wrong.

EXAMPLE:

Peter, a licensed concealed handgun owner, decides to get some lunch, so he pulls into a local burger joint to eat. He parks and exits his vehicle whereupon he witnesses a man walking out of the restaurant and across the parking lot. Suddenly, another man comes running up and points a gun in the first man's face. Peter, not wanting to become a victim of a robbery, drops to one knee while drawing his handgun. Still seeing the gun pointed at the first man, Peter decides to protect the would-be victim of robbery and fires his gun striking the robber.

If there was in fact an armed robbery taking place, Peter's use of deadly force is likely legally justified, because if we put Peter in the shoes of the third person (the first man in the example), Peter would be legally justified in using deadly force to stop the aggravated robbery. Thus, the law will deem Peter's belief that the use of deadly force was immediately necessary as reasonable. But, what if there was no armed robbery?

In fact, what would happen if in the instant after Peter fires his gun, the man Peter sought to protect immediately turns to help the wounded suspected robber yelling "murderer!" at Peter while screaming in fear and grief, "why did you shoot my friend?" It turns out that it was not a robbery, just a couple of fellows pranking each other, and the gun Peter saw was a toy. How does the law deal with this scenario?

In such a situation, Peter's perspective and knowledge of the situation are very different from the person he sought to defend. The man clearly knew there was no robbery in progress since he recognized his friend, and that it was a prank. In this situation, if Peter's belief that an aggravated robbery was in progress was reasonable, then Peter will be legally justified. However, if a jury finds that his belief was unreasonable, Peter will not be legally justified and likely guilty of aggravated assault.

C. Do I have a duty to report a crime?

Under Louisiana law, there is no requirement that one report a crime of which they have become aware. There is no legal duty or obligation to be a "Good Samaritan."

➢ CHAPTER SIX ➢

WHEN CAN I LEGALLY USE MY GUN: PART III UNDERSTANDING WHEN DEADLY FORCE Can Be Used Against Animals

I. CAN I LEGALLY USE DEADLY FORCE AGAINST ANIMALS?

When it comes to the law of use of force and deadly force to defend yourself, others, or property from animal attacks, Louisiana law is not very helpful and is limited only to defense against "vicious dogs."

A. No general defense against animals statute

Louisiana has no general self-defense or defense of others statute that deals with all animals. However, according to La. Rev. Stat. Ann.

§ 3:2773(D). "Any citizen or officer may kill any dangerous or vicious dog, and no citizen or officer shall be liable for damages or to prosecution by reason of killing any dangerous or vicious dog." Although the statute only addresses dogs specifically, it is safe to assume that a vast majority of incidents where deadly force is used against an animal will involve a dog. Thus, this statute affords protection against criminal and civil liability for the killing of a "dangerous or vicious dog."

The test as to whether a dog is "dangerous" is whether a reasonable person under similar circumstances would have concluded that the dog is dangerous. *Chiasson v. Widman*, 376 So. 2d 350 (La. App. 3d Cir. 1979). An example is the case of *Collier v. Hoffman*, 482 So. 2d 922, 923 (La. Ct. App. 2d Cir. 1986). In *Collier*, four German Shepherds were attempting to break into the defendant's rabbit pen. The defendant grabbed his shotgun and ran yelling at the dogs in an unsuccessful attempt to scare them off. He then fired the gun into the air and succeeded in scaring off two of the dogs. The remaining two, however, continued their attack. Defendant shot the first dog when it had what defendant described as half of its body through the wire and into the pen attempting to bite a cornered rabbit. Defendant shot the second dog when it then approached defendant with its teeth bared as if to attack. The dogs were grown German Shepherds that were leased by their owner as security dogs. The court concluded that the two dogs that were shot were dangerous and absolved the defendant of liability. The court also noted that, in Louisiana, a defendant is not required to show prior vicious tendencies of the dog to claim the benefit of the statute.

But if an animal other than a dog is attacking you, and you have to shoot it, no provision of the Louisiana Criminal Code exists that specifically justifies the use of deadly force. The typical laws you would expect to find such as self-defense against an animal attacking a human being don't exist under Louisiana law at all. What this means is that one may not find specific legal justification for using force or deadly force against an animal that is attacking if the animal is not a dog. Under this condition, a person may be forced to argue the general law of necessity. In this situation, persons will be forced to rely generally on the defense of justification because the action was necessary. The remaining portion of this chapter will examine the laws that do exist relating to the use of deadly force, generally, and how your right to self-preservation can best be accomplished against an animal.

B. The doctrine of necessity

Because there is no specific Louisiana law that allows a person to use deadly force against an animal in self-defense, other than a dangerous or vicious dog, often the best claim a person can make in a court is one of legal justification by necessity.

INQUIRY INTO THE NECESSITY OF FORCE OR DEADLY FORCE: LOUISIANA CASE LAW

"In a non-homicide situation, the defense of justification requires a dual inquiry: (1) an objective inquiry into whether the force used was reasonable under the circumstances; and (2) a subjective inquiry into whether the force was apparently necessary." *State v. Canales*, 2014-0663 (La. App. 4th Cir. 12/10/14); 156 So.3d 1183, 1191, quoting *State v. Cooks*, 11-0342, p. 11 (La. App. 4 th Cir. 12/14/11); 81 So. 3d 932, 939.

"The determination of [whether a defendant killed in self-defense] focuses on . . . whether the defendant could reasonably have believed his life to be in imminent danger, and whether deadly force was necessary to prevent the danger." *State v. Toussaint*, 98-1214 (La. App. 5th Cir. 05/19/99); 734 So. 2d 961, 963.

As this law applies to animal attacks, a person may be legally justified in using force or deadly force (such as firing a gun) against an attacking animal if that person has a reasonable belief that force or deadly force is apparently necessary to avoid imminent danger. Further, there are no legal presumptions of reasonableness such as ones that exist when there are human-on-human attacks. So, how does this all work in practice?

EXAMPLE:

Jim is walking in his neighborhood when out of nowhere, three large boars spot him and immediately begin running toward him, barking with sharp tusks showing. Jim barely has time to draw and fire his .40 caliber Glock at the lead hog just before it lunges at him.

If, for some reason, Jim finds himself charged with any form of crime for his shooting of the hog (this could be anything from cruelty to animals to discharge of a firearm in city limits, *etc*.), Jim will not be able to rely on a specific statute for self-defense because none exists. Rather, Jim will have to rely on the general legal doctrine of necessity as described above.

This means that a jury would ultimately decide whether Jim's conduct met the requirements of the defense of justification. First, did Jim "reasonably" believe his conduct (in this case, drawing and firing his gun) was necessary to avoid imminent danger (being bitten, mauled, *etc*.)? As was covered in Chapter Four, any time a reasonable person standard is used, it will be an issue for the jury. Further, without legal presumptions available under either of the Louisiana versions of "Castle Doctrine" or "Stand Your Ground" type laws, a prosecutor will fully be able to argue that Jim should have retreated, that he used too much force, or that the threat really was not reasonable.

C. When is force used against an animal not justified?

Louisiana case law sheds some light on instances where courts have found actions justified, and when courts have found action not justified.

EXAMPLE:

A man was not justified and was therefore guilty of animal cruelty, in the shooting of a dog that had been attacking his ducks. The dog had evidenced no viciousness toward any person and had retreated from the attack on the ducks. *State in Interest of Rowland*, 509 So.2d 779 (La. App. 2nd Cir. 1987).

EXAMPLE:

A jury found the actions of a man to be prudent and reasonable under the circumstances when he shot and killed a dog after his son ran terrified and screaming into his home as a result of being chased by the dog. The dog had previously attacked the man and had been shot by him on a prior occasion. *Chiasson v. Widman*, 376 So.2d 350 (La. App. 3rd Cir. 1979).

D. Federal law defenses

The federal law, in a comprehensive fashion, has actually had the foresight to specifically provide that a person may kill some animals protected by federal law in self-defense, such as the wolves, grizzly bears, and bats. *See* 50 C.F.R. § 17.84 and 50 C.F.R. § 17.40. Therefore, if you are carrying a firearm in a National Park (*see* Chapters 9 and 10), and you find yourself face to face with, for example, a grizzly bear, you will have a legal defense for protecting yourself.

PRACTICAL LEGAL TIP

Beware! Using deadly force against a dog or cat that is only digging into your flowerbed or getting into your garbage may not be justified even under the doctrine of necessity.

Note, however, that "[u]nless authorized, the use or discharge of a firearm within a [National] park area is prohibited." *See* 36 C.F.R. §§ 2.4(b) and 13.30(c). In parks where hunting is specifically authorized by federal statute, firearms may be used to hunt, but only in accordance with National Park Service ("NPS") regulations and state laws. 36 C.F.R § 2.2. Basically, it might be prudent to avoid shooting an animal on federal land without express permission or a permit if at all possible, as it is conceivable that you could still be charged with illegal discharge even if it was done in self-defense. The NPS specifically states that "Visitors should not consider firearms as protection from wildlife." *See Firearms in National Parks* at https://www.nps.gov/articles/firearms-in-national-parks.htm. Bear spray, however, is an effective deterrent. There are legal risks for defending oneself on federal property against animals, but there are also some protections afforded to civilians. In a nutshell, it would be prudent to make sure that using a firearm on federal land is a true last-ditch option for defense of your life, as you will likely be charged with illegal discharge of your firearm.

➢ CHAPTER SEVEN ⮜

WHEN CAN I LEGALLY USE MY GUN: PART IV UNDERSTANDING WHEN DEADLY FORCE Can Be Used To Protect Property

I. OVERVIEW AND LOCATION OF THE LAW TO PROTECT PROPERTY

Louisiana law allows a person to protect, with force, property in their lawful possession against a forcible offense or trespass, provided that the force or violence used is reasonable and apparently necessary to prevent such offense. The statute in the Louisiana Criminal Code dealing with legally justified force to defend property is § 19: Use of Force or Violence in Defense.

Protection of property is analyzed under the same "reasonable person" standard discussed in Chapters 4 and 5 and has the same requirements for a person who reasonably believes that the force or deadly force used was "apparently necessary." In addition to the above sections, Louisiana case law also addresses the legality of using mechanical devices to protect property.

II. WHEN IS SOMEONE LEGALLY JUSTIFIED TO USE "FORCE" BUT NOT "DEADLY FORCE" TO PROTECT THEIR OWN PROPERTY?

Section 19 of the Louisiana Criminal Code provides that force or violence used against another is justifiable when used to prevent a forcible offense or trespass against property in one's lawful possession, provided that the force or violence is reasonable and apparently necessary to prevent such offense.

JUSTIFIED USE OF FORCE TO PROTECT YOUR PROPERTY: LOUISIANA CRIMINAL CODE § 19(A)(1)(A)

"The use of force or violence upon the person of another is justifiable . . . [w]hen committed for the purpose of preventing a forcible offense . . . or trespass against property in a person's lawful possession, provided that the force or violence used must be reasonable and apparently necessary to prevent such offense."

A. What is trespassing?

Black's Law Dictionary defines trespass as "an unlawful interference with one's person, property, or rights." This definition has been expanded to refer typically to "any unauthorized intrusion or invasion of private premises or land of another." Black's Law Dictionary, 6th ed. This commonly understood definition of trespass is similar to the offense of criminal trespass found in subpart A, section 63 of the Louisiana Criminal Code. A criminal trespass occurs whenever:

> a person enters upon or . . . "remain[s] in or upon property, movable or immovable, owned by another without express, legal, or implied authorization." *See* La. Rev. Stat. Ann. §§ 14:63.

Like the common definition of trespass, a person becomes a trespasser whether they realize it or not (unwittingly walking across the King's hunting grounds, for instance).

B. Trespass for legal justification is not just "criminal trespass"

How, then, is "trespasser" defined by Louisiana law? "A trespasser is one who goes upon another's property without his consent." *Powell v. Dorris*, 35510 (La. App 2nd Cir. 4/5/02); 814 So. 2d 763, 767, quoting *Davis v. Culpepper*, 34763 (La. App. 2nd Cir.); 794 So. 2d 68, 75. The plain language of section 19(a)(1)(A) refers only to a "trespass against property" and does not reference a "criminal trespass." It is clear that the statute intends to follow a broader definition of trespass than just the offense of criminal trespass found in Section 63 of the Louisiana Criminal Code. In other words, a person may be potentially legally justified in using force against a person found trespassing on their land—even if that person has not committed the crime of criminal trespass, but only so long as the use of force is accompanied with a reasonable belief that it is apparently necessary to protect the property against the trespass. In the vast majority of cases, a jury will be the ultimate arbiter of whether or not a person had a reasonable belief that it was apparently necessary to protect his or her property against another person's trespass on the land.

C. What is a forcible offense against property?

You have a legal right to use force or violence to prevent a "forcible offense or trespass against property," but what does this mean? A forcible offense or trespass can be a theft, destruction, vandalism, or anything else that diminishes a person's right to their property. Whether particular conduct rises to "a forcible offense or trespass against property" is an issue that a jury decides.

D. Is there a statutory minimum value for property before force may be legally used to protect it?

No. There exists no statutory minimum value for property before force may be used to protect it. Section 19 does not specify that property a person seeks to protect must be of a certain minimum dollar value in order for a person to protect it. Having said that, the Louisiana Criminal Code does specify that a person must have a reasonable belief that the use of force is reasonable and apparently necessary to prevent such offense.

Realistically, even though a person may be in the process of committing a trespass or other forcible offense against property, some property may be of so little value that the use of force to protect or recover it would not be deemed reasonable by a reasonable person (people on a jury).

EXAMPLE:

One day at work, Fred walks into Ricky's office and takes a half-eaten bag of chips off of Ricky's desk and walks away. Ricky, upset at having his favorite chips pilfered from his desk, jumps up, chases Fred down, shoves him to the ground, and starts beating on Fred to recover his chips. On his way to chase Fred, Ricky also passes the office kitchen where identical bags of chips are available for community consumption.

Was Ricky's use of force against Fred legally justified? Unlikely. It may be a very hard sell to a jury that a person was justifiably beat up over potato chips (although, as we all know, trespass against Zapp's Cajun Crawtators might warrant some form of retaliation). But what if a thief is stealing irreplaceable family photos? There's no monetary value there—only personal sentiment. Again, the law is silent on the subject of any monetary value of property to be defended.

The point to be made here is that some items simply may not have enough value (financial, sentimental, or otherwise) to provide a person with a reasonable belief that the use of force is necessary to protect or recover the item. Remember, your conduct will always be evaluated under a reasonable person standard.

PRACTICAL LEGAL TIP

There are plenty of clever signs and bumper stickers out there advocating the use of a firearm. "Keep honking, I'm reloading," and even "Tresspassers Will Be Shot" are seen often on the bumpers of Louisiana cars and the fence posts of Louisiana homeowners. But these signs are not a good idea, at least from a legal perspective. Even if meant only to prompt a laugh, if you are forced to use your firearm to defend yourself and end up in court, you can bet that the prosecutor will bring these signs up to the jury for consideration. Remember, a prosecutor will use every avenue to paint you in the worst light possible.

III. WHEN IS SOMEONE LEGALLY JUSTIFIED IN USING "DEADLY FORCE" TO PROTECT OR RECOVER THEIR OWN PROPERTY?

The short answer is: it depends. You can legally use force reasonably necessary to protect your property, but you are not justified in taking the life of another in defense of property to prevent mere trespass or larceny. *State v. Plumlee*, 177 La. 687, 149 So. 425 (1933). A homicide is justifiable in several situations to protect persons and property. Specifically under Section 14:20, you may use deadly force against someone you reasonable believe is likely to use unlawful force against a person present in a dwelling or place of business, or against a person present in a motor vehicle, while attempting to commit a burglary or robbery of such dwelling, business, or motor vehicle. The statute also allows you to use deadly force against someone who is attempting to make an unlawful entry into a dwelling, place of business, or motor vehicle, when you reasonably believe the that the use of deadly force is necessary to prevent the entry or compel the intruder to leave the dwelling, place of business, or motor vehicle. *State v. Ingram*, 45546 (La. App. 2nd Cir. 6/22/11); 71 So. 3d 437.

EXAMPLE:

After a long day at work, Gordon finally pulls into his driveway just in time to see two masked men running out of his front door with his favorite television in one man's arms and his grandfather's expensive watch on one the other man's wrist. Gordon gets out of his car and demands that the men stop where they are, but they ignore him and attempt to run away. Gordon pulls his Glock 17 and fires at the fleeing men, killing one and injuring the other.

Was Gordon justified under section 20 of the Louisiana Criminal Code to use deadly force? No. Gordon's actions seem to satisfy the first prong of the requirement to justify the use of deadly force: it is reasonable to believe that the victims had made an unlawful entry into his home, as they were carrying things retrieved from inside. However, Gordon likely falls short on the second prong of the requirement: there is no evidence that it was reasonable to believe deadly force was necessary to prevent the entry or to compel the victims to leave. The victims had left the home and were running away when they were shot. It is unlikely a jury will find the homicide to be justified because Gordon's actions did not meet both prongs of this requirement. Gordon's actions would also not be justified under the other prong of the requirement, as there is no evidence that Gordon reasonably believed the victims were likely to use unlawful force against a person in Gordon's home.

IV. CAN I PROTECT ANOTHER PERSON'S PROPERTY?

JUSTIFIED USE OF FORCE TO PROTECT ANOTHER: LOUISIANA CRIMINAL CODE § 22

> "It is justifiable to use force or violence or to kill in the defense of another person when it is reasonably apparent that the person attacked could have justifiably used such means himself, and when it is reasonably believed that such intervention is necessary to protect the other person."

In general, if you place yourself in the shoes of the third person, and the law would allow the third person to use force or deadly force to protect themselves, then you are legally justified to use the same level of force to protect the third person. Section 22 applies the same legal analysis for self-defense to defense of third persons.

Therefore, the same legal justifications and presumptions of "reasonableness" for self-defense are also available for the defense of third persons. However, Section 22 makes no mention of a justification for force or violence used in the protection of the property of another, and only justifies conduct that a person "reasonably believed" was "necessary to protect the other person." La. Rev. Stat. Ann. § 14:22. A strict reading of the statute tells us that justification is not a defense for force or violence used to protect the property of another.

Let's return to our earlier example with Gordon and see how things would play out if another person's property was involved.

EXAMPLE:

After a long day at work, Gordon pulls into his own driveway one night and witnesses two men climbing out of his neighbor's window, which appears to be broken, and with what looks to be his neighbor's television. Gordon exits his vehicle, gun drawn, and demands the two men stop. When the men ignore his command, Gordon shoots and wounds both men.

Is Gordon legally justified in using deadly force under this scenario? No. Even if Gordon reasonably believed his neighbor was home and his neighbor would have been justified in using deadly force while the crime was occurring inside the home, the fact that the two men were leaving the home and running away renders Gordon's actions unjustified.

V. HOW ARE THE CRIMES ASSOCIATED WITH DEFENDING PROPERTY DEFINED UNDER LOUISIANA LAW?

In previous sections, we discussed that force may be used to prevent "forcible offenses" against property. What are some possible "forcible offenses," and how does Louisiana law define them?

1. Arson

"The intentional damaging by any explosive substance or the setting fire to any property of another, without the consent of the owner[.]" La. Rev. Stat. Ann. § 14:52(A)(1).

2. Burglary

"[T]he unauthorized entering of any dwelling, vehicle, watercraft, or other structure, movable or immovable, or any cemetery, with the intent to commit a felony or any theft therein[.]" La. Rev. Stat. Ann. § 14:62(A).

3. Robbery

"[T]he taking of anything of value belonging to another from the person of another or that is in the immediate control of another, by use of force or intimidation[.]" La. Rev. Stat. Ann. § 14:65(A).

4. Theft

"[T]he misappropriation or taking of anything of value which belongs to another, either without the consent of the other to the misappropriation or taking, or by means of fraudulent conduct, practices, or representations. An intent to deprive the other permanently of whatever may be the subject of the misappropriation or taking is essential." La. Rev. Stat. Ann. § 14:67(A).

5. Criminal Mischief

"[T]he intentional performance of any of the following acts:

- Tampering with any property of another, without the consent of the owner, with the intent to interfere with the free enjoyment of any rights of anyone thereto, or with the intent to deprive anyone entitled thereto of the full use of the property.
- Giving of any false alarm of fire or notice which would reasonably result in emergency response.
- Giving of any false report or complaint to a sheriff, or his deputies, or to any officer of the law relative to the commission of, or an attempt to commit, a crime.
- Throwing any stone or other missile in any street, avenue, alley, road, highway, open space, public square, or enclosure, or throwing any stone, missile, or other object from any

place into any street, avenue, road, highway, alley, open space, public square, enclosure, or at any train, railway car, or locomotive.

- The discharging of any firearm at a train, locomotive, or railway car." La. Rev. Stat. Ann. § 14:59(A).

VI. HOW CAN I ASSIST LAW ENFORCEMENT?

Almost without fail, as attorneys we are regularly asked about whether you can make a citizen's arrest, and how you can best assist law enforcement in dicey situations. Every legal situation is unique, under Article 214 of the Louisiana Code of Criminal Procedure, the law governing citizen's arrest states that "[a] private person may make an arrest when the person arrested has committed a felony, whether in or out of his presence." La. Code Crim. Proc. Ann. art. 214.

The law does not, however, permit a private citizen to arrest another "without a warrant when the person arrested is engaged in an act which could constitute at most an element of a misdemeanor." *Girlinghouse v. Zwahlen*, 3 La. App. 720, 722 (Ct. App. 2nd Cir. 1926).

EXAMPLE:

A 15-year-old boy disturbing a fair ride operator with his behavior "could hardly be considered a misdemeanor," so a citizen's arrest of the boy would be unlawful. *Pohl v. Licata*, 236 So. 2d 259 (La. Ct. App. 4th Cir. 1970). In contrast, where a cashier of a store was robbed, the pursuit and citizen's arrest of the robber was valid because first-degree robbery is a felony. *State v. Jackson*, 584 So. 2d 266, (La. Ct. App. 1st Cir. 1991).

A. Detaining potential thieves

The Louisiana Code of Criminal Procedure grants a person authority to detain a person in order to investigate potential theft:

> **DETENTION AND ARREST OF SHOPLIFTERS:**
> **LOUISIANA CODE OF CRIMINAL PROCEDURE ARTICLE 215**
>
> An "officer, merchant, or authorized employee [] of a merchant, may use reasonable force to detain a person for questioning on the merchant's premises, for a length of time not to exceed sixty minutes . . . when he has reasonable cause to believe that the person has committed a theft of goods . . . regardless of the actual value of the goods. The merchant or his employee [] may also detain such a person for arrest by a peace officer."

The most common application of this particular statute is in the retail-store setting. Common scenarios include when a loss prevention official for the store will take a person into some type of custody while they investigate whether an item was stolen from their business.

VII. WHAT CRIMES CAN I BE CHARGED WITH WHEN MY USE OF DEADLY FORCE IS NOT JUSTIFIED?

We've reached the end of our discussion on when you may be justified to use a weapon in defense of your person or property. Now it's time to give a brief summary of where you'll find yourself in legal trouble if you don't meet the elements of justification as we've described throughout this book. The following tables list some of the crimes involving the use of deadly force or a firearm and where relevant provisions may be found in Louisiana law.

CRIMES INVOLVING DEADLY FORCE OR A FIREARM:

1. Murder: *see* La. Rev. Stat. Ann. § 14.30.
2. Manslaughter: *see* La. Rev. Stat. Ann. § 14.31.
3. Aggravated Assault: *see* La. Rev. Stat. Ann. § 14.37.

CRIMES AGAINST THE PUBLIC INVOLVING A FIREARM:

a. Reckless discharge of a firearm at a parade or demonstration: "the reckless or criminally negligent discharge of a firearm within one thousand feet of any parade, demonstration, or gathering for which a permit is issued by a governmental entity." La. Rev. Stat. Ann. § 14:95.2.2.

b. Negligent carrying of a concealed handgun: the intentional or criminally negligent carrying of a concealed handgun causing others to believe a crime is being committed or the handgun will be discharged.

c. Schools and other firearm-free zones: carrying a firearm or dangerous weapon on school property, at a school sponsored function, or in a firearm-free zone is unlawful. This includes firearms carried on one's person at any time while on a school campus, on school transportation, or at any school sponsored function in a specific designated area. La. Rev. Stat. Ann. § 14:95.2.

OTHER CRIMES INVOLVING DEADLY FORCE OR A FIREARM:

a. Possession of a firearm on alcoholic beverage outlet premises: no person shall possess a firearm while on the premises of an alcoholic beverage outlet (in which alcohol is sold in individual servings for consumption on the premises). La. Rev. Stat. Ann. § 14:95.5.

b. Juveniles: it is unlawful for any person 17 years or younger "knowingly to possess any handgun on his person." La. Rev. Stat. Ann. § 14:95.8.

Note: the discharge of a firearm within city limits may be a crime under specific city ordinances (check your local statutes).

WHAT DO I DO IMMEDIATELY AFTER I USE MY FIREARM?

1. Make sure that the threat is contained or neutralized;
2. Return your firearm to safekeeping;
3. Call 911 and tell them you (or another person) has been the victim of a crime. Give the operator your location and description. Avoid giving any unnecessary information and avoid telling them you shot someone. It may be wise to suggest an ambulance is needed. Then hang up with 911.
4. Call the Louisiana LawShield Emergency Hotline and follow the instructions your program attorney gives you;
5. Wait for police and do not touch any evidence;
6. If directed by your attorney, provide police only simple details of the crime against you; and
7. Be careful of police questions and always be ready to invoke your right to silence and your right to counsel at any time.

➢ CHAPTER EIGHT ≺

LAW OF CONCEALED CARRY: PART I

THE LICENSE

Qualifications, Requirements, Appeals, And Regulations

In 1996, the Louisiana Legislature passed a law allowing for the issuance of Concealed Handgun Permits (CHPs). In Louisiana, qualified individuals may obtain a CHP, which allows the carrying of a concealed handgun on their person for any lawful purpose. To obtain a CHP a person must meet certain requirements and submit an application to the Louisiana Department of Public Safety. This Chapter deals exclusively with the licensed carrying of a handgun in Louisiana. A CHP only allows for the lawful carry of handguns; the license does not cover long guns or any other type of weapon.

I. THE EVOLUTION OF THE LOUISIANA CONCEALED CARRY LAW

Despite Louisiana's reputation as being "gun-friendly," it wasn't until 1996 that the Legislature finally passed a "shall-issue" concealed carry law. There have been several attempts at passing legislation allowing "permitless concealed carry," but all have failed.

Louisiana Revised Statutes Annotated 40:1379.3, titled "Statewide Permits for Concealed Handguns," contains the law on how concealed handgun permits are administered in Louisiana. Throughout this Chapter we will discuss the requirements and the application process, as well as the rights given to CHP holders for carrying a handgun in the State of Louisiana.

II. QUALIFICATIONS FOR AND STEPS TO GET A CHP

A. Persons who are legally qualified to obtain a CHP

In this section we will discuss the requirements to apply for a Louisiana CHP, as well as potential disqualifications. In addition to the requirements listed below, applicants must also complete state-mandated education with a CHP instructor certified by the Louisiana State Police and demonstrate competence with a handgun by either completing:

- Any NRA handgun safety/ training course or an NRA Personal Protection course;
- Any law enforcement firearms safety or training course approved by the Department of Public Safety and Corrections in the preceding 12 months;
- Possession of a current valid license to carry a concealed weapon issued by a parish law enforcement officer;
- Completion of any firearms training or safety course or class approved by the Department of Public Safety and Corrections within the preceding 12 months;

- Completion of a law enforcement training academy program certified by the Council on Peace Officer Standards and Training (or, for retired law enforcement, a showing that they were properly certified upon retirement); or
- Completion of small arms training within the preceding 60 months while serving with the armed forces of the United States.

See La. Rev. Stat. Ann. §§ 40:1379.3(D)(1)(a)-(i).

Section 40:1379.3(C) of the Louisiana Revised Statutes Annotated states that to be eligible for a CHP in Louisiana, an individual must:

(1) Make sworn application to the deputy secretary of public safety services of the Department of Public Safety and Corrections;

(2) Agree in writing to hold harmless and indemnify the department, the state, or any peace officer for any and all liability arising out of the issuance or use of the concealed handgun permit;

(3) Be a [Louisiana] resident;

(4) Be 21 years of age or older;

(5) Not suffer from a mental or physical infirmity due to disease, illness, or intellectual disability which prevents the safe handling of a handgun;

(6) Not be ineligible to possess a firearm by virtue of having been convicted of a felony;

(7) Not have been committed, either voluntarily or involuntarily, for the abuse of a controlled dangerous substance, . . . or been found guilty of, or entered a plea of guilty or nolo contendere to a misdemeanor under [Louisiana law] or similar laws of any other state relating to a controlled dangerous substance within a five-year period preceding the

date on which the application is submitted, or be presently charged [with] such an offense;

(8) Not chronically and habitually use alcoholic beverages to the extent that his normal faculties are impaired;

(9) Not have entered a plea of guilty or nolo contendere to or been found guilty of a crime of violence as defined in 14:2 at the misdemeanor level, unless five years have elapsed since completion of sentence or any other conditions set by the court have been fulfilled, or unless the conviction was set aside and the prosecution dismissed, prior to the date on which the application is submitted;

(10) Not have been convicted of, have entered a plea of guilty or nolo contendere to, or not be charged [with] any crime of violence or any crime punishable by imprisonment for a term of one year or greater;

(11) Not be a fugitive from justice;

(12) Not be an unlawful user of, or addicted to, marijuana, depressants, stimulants, or narcotic drugs;

(13) Not have been adjudicated to be mentally deficient or been committed to a mental institution, unless the resident's right to possess a firearm has been restored pursuant to R.S. 28:57;

(14) Not be an illegal alien in the United States;

(15) Not have been discharged from the Armed Forces of the United States with a discharge characterized as "Under Other than Honorable Conditions", a "Bad Conduct Discharge", or a "Dishonorable Discharge";

(16) Not have a history of engaging in violent behavior;

(17) Not be ineligible to possess or receive a firearm under 18 U.S.C. 922(g) or (n);

(18) Not have had a permit denied within one year prior to the most recent application; and

(19) Not have had a permit revoked within four years prior to the most recent application.

B. What does it mean to "chronically and habitually" use alcoholic beverages so as to be disqualified from receiving a CHP?

A person is legally disqualified from receiving a CHP if that person "chronically and habitually" uses alcoholic beverages to the extent that his normal faculties are impaired. There exists a presumption under Louisiana Revised Statutes Annotated 40:1379.3(C)(8) that "an applicant or permittee chronically and habitually uses alcoholic beverages to the extent that his normal faculties are impaired if the applicant has been found guilty of, entered a plea of guilty or nolo contendere to operating a vehicle while intoxicated, or has been admitted, either voluntarily or involuntarily, for treatment as an alcoholic, within the five-year period immediately preceding the date on which the application is submitted, or at any time after the application has been submitted."

C. What does it mean to "have a history of engaging in violent behavior" so as to be disqualified from receiving a CHP?

Louisiana Revised Statutes Annotated 40:1379.3(C)(16) includes "a rebuttable presumption that an applicant has a history of engaging in violent behavior upon proof that, within a ten-year period immediately preceding the date of the application, the applicant has been arrested or charged on three or more occasions for any crime of violence as defined in R.S. 14:2(B) or has been arrested or charged on two or more occasions for any crime of violence that may be punished by death." Having a history of violent behavior prohibits you from obtaining a Louisiana CHP.

D. If you present false information, you can expect your application to be delayed or denied

The qualifying factor that probably delays the majority of applications revolves around when a person fails to make a full disclosure of material facts. To qualify for a Louisiana CHP, a person must make a sworn application to the deputy secretary of public safety services of the Department of Public Safety and Corrections. Providing false or misleading information on the application or any documents submitted with the application shall be grounds for the denial or revocation of a CHP. Most often, this is due to a person failing to disclose a criminal conviction of one nature or another. *See* La. Rev. Stat. Ann. § 40:1379.3(C)(1)(a).

Additionally, Louisiana law makes it "illegal to intentionally present false, fraudulent, altered, or counterfeit documents to prove training in handguns in order to obtain a concealed handgun permit." *See* La. Rev. Stat. Ann. § 40:1379.3(E)(2).

Many applicants forget about things that may have happened many years ago, but which require disclosure in the application. The best practice is: when in doubt, disclose! Otherwise, a person may face unwanted delays or even a denial of their application.

Note: be very careful in the wording of your disclosures. We have seen many applicants encounter difficulties in not using precise descriptions of their legal history, medical condition, *etc*. Be careful with your words.

E. What if I received an "expungement?" Can I get a CHP?

If a person received an "expungement" as a result of a criminal charge, that person may still be eligible for a CHP under specific conditions. Generally, a person convicted of a felony is ineligible to possess a firearm and by virtue, a CHP. However, Louisiana Revised Statutes Annotated 40:1379.3 states that certain crimes—including felonies—will not prevent a person from possessing a CHP if they meet certain requirements.

If a person has been convicted of a felony offense which was expunged prior to August 1, 2014 pursuant to R.S. 44:19 or on or after August 1, 2014 pursuant to Title XXXIV of the Code of Criminal Procedure, his or her felony offense will not be considered a conviction for qualification purposes on an application for a CHP, if 10 years have elapsed since the completion of the applicant's probation, parole, or suspended sentence and the offense for which the person received the expungement was not one of the following offenses. Persons who received an expungement for any of the following "violent crimes" are permanently barred from holding a concealed handgun permit:

1. Solicitation for murder;
2. First degree murder;
3. Second degree murder;
4. Manslaughter;
5. Aggravated battery;
6. Second degree battery;
7. Aggravated assault;
8. Aggravated or first degree rape;
9. Forcible or second degree rape;
10. Simple or third degree rape;
11. Sexual battery;
12. Second degree sexual battery;
13. Intentional exposure to AIDS virus;
14. Aggravated kidnapping;

15. Second degree kidnapping;
16. Simple kidnapping;
17. Aggravated arson;
18. Aggravated criminal damage to property;
19. Aggravated burglary;
20. Armed robbery;
21. First degree robbery;
22. Simple robbery;
23. Purse snatching;
24. Assault by drive-by shooting;
25. Aggravated crime against nature;
26. Carjacking;
27. Terrorism;
28. Aggravated second degree battery;
29. Aggravated assault upon a peace officer;
30. Aggravated assault with a firearm;
31. Armed robbery; use of firearm;
32. Second degree robbery;
33. Disarming of a peace officer;
34. Stalking;
35. Second degree cruelty to juveniles;
36. Aggravated flight from an officer;
37. Battery of a police officer;
38. Trafficking of children for sexual purposes;
39. Human trafficking;
40. Home invasion;
41. Domestic abuse aggravated assault;
42. Vehicular homicide, when the operator's blood alcohol concentration exceeds 0.20 percent by weight based on grams of alcohol per 100 cubic centimeters of blood; and
43. Aggravated assault upon a dating partner.

See La. Rev. Stat. §§ 40:1379.3(C)(6) and 14:2(B)(1)-(47).

What this means is that persons who have received an expungement for felony offenses not listed above may be eligible to apply for and possess a Louisiana CHP after 10 years from the date of their completion of probation, parole, or suspended sentence.

However, a person who has entered a plea of guilty or nolo contendere to or has been found guilty of a crime of violence as defined in R.S. 14:2 at the misdemeanor level, may be eligible to apply for a CHP if 5 years have elapsed since completion of his or her sentence or any other conditions set by the court have been fulfilled, or if the conviction was set aside and the prosecution dismissed it, before the application is submitted.

F. Suspension and revocation of a CHP

1. What is the difference between suspension and revocation?

To begin, it is important to know that there is a difference between a suspension and a revocation of a person's CHP. A suspension is only temporary, and a person's license may be reinstated without the necessity of submitting a new application for a CHP. This means that a person will not have to go through the rigors of the application process or the classroom requirements again in order to regain their CHP. On the other hand, a revocation means that the Louisiana Department of Public Safety and Corrections has decided that a person's CHP shall be terminated, and in order for the person to ultimately regain the CHP, they must reapply from step one by attending a CHP class and submitting the application with the applicable fees.

2. Under what circumstances can the Louisiana DPS revoke a CHP?

Louisiana Revised Statutes Annotated 40:1379.3 governs CHPs and their revocation and suspension. It states that a person's CHP may be revoked for any of the following reasons:

a. Providing false or misleading information on the application or any documents submitted with the application;
b. If "the superintendent of state police or his designee determines conditions and/or circumstances are such that the holder of the CHP can no longer show need or when the holder commits acts contrary to law or uses the permit for self aggrandizement or in an unreasonable and imprudent manner;
c. Failure to inform the Department in writing of any handgun related accident, discharge, incident, injury, or death involving the permittee;
d. Failure to comply with the qualifications required to obtain a CHP discussed earlier in this Chapter and found in Louisiana Revised Statutes Annotated 40:1379.3(C);
e. When the permittee is carrying a concealed handgun and
   (1) The blood alcohol reading of the permittee is .05% or greater by weight of alcohol in the blood;
   (2) A permittee's blood test or urine test shows the confirmed presence of a controlled dangerous substance as defined in Louisiana Revised Statutes 40:961 and 964; or
   (3) A permittee refuses to submit to a department-certified chemical test when requested to do so by a law enforcement officer; or
f. An individual is found guilty of negligent carrying of a concealed handgun as provided for in Louisiana Revised Statutes Annotated 40:1382.

3. Under what circumstances can the Louisiana DPS suspend a CHP?

Louisiana Revised Statutes Annotated 40:1379.3 states that a person's CHP may be suspended for any of the following reasons:

a. Failure to timely notify the Department of Public Safety about a name or address change;
b. While permittee is under the influence of drugs or alcohol, the license is automatically suspended and is not valid;
c. Failure to notify any police officer who approaches the permittee in an official manner or with an identified official purpose that he has a weapon on his person, submit to a pat down, and allow the officer to temporarily disarm him;
d. Failure to notify the Deputy Secretary of Public Safety, within 15 days, of a misdemeanor or a felony arrest other than a minor traffic violation, in Louisiana or any other state, by certified mail;
e. When the superintendent of state police or his designee determines conditions and/or circumstances are such that the holder of such permit can no longer show need or when the holder commits acts contrary to law or uses the permit for self aggrandizement or in an unreasonable and imprudent manner;
f. Failure to inform the Department in writing of any handgun related accident, discharge, incident, injury, or death involving the permittee;
g. The permittee is the subject of any preliminary or permanent injunction in any family or domestic dispute or any other protective order;
h. Failure to pay fines levied by the Department within 15 days of judgment; or
i. Providing false or misleading information or improper notarization on the application or any documents submitted with the application.

For lifetime concealed handgun permit holders (*see* La. Rev. Stat. Ann. § 40:1379.3) the permit can be suspended for any of the following reasons:

a. Failure to submit proof of completion of the educational training; or
b. When the permit holder becomes a resident of another state.

4. Procedure for revocation or suspension of a CHP

In accordance with Louisiana Revised Statutes Annotated 40:1379.3(I)(5), "[w]henever a peace officer determines that grounds . . . exist for the revocation of a concealed handgun permit, he [or she] shall prepare an affidavit, on a form provided by the Department of Public Safety and Corrections, indicating the reasons for the revocation and all other information regarding the revocation available to the officer. A copy of the peace officer's report relating to the incident shall be attached to the affidavit when submitted to the department."

III. THE CHP APPLICATION AND PROCESS

A. The CHP application

A Louisiana CHP application packet containing all required information is necessary to obtain a license. The packet must be completed and submitted to the Louisiana State Police. The packet can be completed in any of the following ways:

a. Complete and submit the online Concealed Handgun Permit Application at http://chp-web.dps.louisiana.gov;
b. Download a Concealed Handgun Permit Application and complete the instructions found on pages one and two of the application; or
c. Obtain an application at the State Police Headquarters (7919 Independence Blvd., Baton Rouge, LA 70806).

Applicants must also provide all necessary documentation pertaining to training, arrest dispositions, medical summary dispositions, and divorce decrees (if applicable). New fingerprints must be submitted for original/first time applicants. Old fingerprints on file will not be accepted. Fingerprinting at State Police Headquarters requires a $10.00 money order or can be paid using a debit/credit card. Prints must be submitted on an FBI Applicant Fingerprint Card.

Paper applications, fingerprint cards, and/or other documentation must be submitted to:

Louisiana State Police
Concealed Handgun Permit Unit
PO Box 66375
Baton Rouge, LA 70896

B. CHP class and shooting test

In addition to meeting the qualifications in Louisiana Revised Statutes Annotated 40:1379.3(C), for a concealed handgun permit, an applicant must demonstrate competence with a handgun by completion of an approved firearms safety or training course taught by an NRA or P.O.S.T. certified instructor that is registered with State Police, or completion of small arms training while serving in the military, as evidenced by a DD-214 (active service members, reservist, and national guard members must include a clear photocopy of their military ID (front & back) with a copy of their last qualification record from their 201 file), or possession of a current valid license to carry a concealed weapon issued by a parish law enforcement officer. Lifetime permit holders are required to complete refresher training every five years. *See* La. Rev. Stat. Ann. § 40:1379.3(V)(4).

➢ CHAPTER NINE ➣

LAW OF CONCEALED CARRY: PART II
WHAT, HOW, AND WHERE
You Can Legally Carry With A CHP

I. WHERE CAN A CHP HOLDER LEGALLY CARRY A CONCEALED HANDGUN?

A person in possession of a CHP may legally carry their handgun concealed in any place where it is not illegal for them to possess a concealed handgun under either state or federal law (*see* La. Rev. Stat. Ann. § 40:1379.3(M)). However, a CHP holder may not legally carry a concealed handgun if their actions constitute the negligent carrying of a concealed weapon pursuant to Louisiana Revised Statutes Annotated § 40:1382(A):

(1) "When it is foreseeable that the handgun

may discharge, or when others are placed in reasonable apprehension that the handgun may discharge; or

(2) When the handgun is being carried, brandished, or displayed under circumstances that create a reasonable apprehension on the part of members of the public or a law enforcement official that a crime is being committed or is about to be committed."

The places prohibited under Louisiana law are located in Louisiana Revised Statutes Annotated § 40:1379.3(N). In addition, because a CHP is issued by the State of Louisiana and not the federal government, a CHP holder may not legally carry their concealed handgun on federal property unless specifically authorized by federal law.

A. Prohibited places for CHP holders

(1) "A law enforcement office, station, or building.

(2) A detention facility, prison, or jail.

(3) A courthouse or courtroom provided that a judge may carry such a weapon in his or her own courtroom.

(4) A polling place.

(5) A meeting place of the governing authority of a political subdivision.

(6) The state capitol building.

(7) Any portion of an airport facility where the carrying of firearms is prohibited under federal law, except that no person shall be prohibited from carrying any legal firearm into the terminal, if the firearm is encased for shipment, for the purpose of checking such firearm as lawful baggage.

(8) Any church, synagogue, mosque, or other similar place of worship

(9) A parade or demonstration for which a permit is issued by a governmental entity.

(10) Any portion of the permitted area of an establishment that has been granted a Class A-General retail permit . . . to sell alcoholic beverages for consumption on the premises: [Or]

(11) Any school, school campus, or school bus."

See La. Rev. Stat. Ann. § 40:1379.3(N).

B. Any place where the property owner prohibits the carrying of concealed weapons

In accordance with Louisiana Revised Statutes Annotated § 40:1379.3(O), property owners, lessees, or other lawful custodians have the right to prohibit or restrict the access of those who possess a concealed handgun, even if they possess a valid concealed handgun permit.

Additionally, one cannot carry a concealed handgun into the private residence of another without first receiving the consent of that person. *See* La. Rev. Stat. Ann. § 40:1379.3(O).

1. Correctional facilities

STATEWIDE PERMITS FOR CONCEALED HANDGUNS: LOUISIANA REVISED STATUTES ANNOTATED § 40:1379.3(N)(2)
"No concealed handgun may be carried into . . . : (2) A detention facility, prison, or jail."

A CHP holder is not permitted to carry a concealed handgun into a correctional facility under Louisiana law.

2. Meetings of governmental entities

STATEWIDE PERMITS FOR CONCEALED HANDGUNS: LOUISIANA REVISED STATUTES ANNOTATED § 40:1379.3(N)(5)

"No concealed handgun may be carried into . . . :

(5) A meeting place of the governing authority of a political subdivision."

This means that a CHP holder is not permitted to carry at a city council meeting or other meetings of governmental entities.

3. When a license holder is intoxicated

STATEWIDE PERMITS FOR CONCEALED HANDGUNS: LOUISIANA REVISED STATUTES ANNOTATED § 40:1379.3(I)(1)

"While a permittee is under the influence of alcohol or a controlled dangerous substance, an otherwise lawful permit is considered automatically suspended and is not valid."

No CHP holder may carry a concealed handgun while under the influence of alcohol or a controlled dangerous substance.

What is "under the influence?"

Louisiana Revised Statutes Annotated § 40:1379.3(I)(1) states that a person cannot be under the influence while in the possession of their concealed handgun. It does not say that a person cannot consume alcohol while carrying their gun, merely that the person cannot consume so much alcohol or other substance that they are considered "under the influence" for the purpose of the statute.

"A permittee shall be considered under the influence as evidenced by a blood alcohol reading of .05 percent or greater by weight of alcohol in the blood, or when a blood test or urine test shows any confirmed presence of a controlled dangerous substance." La. Rev. Stat. Ann. § 40:1379.3(I)(1).

As can be seen from these provisions, an individual is considered under the influence when an individual consumes a controlled dangerous substance, or enough alcohol that an individual has a blood alcohol concentration of .05% or greater. It is hard to imagine that one beer or glass of wine with dinner would cause someone to have a blood alcohol concentration of .05% or greater. But, it should be well-noted that people react to alcohol or medication differently.

A CHP cannot be issued to one who "chronically and habitually use[s] alcoholic beverages to the extent that his or her normal faculties are impaired" under Louisiana law. *See* La. Rev. Stat. Ann. § 40:1379.3(C)(8). There exists a presumption "that an applicant . . . chronically and habitually uses alcoholic beverages to the extent that his or her normal faculties are impaired if he or she has been found guilty of, entered a plea of guilty or nolo contendere to operating a vehicle while intoxicated, or has been admitted, either voluntarily or involuntarily, for treatment as an alcoholic, within the five-year period immediately preceding the date on which the application is submitted, or at any time after the application has been submitted." La. Rev. Stat. Ann. § 40:1379.3(C)(8).

C. Employer/employee parking lot rules

In addition, under Louisiana Revised Statutes Annotated § 32:292.1(A), most license holders are allowed to conceal their handgun within their locked, privately-owned motor vehicle in an employee parking lot, garage, or other parking area provided by an employer. The statute states:

> "[A] person who lawfully possesses a firearm may transport or store such firearm in a locked, privately-owned motor vehicle in any parking lot, parking garage, or other designated parking area."

However, please note that there are exceptions. In particular, subsection (C) provides that: "Nothing in this Section shall prohibit an employer or business entity from adopting policies specifying that firearms stored in locked, privately-owned motor vehicles on property controlled by an employer or business entity be hidden from plain view or within a locked case or container within the vehicle."

Moreover, the right to keep a firearm in your vehicle does not apply to the following situations:

"(1) Any property where the possession of firearms is prohibited under state or federal law.

(2) Any vehicle owned or leased by a public or private employer or business entity and used by an employee in the course of his employment, except for those employees who are required to transport or store a firearm in the official discharge of their duties.

(3) Any vehicle on property controlled by a public or private employer or business entity if access is restricted or limited through the use of a fence, gate, security station, signage, or other means of restricting or limiting general public access onto the parking area, and if one of the following conditions applies:

   (a) The employer or business entity provides facilities for the temporary storage of unloaded firearms.

   (b) The employer or business entity provides an alternative

> parking area reasonably close to the main parking area in which employees and other persons may transport or store firearms in locked, privately-owned motor vehicles."

Therefore, while there is legal protection permitting legal firearm owners to keep a firearm in their vehicle at work, this protection is not absolute and does not apply to a few certain circumstances.

D. Automobiles, watercrafts, and other places

1. May a CHP holder carry a concealed handgun in an automobile?

Yes. A CHP holder in Louisiana can legally carry a concealed handgun in their vehicle.

2. May a person legally carry a concealed handgun in a commercial vehicle?

Louisiana Revised Statutes Annotated §§ 32:292.1(A) and (C) state that it is legal to "transport or store [a] firearm in a locked, privately-owned motor vehicle in any parking lot, parking garage, or other designated parking area[,]" and that "[n]o property owner, tenant, public or private employer, or business entity shall prohibit any person from" doing so. This section, however, does not apply to "[a]ny vehicle owned or leased by a public or private employer or business entity and used by an employee in the course of his employment, except for those employees who are required to transport or store a firearm in the official discharge of their duties." La. Rev. Stat. Ann. § 32:292.1(D)(2). Thus, if a CHP holder is driving a commercial vehicle, his or her employer may limit the ability to carry a concealed weapon onboard. *See* La. Rev. Stat. Ann. § 32:292.1.

3. May a person carry a concealed handgun on a boat or watercraft?
Louisiana law is silent on the concealed carrying of a handgun, or any type of gun, onboard a boat or other watercraft.

4. May a person with a CHP carry a concealed handgun in a state park?
Yes. According to Louisiana Revised Statutes Annotated § 56:1691, "[a] person who lawfully possesses a firearm may possess or transport such firearm within the boundaries of a state park, state historic site, state preservation area, wildlife management area, or wildlife refuge."

5. Can a CHP holder carry in a restaurant?
Under Louisiana law, CHP holders are prevented from carrying in:

> "Any portion of the permitted area of an establishment that has been granted a Class A-General retail permit . . . to sell alcoholic beverages for consumption on the premises."

La. Rev. Stat. Ann. § 40:1379.3(N)(10).

A Class-A General retail permit is granted to "retail outlet[s] where beverage alcohol is sold on the premises for consumption on the premises by paying customers. Such an establishment must be equipped with a permanent wet bar equipped with a non-movable sink and a backbar or similar equipment for public display and to inform the public of brands and flavors offered for sale." *See* La. Rev. Stat. Ann. § 26:71.1(1)(a).

If a restaurant meets this requirement, the carrying of a concealed handgun is prohibited in both the restaurant portion and the bar portion of the building. Likewise, if a restaurant has posted a "firearms prohibited" sign, the carrying of a concealed handgun by a license holder is prohibited. However, if neither of these are applicable, then a license holder is legally able to carry their concealed handgun in a restaurant.

6. Can a person have their gun in a hotel?

Hotels are permitted to follow the same guidelines for other businesses in that they can prohibit firearms on the premises. However, if there is no such prohibition, Louisiana law does not prevent the carrying of firearms on hotel property.

E. Federal Property

A CHP and its rights are a product of state law and convey no rights to the CHP holder that have been recognized under federal law. *See* La. Rev. State. Ann. § 40:1379.3(M). However, in certain instances, the federal government recognizes these state rights on certain federal property.

1. Federal buildings: firearms are prohibited

FIREARMS PROHIBITED IN FEDERAL FACILITIES:
18 U.S.C. § 930(A)

". . .whoever knowingly possesses or causes to be present a firearm or other dangerous weapon in a Federal facility (other than a Federal court facility), or attempts to do so, shall be fined under this title or imprisoned not more than 1 year, or both."

Under this statute, a "federal facility" refers to any building or part of a building that is owned or leased by the federal government and is a place "where Federal employees are regularly present for the purpose of performing their official duties." *See* 18 U.S.C. § 930(g)(1). However, this statute does not apply to "the lawful performance of official duties by an officer, agent, or employee of the United States, a State, or a political subdivision thereof, who is authorized by law to engage in or supervise the prevention, detection, investigation, or prosecution of any violation of law[,]" nor does it apply to federal officials or members of the armed forces who are permitted to possess such a firearm by law, or the lawful carrying of a firearm incident to hunting or "other lawful purposes." 18 U.S.C. § 930(d). This statute does not govern the possession of a firearm in a federal court facility.

2. National parks

CHP holders are permitted to carry in Louisiana National Parks, but not buildings within the parks, such as ranger stations, because these are federal buildings. Under federal law, for firearms purposes, all federal parks are subject to the state law of the state in which the park is located. *See* 16 U.S.C. § 1a-7b. A CHP holder may, therefore, carry a handgun concealed in a federal park, but not in federal buildings in the park.

3. VA Hospitals: firearms prohibited

FIREARMS PROHIBITED AT VETERANS AFFAIRS HOSPITALS: 38 C.F.R. § 1.218(A)(13)

"No person while on property shall carry firearms, other dangerous or deadly weapons, or explosives, either openly or concealed, except for official purposes."

One place where many law-abiding CHP holders fall victim is at the VA Hospital. The VA Hospital system is governed by federal law, which prohibits the carrying of any firearm while on VA property. This includes the parking lot, sidewalk, and any other area that is the property of the VA.

Under federal law, 38 C.F.R. § 1.218(a)(13) states that "[n]o person while on property shall carry firearms, other dangerous or deadly weapons, or explosives, either openly or concealed, except for official purposes." The "official purposes" specified refer specifically to the VA Hospital Police. The area where this specific law gets good people in trouble is that the Department of Veterans Affairs has its own set of laws and guidelines and is not controlled strictly by the Gun Control Act and the general provisions regarding the prohibition of firearms on federal property. The VA law is much more restrictive, and many veterans have found themselves in trouble when they valet-park their vehicle and the valet discovers a concealed handgun in the console or concealed in the door storage area. How rigidly this law is enforced is determined by the individual hospital administrators as described in 38 C.F.R. § 1.218(a), however, regardless of how strictly the law is enforced firearms are still prohibited under the law and the VA police are very aggressive in enforcing them.

4. United States Post Offices: firearms prohibited

FIREARMS PROHIBITED AT POST OFFICES:
39 C.F.R. § 232.1(L)

"Notwithstanding the provisions of any other law, rule or regulation, no person while on postal property may carry firearms, other dangerous or deadly weapons, or explosives, either openly or concealed, or store the same on postal property, except for official purposes."

Under this regulation, firearms or other deadly weapons are prohibited on postal property, which includes not only the building, but all property surrounding the building where a post office is located. This includes the parking lot (*e.g.*, a person's vehicle where a firearm may be stored), as well as the sidewalks and walkways.

5. Military bases and installations: firearms generally prohibited

Military bases and installations are treated much like the VA Hospital and US Post Offices in that they have, and are governed by, a separate set of rules and regulations with respect to firearms on the premises of an installation or base and are generally prohibited. Military installations are governed by the federal law under Title 32 of the Code of Federal Regulations. Moreover, the sections covering the laws governing and relating to military bases and installations are exceedingly numerous. There are, in fact, sections that are dedicated to only certain bases, such as 32 C.F.R. § 552.98, which only governs the "possessing, carrying, concealing, and transporting of firearms . . . on Fort Stewart/Hunter Army Airfield[.]"

F. Can municipalities restrict firearms rights?

1. Can cities or other governmental agencies enact firearms laws or regulations regarding the carrying of a concealed handgun by CHP holders that are more restrictive than state laws?

No. The Louisiana Legislature can and does prohibit local municipalities from making certain gun laws by the legal doctrine known as "preemption." A preemption statute is a mechanism by which the Louisiana legislature sets certain areas off limits to local governments, which helps ensure the uniformity of law across the state, in this case, firearms law.

The Louisiana preemption statute can be found in Louisiana Revised Statutes Annotated § 40:1796(A). It states that "[n]o governing authority . . . shall enact after July 15, 1985, any ordinance or regulation more restrictive than state law concerning in any way the sale, purchase, possession, ownership, transfer, transportation, license, or registration of firearms, ammunition, or components of firearms or ammunition." For a complete discussion, *see* Chapter 1.

G. How big of a handgun can a CHP holder legally carry?

As we mentioned in Chapter 2, federal law dictates that any firearm which has any barrel with a bore of more than one-half inch in diameter (.50 caliber) is a "destructive device" and is subject to the National Firearms Act (except for certain shotguns). Possession of any such firearm without the proper paperwork associated with NFA firearms is illegal whether a person is a CHP holder or not. For more information on destructive devices and the NFA, *see* Chapter 14.

Louisiana law doesn't specify a size of handgun to be carried legally with a CHP, but does define "handgun" as any "pistol or revolver originally designed to be fired by the use of a single hand and which is designed to fire or is capable of firing fixed cartridge ammunition." *See* La. Rev. Stat. Ann. § 40:1379.3(J)(3).

II. CHP HOLDERS DEALING WITH LAW ENFORCEMENT

A. Do I legally have to present my CHP to a police officer if they ask for my identification and I am carrying my gun?

Yes. Louisiana Revised Statutes Annotated § 40:1379.3(I)(2) states that "[a] permittee armed with a handgun in accordance with [a Louisiana CHP] shall notify any police officer who approaches a permittee in an official manner or with an identified official purpose that they have a weapon on their person, submit to a pat down, and allow the officer to temporarily disarm them."

B. Can a police officer legally take a CHP holder's handgun away?

Yes. "Whenever a law enforcement officer is made aware that an individual is carrying a concealed handgun and the officer has reasonable grounds to believe that the individual is under the influence of either alcohol or a controlled dangerous substance, the officer may take temporary possession of the handgun and request submission of the individual to a department certified chemical test for determination of the chemical status of the individual. Whenever [an] . . . officer is made aware that an individual is behaving in a criminally negligent manner . . . or is negligent in the carrying of a concealed handgun . . . the officer may seize the handgun." La. Rev. Stat. Ann. § 40.1379.3(I)(2).

PRACTICAL LEGAL TIP

Having a Concealed Handgun License can make you feel safer as you are out and about. But remember, a CHP is a license to protect against trouble–not to go looking for it!

C. Can I carry a concealed handgun in other states if I have a Louisiana CHP?

Yes. Check the Louisiana State Police website at lsp.org/handguns for an up-to-date list of "reciprocal" states that honor Louisiana permits.

Every state has the authority to determine whether or not their state will recognize a carry license or permit issued by another state. Reciprocity is where states enter into an agreement with each other, in this case, to recognize each other's carry licenses. However, states are not required to have reciprocity with one another, nor are they required to recognize another state's carry license.

There are many states that issue their own licenses, but refuse to recognize a carry license from another state. Conversely, there are states that choose to recognize some or all other states' carry licenses. Louisiana gives the Deputy Secretary of Public Safety authority to negotiate reciprocity agreements with other states. Louisiana recognizes the concealed carry permits of states that recognize Louisiana concealed carry permits. As of the date of writing, a Louisiana CHP is recognized by 37 other states and Louisiana recognizes the handgun licenses issued in the same 37 states.

D. What out-of-state handgun licenses does Louisiana NOT recognize?

At the time of writing, Louisiana does not recognize handgun licenses issued by the following states:

California	Connecticut	Delaware
District of Columbia	Hawaii	Illinois
Maryland	Massachusetts	New Jersey
New Mexico	New York	Oregon
Rhode Island		

However, again, check the Louisiana State Police website for a current listing. An out-of-state concealed carry license holder must follow Louisiana law while in Louisiana, just like a Louisiana CHP holder must follow the laws of the state he or she is located in when traveling. For example, a Florida Concealed Weapons or Firearms License will allow a person to carry a concealed handgun, knife, electric weapon, billy club, and tear-gas gun while in Florida. However, a person with a Florida license will only be allowed to carry a concealed handgun in Louisiana and not be legally allowed to carry other forms of weapons pursuant to Florida's license.

E. What state's laws apply to me when using my Louisiana CHP in another state?

Anytime a CHP holder is in another state, even if that state recognizes a Louisiana CHP, the law of the state where the person is currently located will be the law which governs that person's firearms possession and use. If a person is traveling to another state, they must abide by that state's laws. Just like a non-Louisianan visiting Louisiana must follow Louisiana law. Most common laws Louisianans should be aware of are the requirement to present a license and the places that are off-limits to CHP holders, as most of the time they vary from state to state. For example, while having a handgun will get a license holder quick entry into the Texas Capitol, having a handgun at the Louisiana capitol will get a person carrying a quick trip to jail in Louisiana.

F. Can persons who are not Louisiana residents obtain a Louisiana CHP?

No. According to Louisiana Revised Statutes Annotated § 40:1379.3(C):

> "[t]o qualify for a concealed handgun permit, a Louisiana resident shall: . . .
>
> (3) Be a resident of the state."

As soon as a CHP holder ceases to reside in the State, the CHP becomes automatically invalid. "Resident" is defined by the statute as "a person who is legally domiciled in Louisiana." La. Rev. Stat. Ann. § 40:1379.3(J)(4). One can prove his legal domicile by providing a copy of a valid Louisiana driver's license or an official Louisiana identification card. A person who maintains a home in Louisiana but is residing elsewhere as a member of the United States military or as a student is still considered to be a resident for the purposes of concealed carry permits. *See* La. Rev. Stat. Ann. § 40:1379.3(J)(4).

➢ CHAPTER TEN ≺

POSSESSING, CARRYING, AND TRANSPORTING FIREARMS WITHOUT A CHP

This chapter deals with when and where a person may possess, carry, or transport a firearm if they are not a concealed handgun permit holder or someone with a Louisiana-recognized concealed carry permit. Louisiana is an open-carry state, meaning that as long as your firearm is visible, you can carry it anywhere with a few exceptions.

The law discussed in this chapter is based primarily on Article 1, Section 11 of the Louisiana State Constitution which states: "[t]he right of each citizen to keep and bear arms is fundamental and shall not be infringed. Any restriction on this right shall be subject to strict scrutiny." Case law, as we will discuss, has interpreted this to mean that Louisiana citizens, with a few exceptions, have the right to openly carry firearms.

I. WHERE ARE FIREARMS (LONG GUNS OR HANDGUNS) PROHIBITED UNDER LOUISIANA LAW?

A. What are prohibited places in Louisiana?

Under Louisiana law, there are certain places where all firearms, including long guns and handguns, as well as other prohibited weapons, such as illegal knives, clubs, and the weapons listed in La. Rev. Stat. Ann. § 14:95 of the Louisiana Criminal Code, are forbidden. Firearms can be openly carried anywhere except: school zones (unless in your vehicle or on private property) (*see* La. Rev. Stat. Ann. § 14.95.2(C)(4)&(5)), local and state government buildings, any place that sells alcohol for consumption on the premises (those with a Class A-Restaurant permit) (*see* La. Rev. Stat. Ann. § 14:95.5(C)(2)), and any private property that posts signs expressly forbidding the carrying of firearms as discussed in the last chapter.

1. Schools and educational institutions

FIREARM-FREE ZONES LOUISIANA CRIMINAL CODE § 14:95.2

"Carrying a firearm or dangerous weapon . . . by a student or nonstudent on school property, at a school sponsored function, or in a firearm-free zone is unlawful[.]" This includes "any firearm or dangerous weapon, on one's person, at any time while on a school campus, on school transportation, or at any school sponsored function in a specific designated area including but not limited to athletic competitions, dances, parties, or any extracurricular activities, or within one thousand feet of any school campus."

This prohibition applies to the physical premises of a school campus, as well as any grounds or buildings where a school sponsored function is taking place, and on any form of school transportation. This means that if the marching band is practicing in a parking lot more than 1000 feet from the school—a place where a firearm is otherwise permitted—then while the band is participating in its activity, firearms and other weapons are prohibited. "School" includes any public or private elementary, secondary, high school, or vocational-technical school, college, or university. *See* La. Rev. Stat. Ann. § 14:95.2(B)(3). For more information on firearms in Gun-Free School Zones, see Section VII of this Chapter.

2. Polling places

Under the Louisiana Code, it is an offense for any person (other than a peace officer in the performance of his official duties) to carry a firearm while present at a polling place. *See* La. Rev. Stat. Ann. §§ 18:1461.7(C)(3); 40:1379.3(N)(4). It is important to note that many polling locations are often places where firearms are already prohibited, such as schools and government buildings, so, be doubly cautious about disarming before going to your local polls.

3. Various government buildings

Under Louisiana law, individuals are not permitted to possess firearms or other weapons in several kinds of state or local government buildings, including law enforcement offices, stations, or buildings, a courthouse or courtroom, the meeting place of the governing authority of a political subdivision, or the state capitol building. *See* La. Rev. Stat. Ann. § 40:1379.3(N)(1)(3)(5) & (6).

4. Defenses and exceptions to prohibited places

There are, of course, certain exceptions to possessing firearms and other weapons in the places listed above. Most of these defenses and exceptions are in line with a person acting within the scope of their employment.

School firearm-free zones

There are exceptional situations in which the carrying of firearms in the firearm-free zone of a school is not unlawful. These exceptions are laid out in Section 14:95.2(C):

"(1) A federal law enforcement officer or a Louisiana-commissioned state or local Post Certified law enforcement officer who is authorized to carry a firearm;

(2) A school official or employee acting during the normal course of his employment or a student acting under the direction of such school official or employee;

(3) Any person having the written permission of the principal.

(4) The possession of a firearm occurring within one thousand feet of school property and entirely on private property, or entirely within a private residence;

(5) A firearm contained entirely within a motor vehicle;

(6) Any student carrying a firearm to or from a class, in which he is duly enrolled, that requires the use of the firearm in the class;

(7) A student enrolled or participating in an activity requiring the use of a firearm including but not limited to any ROTC function under the authorization of a university;

(8) A student who possesses a firearm in his dormitory room or while going to or from their vehicle or any other person with permission of the administration; or

(9) Any person who has a valid concealed handgun permit issued pursuant to La. Rev. Stat. Ann. § 40:1379.1 or 1379.3 and

who carries a concealed handgun within one thousand feet of any school campus."

B. Can a person legally carry a firearm while in a vehicle?

Under most circumstances, the vehicle carry of a firearm by someone lawfully entitled to possess it is legal. Exceptions include situations wherein the firearm has been used in the commission of a crime (La. Rev. Stat. Ann. § 14:95(B)), the firearm's serial numbers have been obliterated (La. Rev. Stat. Ann. § 14:95.7), or the person in control of the vehicle has been convicted of a felony. (La. Rev. Stat. Ann. § 14:95.1). Additionally, under Louisiana law, "a person who lawfully possesses a firearm may transport or store such firearm in a locked, privately-owned motor vehicle in any parking lot, parking garage, or other designated parking area." La. Rev. Stat. Ann. § 32:292.1(A).

PRACTICAL LEGAL TIP

If you carry a handgun in your vehicle, don't allow yourself to be drawn into a road-rage incident, no matter how minor. Someone who calls 911 to report that you pointed a gun at them, even though it was really just your middle finger, may get you arrested and charged with a crime. So, if you carry a gun in the car, forget how to flip the bird!

1. May I keep a handgun in my vehicle if there are children in the car?

Yes, having children in the car does not change the law on whether a person is able to legally possess a firearm in the vehicle.

2. Is it legal for a passenger in a vehicle or watercraft without a CHP to have a handgun?

Because Louisiana is an open carry state, the open carrying of a firearm is legal in most public places (except for the exceptions discussed above). This includes when you are a passenger in a motor vehicle or watercraft so long as the owner of the vehicle or watercraft has not prohibited passengers from carrying firearms aboard.

3. Is it legal for an owner of a vehicle to possess a handgun when a passenger in the vehicle is a felon or is otherwise disqualified from possessing firearms?

Yes, so long as the felon (or person disqualified) never constructively possesses or has dominion or control over the firearm. This can be tricky, and because the law is not explicit, what one person views as constructive possession might not always be true for another viewing the same set of facts.

EXAMPLE:

Mark arrives to pick up his brother John, who is being released from prison after completing his 5-year sentence. Mark always keeps a handgun under the driver seat of his vehicle. When John gets in the car, he sits in the front-passenger seat.

Has Mark violated the law? No, because Mark still has possession of the firearm. It is a crime to affirmatively give a handgun to a disqualified individual—like a felon—but it is not a crime to possess a handgun around such an individual. *See* La. Rev. Stat. Ann. § 14:95.1.1.

Has John violated the law? Not likely. Because he did not have control and dominion over the firearm, there will probably not be sufficient evidence to show he constructively possessed a firearm as a felon.

The law here revolves around whether the prohibited person possesses the firearm, not whether a firearm is nearby. For instance, if we change the example to a person who hands a recently-released felon a handgun in the car and asks the felon to "put it under the seat," then the person has committed a crime. However, in the real world, the legal fight will be over who was actually in possession of the firearm. This issue may ultimately be for the jury to decide.

ILLEGALLY SUPPLYING A FELON WITH A FIREARM
LOUISIANA CRIMINAL CODE § 14:95.1.1

"Illegally supplying a felon with a firearm is the intentional giving, selling, donating, providing, lending, delivering, or otherwise transferring a firearm to any person known by the offender to be a person convicted of a felony and prohibited from possessing a firearm[.]"

C. May a person keep a firearm in their hotel room?

Yes. Louisiana is an open carry state, and the open carrying of firearms is permitted in most public places, save the few exceptions discussed above. This includes hotel rooms. However, a hotel, or any private business, has the right and ability to prohibit the possession of firearms in or on their property. La. Rev. Stat. Ann. § 40:1379.3(O).

II. TRAVELING ACROSS STATE LINES WITH FIREARMS

Many people vacation and travel outside of Louisiana. Naturally, no one wants to travel unarmed if they can help it, but, unfortunately, not every state shares the same views on gun ownership and gun rights as we do in Louisiana. This is especially true in the northeast corner and west coast of the United States. How then does a person pass through states that have restrictive firearms laws or those different from Louisiana? For example, how does a person legally pass through a state that prohibits the possession of a handgun without a license from that state? The answer: safe-passage legislation.

A. Federal law: qualifying for firearms "Safe Passage"

Traveling across state lines with a firearm means that a person may need to use the provisions of the federal law known as the "Safe Passage" provision. Federal law allows individuals who are legally in possession of firearms in their state (the starting point of traveling) to travel through states that are not as friendly. This protection is only available under federal law to transport such firearms across state lines for lawful purposes, as long as they comply with the requirements of the Firearm Owners Protection Act, 18 U.S.C. § 926A, nicknamed the "Safe Passage" provision. The first requirement to qualify for the Federal "Safe Passage" provision is that throughout the duration of the trip through the anti-firearm state, the firearm must be unloaded and locked in the trunk, or locked in a container that is out of reach or not readily accessible from the passenger compartment. The ammunition also must be locked in the trunk or a container. Note that for the storage of both firearms and ammunition, the glove box and center console compartment are specifically not allowed under the statute.

1. "Safe Passage" requires legal start to legal finish

To get protection under federal law, a gun owner's journey must start and end in states where the traveler's possession of the firearm is legal; for instance, a person traveling with their Glock 17 starting in Louisiana and ending in Vermont. Even though a person must drive through New York or Massachusetts to get to Vermont, as long as the person qualifies under the "Safe Passage" provision, then they may legally pass through. However, if the start point was Louisiana and the end point was New York (a place where the handgun would be illegal), there is no protection under the federal law. Safe-passage requires legal start and legal finish.

Although traveling across state lines naturally invokes federal law, it is important to remember that whenever a person finally completes their journey and reaches their destination state, the laws of that state control the possession, carrying, and use of the firearm. Federal law does not make it legal or provide any protection for possession of a firearm that is illegal under the laws of the destination state (*i.e.*, the end state of your travels).

2. What is the definition of "traveling" for "Safe Passage" provisions?

The final requirement for protection under the federal law is that individuals MUST be "traveling" while in the firearm hostile state. The legal definition of "traveling" is both murky and narrow. The "Safe Passage" provision protection has been held in courts to be limited to situations that strictly relate to traveling and nothing more. Traveling is a term that is not defined in the federal statute; however, it has received treatment in the courts that is indicative of what one can expect. Generally speaking, if a person stops somewhere for too long, they cease to be "traveling" and, therefore, lose their protection under the "Safe Passage" provision. How long this time limit is has not been determined either statutorily or by case law with any definitiveness.

While stopping for gas or restroom breaks may not disqualify a person from the "traveling" protection, any stop for an activity not directly related to traveling could be considered a destination and thus, you would lose the legal protection. For example, in Chicago, anyone in the city for more than 24 hours is not considered to be traveling under local policy. In an actual case, stopping for a brief nap in a bank parking lot in New Jersey caused a Texan driving back home from Maine to lose the "traveling" protection. He received 5 years in prison for possession of weapons that are illegal under New Jersey law. Of course, if the driver would have made it to Hershey, Pennsylvania, he would have been safe. The moral of the story is to travel through these gun-unfriendly states as fast as you can (without breaking the speed limit, of course)!

3. Protection under federal law does not mean protection from prosecution in unfriendly states

To make matters even worse for firearms travelers, even if a person qualifies for protection under the federal "Safe Passage" provision, New Jersey and New York seem quite proud to treat this protection as an affirmative defense. This means that someone can be arrested even though he or she met all of the requirements of the federal statute. Then, they would have to go to court to assert this defense. In other words, while a person could beat the rap, they will not beat the ride! This becomes even more troublesome in the instance of someone who is legally flying with their firearm, and then due to flight complications, must land in New Jersey or New York, as travelers in this position have been arrested or threatened with arrest.

Once again, the "Safe Passage" provision only applies while a person is traveling; as soon as they arrive at their destination and cease their travels, the laws of that state control a person's actions. Remember: check all applicable state firearms laws before you leave for your destination!

III. AIR TRAVEL WITH A FIREARM

A. How do I legally travel with a firearm as a passenger on a commercial airline?

It is legal to travel with firearms on commercial airlines so long as the firearms transported are unloaded and in a locked, hard-sided container as checked baggage. Under federal law, the container must be completely inaccessible to passengers. Further, under U.S. Homeland Security rules, firearms, ammunition and firearm parts, including firearm frames, receivers, clips, and magazines, are prohibited in carry-on baggage. The Transportation Safety Administration (TSA) also requires that "[r]eplica firearms, including firearm replicas that are toys, may be transported in checked baggage only. Rifle scopes are permitted in carry-on and checked baggage." *See* www.tsa.gov/travel/transporting-firearms-and-ammunition.

PRACTICAL LEGAL TIP

Most people say that the reason they forgot to remove a firearm from their baggage at the airport is because they were in such a hurry to not miss their flight. But, if you do accidentally leave it in your carry-on bags, you can be assured that you will miss your flight! At a very minimum, if TSA finds a gun in your baggage, you will not only cause a scene and miss your flight, but you will also incur a fine from the TSA and possibly be subjected to prosecution by local law enforcement.

1. Firearms must be inaccessible

Federal law makes it a crime subject to fine, imprisonment for up to 10 years, or both, if a person "when on, or attempting to get on, an aircraft in, or intended for operation in, air transportation or intrastate air transportation, has on or about the individual or the property of the individual a concealed dangerous weapon that is or would be accessible to the individual in flight." 49 U.S.C. § 46505(b). Additionally, under 49 U.S.C. § 46303(a) "[a]n individual who, when on, or attempting to board, an aircraft in, or intended for operation in, air transportation or intrastate air transportation, has on or about the individual or the property of the individual a concealed dangerous weapon that is or would be accessible to the individual in flight is liable to the United States Government for a civil penalty of not more than $ 10,000 for each violation."

2. Firearms must be checked in baggage

The following guidelines are put out by the TSA for traveling with firearms on airlines:

"To avoid issues that could impact your travel and/or result in law enforcement action, here are some guidelines to assist you in packing your firearms and ammunition:

- All firearms must be declared to the airline during the ticket counter check-in process.
- The term firearm includes: (Please see, for instance, United States Code, Title 18, Part 1, Chapter 44 for information about firearm definitions.)
- Any weapon (including a starter gun) which will, or is designed to, or may readily be converted to expel a projectile by the action of an explosive.
- The frame or receiver of any such weapon.
- Any firearm muffler or firearm silencer.
- Any destructive device.
- The firearm must be unloaded.
- As defined by 49 CFR § 1540.5, 'A loaded firearm means a firearm that has a live round of ammunition, or any component thereof, in the chamber or cylinder or in a magazine inserted in the firearm.'
- The firearm must be in a hard-sided container that is locked. A locked container is defined as one that completely secures the firearm from being accessed. Locked cases that can be pulled open with little effort cannot be brought aboard the aircraft.
- If firearms are not properly declared or packaged, TSA will provide the checked bag to law enforcement for resolution with the airline. If the issue is resolved, law enforcement will release the bag to TSA so screening may be completed.

- TSA must resolve all alarms in checked baggage. If a locked container containing a firearm alarms, TSA will contact the airline, who will make a reasonable attempt to contact the owner and advise the passenger to go to the screening location. If contact is not made, the container will not be placed on the aircraft.
- If a locked container alarms during screening and is not marked as containing a declared firearm, TSA will cut the lock in order to resolve the alarm.
- Travelers should remain in the area designated by the aircraft operator or TSA representative to take the key back after the container is cleared for transportation.
- Travelers must securely pack any ammunition in fiber (such as cardboard), wood or metal boxes or other packaging specifically designed to carry small amounts of ammunition.
- Firearm magazines and ammunition clips, whether loaded or empty, must be securely boxed or included within a hard-sided case containing an unloaded firearm.
- Small arms ammunition, including ammunition not exceeding .75 caliber for a rifle or pistol and shotgun shells of any gauge, may be carried in the same hard-sided case as the firearm, as long as it follows the packing guidelines described above.
- TSA prohibits black powder or percussion caps used with blackpowder.
- Rifle scopes are not prohibited in carry-on bags and do not need to be in the hard-sided, locked checked bag."

See www.tsa.gov.

B. May I have a firearm in a private aircraft that takes off from Louisiana and lands in another state?

In situations where a private aircraft is taking off from one state and landing in another, the law will simply view this as traveling interstate with firearms. Where no other statutes apply to the person's flight, the person will be subject to the provisions of 18 U.S.C. § 926A regarding the interstate transportation of a firearm: "any person who is not otherwise prohibited by this chapter from transporting, shipping, or receiving a firearm shall be entitled to transport a firearm for any lawful purpose from any place where he may lawfully possess and carry such firearm to any other place where he may lawfully possess and carry such firearm if, during such transportation the firearm is unloaded, and neither the firearm nor any ammunition being transported is readily accessible or is directly accessible from the passenger compartment of such transporting vehicle[.]"

This statute allows a person to transport firearms between states subject to the following conditions: that the person can lawfully possess the firearm at his or her points of departure and arrival, and that the firearm remain unloaded and inaccessible during the trip. However, what if the person is a CHP holder and wants to carry concealed between states? Fortunately, 18 U.S.C. § 927 states that section 926A does not preempt applicable state law. Thus, if a person can lawfully carry a concealed weapon in the state in which he or she boards the aircraft and in the state in which he or she lands, the CHP holder is not subject to the unloaded and inaccessible restrictions of 18 U.S.C. § 926A.

For operations of private aircraft within one state, a person will only be subject to the laws of the state within which he or she is operating. The person will need to review their state's statutes to determine whether they impose any restrictions on possession of firearms within non-secure areas of airports. The person will also need to be familiar with the airports he or she will be visiting to determine whether each airport has any restrictions (*e.g.*, posting to prohibit concealed carry, *etc.*).

IV. UNDERSTANDING FIREARM-FREE SCHOOL ZONE LAWS

The discussion of firearm-free school zones is one that covers many different areas of the law and affects both persons who hold a CHP, as well as persons who do not. That is because the "Firearm-Free School Zone" law and its meaning cause a lot of confusion. Signs warning about being in a firearm-free school zone are common around schools, but what does this mean to people lawfully in possession of firearms? There are actually both Louisiana and federal firearm-free school zone laws, each with very different meanings and consequences. For this reason, we will explain the applicable rules to individuals who possess and do not possess a CHP in this Chapter, even though the Chapter has been dedicated to possessing or carrying a firearm without a license.

A. Louisiana "Firearm-Free Zone" law

The Louisiana "Firearm-Free Zone" law is part of Section 14:95.6. The statute lays out the area considered to be a "firearm-free zone" as "an area inclusive of any school campus and within one thousand feet of any such school campus, and within a school bus[.]"

Louisiana law allows lawful firearms carriers to carry firearms in their vehicles even in "firearm-free zones." The statute says it should not apply to: "[a]ny constitutionally protected activity . . . such as a firearm contained entirely within a motor vehicle." La. Rev. Stat. Ann. § 14:95.6(B)(5).

B. Federal "Gun Free School Zone" law: 18 U.S.C. § 922(q)

The text of the federal "Gun Free School Zone" law is found in 18 U.S.C. § 922(q). This law states that it is a federal crime for a person to possess a firearm that has moved through interstate commerce (this includes virtually all firearms), on the grounds of or within 1,000 feet of a public, parochial, or private school. As surprising as it may seem, under this federal law, the mere possession of a firearm by the occupant of a motor vehicle while driving past a school or dropping off a child, is a federal crime.

However, federal law provides seven exceptions:

1. *Exception one:* if the possession is on private property which is not part of the school grounds. This means that a person living within 1,000 feet of a school can keep a firearm in their house.
2. *Exception two:* if the individual possessing the firearm is licensed to do so by the State in which the school zone is located or a political subdivision of the State, and the law of the State or political subdivision requires that, before an individual obtains such a license, the law enforcement authorities of the State or political subdivision verify that the individual is qualified under law to receive the license. This means that a CHP holder may legally carry a concealed firearm into a gun free school zone. However, there is one important note about the statute: a person can only lawfully carry in a school zone located in the state that issued the firearms license. Therefore, if a person has a Louisiana CHP, they can only carry through Louisiana school zones. If that Louisiana CHP holder is traveling through another state, the exception under federal law does not apply to them, and they are in violation of this law. It also means that a Louisiana resident, who holds a non-resident, non-Louisiana concealed

carry license or permit, does not benefit from this exception and is in violation of the law if they take a firearm into a school zone.

3. *Exception three:* if the firearm is not loaded, and is in a locked container, or a locked firearms rack that is on a motor vehicle. This means that if a firearm is unloaded and carried in a locked case, or other type of locked container, such as a glove box or trunk, there is no violation of the federal law.
4. *Exception four:* if the firearm is carried by an individual for use in a program approved by a school in the school zone. This exception covers school-sponsored shooting activities, such as an ROTC program.
5. *Exception five:* if the firearm is carried by an individual in accordance with a contract entered into between a school in the school zone and the individual or an employer of the individual. This means that school security guards can carry firearms while on the job.
6. *Exception six:* if the firearm is carried by a law enforcement officer acting in his or her official capacity. This exception covers police officers while on-duty only. It does not appear to cover them while they are off-duty, even if they are required by state law to carry while off-duty.
7. *Exception seven:* if the firearm is unloaded and is in the possession of an individual while traversing school premises for the purpose of gaining access to public or private lands open to hunting, if the entry on school premises is authorized by school authorities. This means that if a hunter must cross school property to get to a lawful hunting ground, they must have the permission of the school, and the firearm must be unloaded.

See 18 U.S.C. §§ 922(q)(1)(I)(2)(B)(i)-(vii).

C. Reconciling Louisiana and federal laws on gun-free school zones

The law puts a vast number of unknowing and unsuspecting people in conflict with federal law, while being in full compliance with state law. As a result, it is likely that this law is violated thousands of times a day. However, while this has been federal law since 1996 and its predecessor was the law since 1990, there does not appear to be a wave of federal prosecutions for the mere possession of a firearm by a person who is only driving through a school zone or picking up or dropping off their child. Nevertheless, even though it appears that the federal government is not inclined to enforce some of the provisions of this statute today, the law is on the books right now.

D. Is a person legally permitted to possess a firearm in their vehicle in the parking lot of a college or university?

Yes, according to Section 14:95.6(B)(5), the prohibition on firearms in firearm-free zones surrounding schools does not apply to firearms contained entirely in motor vehicles. Additionally, La. Rev. Stat. Ann. § 14:95.2(C)(8) protects a student who possesses a firearm on campus in their dormitory room or while going to or from their vehicle with such firearm.

➤ CHAPTER ELEVEN ≺

RESTORATION OF FIREARMS RIGHTS: THE LAW OF PARDONS AND EXPUNGEMENTS

I. IS IT POSSIBLE TO RESTORE A PERSON'S RIGHT TO BEAR ARMS?

What happens after a person has been convicted of a crime; is it possible to later clear their name and/or criminal record? If possible, then what is the process for removing a conviction and restoring a person's right to purchase and possess firearms? This Chapter will explain how a person, under very limited circumstances, can have arrest records, criminal charges, and even criminal convictions removed or nullified. But words of caution, success in this arena may be rare. Further, each state has different rules concerning these issues, as well as a completely different set of rules under federal law. Before we begin a meaningful discussion, it is important to explain two terms and concepts: clemency and expungement.

A. What is clemency?

Clemency is the action the government, usually the chief executive (*e.g.*, the President on the federal level or a governor on the state level), takes in forgiving or pardoning a crime or canceling the penalty of a crime, either wholly, or in part. Clemency can include full pardons after a conviction, full pardons after completion of deferred adjudication community supervision, conditional pardons, pardons based on innocence, commutations of a sentence, emergency medical reprieves, and family medical reprieves. Clemency can be granted at both the federal and state level.

B. What is expungement?

Expungement is the physical act of destroying or purging government criminal records, unlike sealing, which is simply hiding the records from the public. Under certain circumstances, a person may have their criminal record either expunged or sealed.

II. FEDERAL LAW

A. Presidential pardon

Under Article II, Section 2 of the United States Constitution, the President of the United States has the power "to grant reprieves and pardons for offenses against the United States, except in cases of impeachment." The President's power to pardon offenses has also been interpreted to include the power to grant conditional pardons, commutations of sentence, conditional commutations of sentence, remission of fines and forfeitures, respites, and amnesties. However, the President's clemency authority only extends to federal offenses; the President cannot grant clemency for a state crime.

1. How does a person petition for federal clemency or a pardon?

Under federal law, a person requesting executive clemency must petition the President of the United States and submit the petition to the Office of the Pardon Attorney in the Department of Justice. The Office of the Pardon Attorney can provide petitions and other required forms necessary to complete the application for clemency. *See* 28 C.F.R. § 1.1. Petition forms for commutation of sentence may also be obtained from the wardens of federal penal institutions. In addition, a petitioner applying for executive clemency with respect to military offenses should submit his or her petition directly to the Secretary of the military branch that had original jurisdiction over the court-martial trial and conviction of the petitioner.

The Code of Federal Regulations requires an applicant to wait five years after the date of the release of the petitioner from confinement, or in a case where no prison sentence was imposed, an applicant is required to wait five years after the date of conviction prior to submitting a petition for clemency. The regulation further states that "[g]enerally, no petition should be submitted by a person who is on probation, parole, or supervised release." 28 C.F.R. § 1.2. With that in mind, the President can grant clemency at any time, whether an individual has made a formal petition or not. For example, President Gerald Ford granted a full and unconditional pardon to former President Richard Nixon prior to any indictment or charges being filed related to his involvement in Watergate.

2. What should a petition for clemency include?

Petitions for executive clemency should include the information required in the form prescribed by the United States Attorney General. This includes information:

1. that the person requesting clemency must state specifically the purpose for which clemency is sought, as well as attach any and all relevant documentary evidence that will support how clemency will support that purpose;
2. that discloses any arrests or convictions subsequent to the federal crime for which clemency is sought;
3. that discloses all delinquent credit obligations (whether disputed or not), all civil lawsuits to which the applicant is a party (whether plaintiff or defendant), and all unpaid tax obligations (whether local, state, or federal); and
4. that includes three character affidavits from persons not related to the applicant by blood or marriage.

See www.justice.gov/pardon/pardon-information-and-instructions.

In addition, acceptance of a Presidential pardon generally carries with it an admission of guilt. For that reason, a petitioner should include in his or her petition a statement of the petitioner's acceptance of responsibility, an expression of remorse, and atonement for the offense. All of the requirements are contained in 28 C.F.R. §§ 1.1-1.11.

3. What happens after a petition for executive clemency is submitted?

All petitions for federal clemency are reviewed by the Office of the Pardon Attorney in the Department of Justice. A non-binding recommendation on an application is made to the President.

Federal regulations also provide for guidelines and requirements to notify victims of the crimes, if any, for which clemency is sought. The President will either grant or deny a pardon. There are no hearings held on the petition, and there is no appeal of the President's decision. *See* www.justice.gov/pardon/commutation-instructions.

4. What is the effect of a Presidential pardon?

A pardon is the forgiveness of a crime and the cancellation of the penalty associated with that crime. While a Presidential pardon will restore various rights lost as a result of the pardoned offense, it will not expunge the record of your conviction. This means that even if a person is granted a pardon, the person must still disclose their conviction on any form where such information is required, although the person may also disclose the fact that the offense for which they were convicted was pardoned.

B. Expungement of federal convictions

1. No law exists for general federal expungement

Congress has not provided federal legislation that offers any comprehensive authority or procedure for expunging criminal offenses. There exist only statues that allow expungement in certain cases for possession of small amounts of controlled substances (see below) and interestingly, a procedure to expunge DNA samples of certain members of the military wrongfully convicted. Because there is no statutory guidance, federal courts have literally made up the rules and procedures themselves, often coming to different conclusions. Some federal court circuits have stated they have no power to expunge records. However, other federal courts have indicated that they do have the power to expunge. The federal Fifth Circuit, which includes Louisiana, has held that under certain limited circumstances, federal courts may order expungement both of records held by other branches of the government (*e.g.*, executive branch), and its own court records. *See Sealed Appellant v. Sealed Appellee*, 130 F.3d 695 (5th Cir. 1997). The Supreme Court has passed on hearing cases that would have resolved the split between the circuits. This issue remains legally murky.

2. Possible procedure for federal expungement

There are no statutory guidelines for how to seek an expungement under federal law, however, the place to start would be to file a motion with the federal court that issued the conviction that a person wants to be expunged. However, federal judges very rarely grant these types of motions. Some circuits, including the Fifth Circuit have adopted a balancing test to decide if a record held by the court may be expunged. The court weighs the interests of the government in keeping open, unredacted records, against the injury to the individual of maintaining a criminal record. The Fifth Circuit, however, has acknowledged that "expungement is 'exceedingly narrow' and is granted only in exceptional circumstances." The court explained "the government cannot and should not be forced to rewrite history" every time a wrongfully accused wanted his record expunged. *Sealed Appellant v. Sealed Appellee*, 130 F.3d 695 (5th Cir. 1997). Some of the areas where expungement has worked are in incidents of extreme police misconduct, or where the conviction is being misused against the person. Unless there exist compelling reasons, a federal judge is highly unlikely to grant expungement.

3. Expungement for drug possession: statutory authority

Under a federal law entitled "special probation and expungement procedures for drug possessors," certain persons are allowed to request a federal court to issue an expungement order from all public records. *See* 18 U.S.C. § 3607. Congress intended this order to restore the person to the status he or she "occupied before such arrest or institution of criminal proceedings." 18 U.S.C. § 3607(c).

In order to qualify for the expungement, you must have been under the age of 21 when you were convicted, you must have no prior drug offenses, and your conviction must have been for simple possession of a small amount of a controlled substance. *See* 18 U.S.C. § 3607.

4. How does a person have firearms rights restored under federal law?

Under the Gun Control Act of 1968, a person who has received a Presidential pardon is not considered convicted of a crime preventing the purchase and possession of firearms subject to all other federal laws. *See* 18 U.S.C. §§ 921(a)(20) and (33). In addition, persons who had a conviction expunged or set aside, or who have had their civil rights restored, are not considered to have been convicted for purposes of the GCA "unless the pardon, expungement, or restoration of civil rights expressly provides the person may not ship, transport, possess, or receive firearms." 18 U.S.C. §§ 921(a)(20) and (33).

The GCA also provides the United States Attorney General with the authority to grant relief from firearms disabilities where the Attorney General determines that the person is not likely to act in a manner dangerous to the public safety and where granting relief would not be contrary to the public interest. *See* 18 U.S.C. § 925(c). The Attorney General has delegated this authority to the ATF. Unfortunately, the ATF reports that it has been prohibited from spending any funds in order to investigate or act upon applications from individuals seeking relief from federal firearms disabilities. This means that until the ATF's prohibition has been lifted, a person's best—and most likely—option to have their firearms rights restored is through a Presidential pardon. *See* www.atf.gov/qa-category/general.

III. LOUISIANA LAW

A. Clemency by Governor and Board of Pardons and Paroles

The Governor of Louisiana possesses the authority to grant executive clemency under Louisiana Revised Statutes Annotated § 15:572(A). The statute states:

> "The governor may grant reprieves to persons convicted of offenses against the state and, upon recommendation of the Board of Pardons . . . may commute sentences, pardon those convicted of offenses against the state, and remit fines and forfeitures imposed for such offenses."

1. Who is eligible for executive clemency in Louisiana?

Executive clemency can be granted if:

1. "You have been convicted of a violation of Louisiana law, either a felony or misdemeanor;
2. You have no pending charges, outstanding detainers, or any pecuniary penalties or liabilities which total more than $1,000 and result from any criminal conviction or traffic infraction;
3. You have paid all court costs which were imposed in connection with the conviction of the crime(s) for which pardon is requested;
4. You have paid all victim restitution, including but not limited to, restitution pursuant to a court or civil judgment or by order of the Committee on Parole;
5. You are not currently in jail or prison;
6. You must have discharged all sentences, including any type of supervision; and
7. You cannot have been considered for a Pardon within the past two years."

See Louisiana Application for Pardon Consideration at www.doc.la.gov/clemency-application-form2.

Note: a first offender who has never been previously convicted of a felony and who was convicted of a non-violent crime or aggravated battery, second degree battery, aggravated assault, mingling harmful substances, aggravated criminal damage to property, purse snatching, extortion, or illegal use of weapons or dangerous instrumentalities is automatically pardoned upon completion of their sentence without a recommendation of the Board of Pardons and without action by the Governor. *See* La. Const. Art. IV, § 5(E)(1).

2. How does a person seek executive clemency in Louisiana?

A person seeking executive clemency in Louisiana is required to complete an application, which is available from the Louisiana Department of Corrections. Once properly submitted, the file of any applicant eligible for clemency will be reviewed by the Board of Pardons, a five-member board whose members are appointed by the Governor.

The Board will review the application in a public hearing, however, the hearing is actually a review of the applicant's file rather than a formal hearing. The Board members vote on case files individually, and an applicant must obtain the favorable vote of 4 out of the 5 members of the Board before the application will be sent to the Governor for a final determination. Applicants are not able to appeal the decision of the Board or the Governor, but can re-apply for clemency after two years, if denied. If four members of the Board recommend clemency be extended to an applicant, the file is sent to the Governor, who may either accept the Board's recommendation and grant clemency or reject the recommendation and deny clemency. For more information on the process, please visit www.doc.la.gov/louisiana-board-of-pardons-and-parole/.

"Before considering the application for pardon of any person the board shall give written notice of the date and time at which the application will be heard and considered, at least thirty days prior to the hearing, to the following:

a) The district attorney, the sheriff of the parish in which the applicant was convicted, and in Orleans Parish, the superintendent of police;
b) The applicant;
c) The victim or the spouse or next of kin of a deceased victim. The notice is not required when the victim, or the spouse or next of kin of a deceased victim, advises the board in writing that such notification is not desired. The notice shall advise the victim, or the spouse or next of kin of a deceased victim, of their rights with regard to the hearing; and
d) Any other interested person on whose behalf a written request for such notification has been made by any other person who has a right, under law, to present testimony."

La. Rev. Stat. Ann. § 15:572.4(B)(1).

Further, it should be noted that:

1) "The victim, or the spouse or next of kin of a deceased victim, shall be allowed to testify at the hearing. The victim, or the spouse or next of kin of a deceased victim, shall be allowed to testify directly, or in rebuttal to testimony or evidence offered by or on behalf of the offender, or both; and
2) The district attorney and any other persons who desire to do so shall be given a reasonable opportunity to attend the meeting and be heard."

La. Rev. Stat. Ann. §§ 15:572.4(B)(2) and (3).

Additionally, before setting a hearing for pardon application or commutation of sentence, "notice of the application to the board for clemency or commutation of sentence shall be published on three separate days within a thirty-day period of time, without cost to the state, in any newspaper recognized, at any time during the six-month period prior to or following the publication of the first notice, as the official journal of the governing authority of the parish where the offense occurred for which the person was convicted." La. Rev. Stat. Ann. § 15:572.4(C).

3. What is the effect of executive clemency in Louisiana?

"[W]here the individual receives a full executive pardon by the governor, upon recommendation of the Department of Corrections, he is restored to the 'status of innocence.'" *State v. Riser*, (La. App. 2 Cir. 12/12/97); 704 So. 2d 946, 949. After a pardon, the conviction cannot be used to enhance punishment for a later crime, but it may be used at trial to impeach the individual as a witness. A full executive pardon also is effective under federal immigration law to avoid deportation and to lift the bar to establish good moral character for purposes of naturalization.

Conversely, a "first offender pardon" merely restores "all rights of citizenship and franchise[.]" La. Rev. Stat. Ann. § 15:572(D). This does not, however, restore the right to run for office (*see Touchet v. Broussard*, 10-0380, (La. 03/03/10); 31 So. 3d 986), relieve the obligation to register as a sex offender (La. Rev. Stat. Ann. § 15:572(B)(2)), restore firearms rights (*see State v. Wiggins*, 432 So. 2d 234 (La. 1983)), nor does it restore the privilege of a liquor license (*see State v. Adams*, 355 So. 2d 917 (La. 1978)). Unlike a federal or executive pardon, a first offender pardon does not prevent the use of the conviction in a later prosecution or sentencing.

See Touchet v. Broussard, 31 So. 3d at 993–94. A first offender pardon is also not considered "full and unconditional" under federal immigration law for purposes of avoiding deportation or for demonstrating good moral character for naturalization.

B. Louisiana expungement

Title 34 of the Louisiana Code of Criminal Procedure controls expungement under Louisiana law. This Chapter provides for when a person is entitled to expungement. The Chapter allows expungement under certain circumstances.

Not all individuals are entitled to an expungement of their record, but Title 34 provides some guidance.

Article 976 covers situations wherein the individual was arrested, but no conviction resulted from that arrest. This Article applies if:

1) "The person was not prosecuted for the offense for which they were arrested, and the limitations on the institution of prosecution have barred the prosecution for that offense;
2) The district attorney for any reason declined to prosecute any offense arising out of that arrest;
3) Prosecution was instituted and such proceedings have been finally disposed of by dismissal, sustaining of a motion to quash, or acquittal; or
4) The person was judicially determined to be factually innocent."

La. Code Crim. Proc. Ann. § art.976(A).

Article 977 governs expungements of misdemeanor arrests and convictions. Expungements may be available if:

1) "The conviction was set aside and the prosecution was

dismissed pursuant to Article 894(B) of [the Louisiana Code of Criminal Procedure]; and

2) More than five years have elapsed since the person completed any sentence, deferred adjudication, or period of probation or parole, and the person has not been convicted of any felony offense during the five-year period, and has no felony charge pending against them."

La. Code Crim. Proc. Ann. § art.977(A).

Expungements of misdemeanors are not available, however, if the arrest was for a sex offense, domestic abuse battery, or stalking. *See* La. Code Crim. Proc. Ann. § art.977(C).

Finally, Article 978 governs expungements of felony offenses. A felony can be expunged if:

1) "The conviction was set aside and the prosecution was dismissed pursuant to Article 893(E) [of the Louisiana Code of Criminal Procedure]; and
2) More than ten years have elapsed since the person completed any sentence, deferred adjudication, or period of probation or parole based on the felony conviction, and the person has not been convicted of any other criminal offense during the ten-year period, and has no criminal charge pending against them."

La. Code Crim. Proc. Ann. § art.978(A).

C. Can you have firearms rights restored under Louisiana law?

Under Louisiana law, restrictions on possessing firearms or carrying concealed weapons apply to any person convicted of a crime of violence, felony weapons or drug offense, or sex offense, and terminate 10 years after completion of sentence, so long as no other felony conviction occurs during that period. *See* La. Rev. Stat. Ann. § 14:95.1(C). An executive or full pardon will restore firearms rights prior to the 10 years, but a first offender pardon will not. *Wiggins, supra,* 432 So. 2d 234.

➤ CHAPTER TWELVE ➤

I'M BEING SUED FOR WHAT? CIVIL LIABILITY

If You Have Used Your Gun

I. WHAT DOES IT MEAN TO BE SUED?

The term "lawsuit" refers to one party's assertion in a written filing with a court that another party has violated the law. In the context of firearms, typically the party suing has been injured and wants a ruling or judgment from the court to that effect that most likely will entitle the person suing to receive money.

A. What is a civil claim or lawsuit?

A civil "lawsuit" or "suit" refers to the actual filing of written paperwork with a court (1) asserting that another party violated the law, and (2) seeking some type of redress. A "claim" can exist without the filing of a lawsuit. A claim is simply the belief or assertion that another party has violated the law. Many parties have claims they never assert, or sometimes parties informally assert the claim in hopes of resolving the disputes without the filing of a lawsuit. Also, another term commonly used is "tort" or "tort claim." A tort is a civil claim arising out of a wrongful act, not including a breach of contract or trust, that results in injury to another's person, property, reputation, or the like. The claims described below are all tort claims.

B. Difference between "civil claims" and "criminal charges"

To start with the basics, there are two different aspects of the legal system that gun owners may face after the use of a firearm: criminal and civil. There are several names and descriptive terms used for each (*e.g.*, civil lawsuit, criminal actions, civil claims, criminal proceedings, *etc.*), but regardless of the terms, the same breakdown applies; most cases are either criminal or civil. There is another subgroup of proceedings called administrative actions. Those actions are not covered by this Chapter, but can sometimes impact CHP holders. For example, appealing the denial of a CHP is an administrative act. *See* Chapters 8 and 9 for more information.

With that said, the three primary differences between a criminal action and a civil proceeding are: (1) who or what is bringing the action or lawsuit, (2) what are they seeking, and (3) what is the burden of proof? These differences are fairly straightforward.

1. State versus individual bringing claims

In a criminal case, the party bringing the action is the "sovereign," meaning the United States, state, municipality, county, *etc.* that believes that a person violated their laws. Even if an individual calls the police, fills out a criminal complaint, or even asks the district attorney to file charges, the party that actually brings a criminal action is the state, county, *etc.*, not the individual.

However, a civil action may be filed by any individual, business, or other entity (partnership, LLC, trust, *etc.*). The entity bringing the claim is called the "plaintiff." Even governmental entities can bring civil claims; *i.e.*, if you negligently shoot a parish propane tank causing a fire, the parish can sue you civilly for those damages. The typical gun case, though, will involve an individual filing a lawsuit against another individual for damages caused by the firearm. If the incident occurs at a place of business, the plaintiff may also sue the business claiming that it is in some way at fault for the incident. The party being sued is typically called the "defendant."

2. Relief sought/awarded

In a criminal case, the entity prosecuting the case is usually seeking to imprison or fine you. Most crimes are punishable by "X" number or days/months/years in prison or jail, and a fine not to exceed "X" dollars.

By contrast, the plaintiff in the civil case is almost always seeking a monetary award. Several other types of relief are available (declaratory, injunctive, specific performance), but for the most part, gun cases will involve the plaintiff seeking monetary damages.

3. Burden of proof

In a criminal case, the standard is "beyond a reasonable doubt." In civil cases, however, a plaintiff must prove a person is liable for damages by a "preponderance of the evidence" standard. A preponderance of the evidence standard is much lower than the criminal standard of beyond a reasonable doubt. It generally means that the party with the greater weight of credible evidence wins that issue. The preponderance of the evidence has been described as more than half, that is, if the evidence demonstrates that something "more likely occurred than not," this meets the burden of proof. Whereas in a criminal case, if there exists any "reasonable doubt," the burden of proof is not met. It does not mean the party with the most exhibits or greater number of witnesses will prevail. One highly credible witness can prevail over the testimony of a dozen biased, shady witnesses.

EXAMPLE:

John mistakes a utility meter reader for a burglar due to his disheveled appearance, tool bag, and because he looks to be snooping around John's house. John fires a shot without warning and injures the meter reader.

Possible criminal liability: the State of Louisiana could bring criminal charges against John for a number of crimes. The State would be seeking to imprison or fine John for his conduct, and it would be required to prove that John committed the crime at issue "beyond a reasonable doubt."

Possible civil liability: the meter reader could also file a civil lawsuit against John alleging that John was negligent or committed the tort of assault. The meter reader would seek monetary damages and be required to prove his claims by a "preponderance of the evidence."

C. Impact of result in one court upon the other

1. Can a result in a criminal trial be used in a civil trial?

Yes, because of the legal doctrines of *res judicata* and collateral estoppel. These two legal doctrines govern the impact of a ruling or judgment in one case upon a separate case involving the same set of facts and circumstances. For the present discussion, if a person is found guilty of a crime in a criminal proceeding, because that court uses a higher standard of "beyond a reasonable doubt" than the civil requirement of "preponderance of the evidence," the finding of the criminal court may be used for purposes of establishing civil liability. Entire chapters in law books have been written on these topics, so, suffice to say, this section is a brief overview of these laws.

The criminal concept of *nolo contendere* or "no contest" often generates confusion in this area. In a criminal case, a plea of *nolo contendere* or no contest means that the defendant does not admit guilt. The plea, however, still results in a judgment that the defendant is guilty of the crime and that judgment can be used to establish the defendant's liability in a separate civil case.

EXAMPLE:

Phil and Jeremy become involved in a road rage incident, and an altercation follows. Phil shoots Jeremy, wounding him. When all is sorted out, Phil is found guilty of criminal assault and receives punishment from the court (remember, criminal trials use the "beyond a reasonable doubt" standard).

If Jeremy later sues Phil from the injuries he received when Phil shot him, Jeremy, in his civil action, will very likely be allowed to use the finding of guilt in the criminal case (because it used the higher standard of reasonable doubt) to establish his burden in the civil case (the lower preponderance of the evidence standard) that he is owed damages or money in the civil case. This is an example of collateral estoppel; Phil will not be permitted to re-litigate his guilt in the civil case.

Both doctrines are based on the concept that a party to a legal proceeding should not be able to endlessly litigate issues that have already been decided by the legal system. At its most basic level, it means that a party to a legal proceeding who receives a final ruling on a particular issue, win or lose, cannot attempt to have another trial court or even the same court decide the same issue.

Note about appeals: this is a different concept than an appeal, or asking the court in the first proceeding to reconsider its ruling, or granting a new trial. An appeal is a request to a higher court to review the decision of a lower court. Likewise, in any given case, the parties will have numerous opportunities to ask the current court to reconsider its rulings, or even ask for a new trial after a trial is completed. Collateral estoppel and *res judicata* come into play after a final judgment that is no longer subject to appeal or revision by the trial court.

EXAMPLE:

Michele is sued for accidentally shooting Nancy. Nancy wins a judgment of $350 against Michele, much less than Nancy believed she was damaged.

In that case, Nancy can appeal the decision, or even ask that trial court for a new trial. However, Nancy cannot file another, or new, lawsuit regarding the same incident and attempt to recover more in the second case because of the doctrine of *res judicata*. In order for the doctrine to apply, the facts, circumstances, and issues must be the same.

EXAMPLE:

Justin fires his hunting rifle from his deer blind, hitting Peter with one round. Peter files a civil suit against Justin and loses at trial. The court awards Peter no damages. Peter appeals and loses the appeal also.

Peter is legally barred from recovering in another lawsuit against Justin involving the same incident. However, Peter is not barred from filing suit against Justin for damages arising out of another set of facts and circumstances: for example, if the two are involved in a car wreck on a different day.

2. Civil case result impact on criminal case

Suppose you lose a civil suit and a judgment is entered against you arising out of a shooting incident. Can that judgment be used to establish that you committed a crime? No. The burden of proof is much higher in the criminal context than the civil case. The plaintiff proved his civil case by a "preponderance of the evidence." This does not mean that he proved his case "beyond a reasonable doubt," meaning a separate criminal trial is required to make that determination.

The one area where a civil case can impact a criminal case is the potential overlapping use of evidence and testimony. Your admission in one case can almost always be used against you in another case. Meaning, your sworn testimony in the civil case ("yes, I shot the guy") can almost always be used against you in the criminal case, and vice versa.

PRACTICAL LEGAL TIP

For capital criminal cases, all twelve jurors must agree to render a verdict. Where punishment by hard labor is necessary, ten of twelve jurors must agree, and for crimes that may be punished by hard labor, only six jurors are required, but all must agree. To prevail in a civil suit in Louisiana, only nine of twelve jurors (or five out of six, depending upon the court where your case is pending), must agree to render a verdict. In a capital case, many times the goal of the defendant is to avoid conviction by convincing a single juror that the State cannot prove its case at the higher "beyond a reasonable doubt" standard. By contrast, in a civil lawsuit, a plaintiff can prevail and recover damages, even if three of the jurors vehemently believe the defendant should prevail, as long as the remaining nine jurors believe that the plaintiff has proven his case by the lower "preponderance of the evidence" standard.

II. WHAT MIGHT YOU BE SUED FOR? GUN RELATED CLAIMS IN CIVIL COURTS

A. Liability for unintentional discharge

This section deals with accidental or unintentional discharges of your firearm. Common unintentional discharges are associated with hunting and cleaning accidents or the mishandling of a weapon.

With that said, the following are the types of civil claims that may be asserted in connection with an unintentional discharge.

1. Negligence/gross negligence

Most civil cases for damages resulting from an accidental discharge will include a negligence or gross negligence claim. What does this mean and what does a plaintiff have to prove before they can win? Under Louisiana law, negligence is defined as the failure to exercise a reasonable amount of care, therefore breaching an inherent duty to keep another person safe from harm. If a person fails to use ordinary care, then they have acted negligently and will be liable for damages resulting from their conduct. Ordinary or reasonable care means that degree of care that would be used by a person of ordinary prudence under the same or similar circumstances. This is an objective standard, meaning that the test is not whether you believed you acted prudently, but whether the judge or jury believes you acted as a person of ordinary prudence would have acted. Of course, this is the definition of negligence in the civil context. There is actually a different definition of criminal negligence, which is beyond the scope of this book's discussion.

What is gross negligence and how is it different than "regular" negligence? Many gun cases will include a claim for "gross negligence" by the plaintiff. The primary reason for this is that if a plaintiff establishes gross negligence by a defendant, the plaintiff may be entitled to additional types or amounts of money that are not legally available if mere negligence is established. The Louisiana Supreme Court has defined gross negligence as "the 'want of even slight care and diligence' and 'the want of that diligence which even careless men are accustomed to exercise.'" *Ambrose v. New Orleans Police Department Ambulance Service*, 93-3099 (La.7/5/94); 639 So. 2d 216, 219. "The difference between ordinary negligence and gross negligence is the level or degree of lack of care shown by the offending party." *Brinkley v. Landry*, 2000-1710 (La. App. 1 Cir. 9/28/01); 811 So. 2d 18, 25-26.

The defendant's state of mind is a key difference between negligence and gross negligence. Negligence involves an objective standard—how would a reasonable person have acted? Gross negligence applies a subjective component—was this particular person actually aware of the risk involved?

EXAMPLE:

Jessica has practiced her shooting at a private range on her country property for 20 years, without incident. Jessica shoots towards an area where she has never seen another person, and she believes the range of her guns cannot reach her property line. One day, a neighbor is hit by a shot as he is strolling through the woods just off of Jessica's property.

Result: Jessica might be liable for negligence if a jury determines, for example, that a reasonably prudent person would have acted differently, tested the range of her guns, or built a different type of back stop or berm, *etc.* However, Jessica was not subjectively aware of an extreme degree of risk, so there would be no evidence of gross negligence. However, change Jessica's awareness and it changes the result.

EXAMPLE:

Jessica has received several complaints over the years about bullets leaving her property and hitting her neighbor's property. Nevertheless, Jessica ignores the complaints and continues practicing in the direction that she typically shoots. One day while practicing, her bullet leaves her property and hits her neighbor. She is later sued by the neighbor for gross negligence.

Result: Jessica may very well be liable for gross negligence because she was subjectively aware that her shots were reaching the neighbor's property and that there were people in the same area (*i.e.*, the folks who reported the shots), and despite that knowledge, she continued to shoot without changing direction or building a back stop or berm and someone was injured as a result.

2. Extraordinary degree of care

Under Louisiana law, those who use or handle dangerous agencies, such as firearms are held to a high degree or extraordinary degree of care. *Gregory v. Guarisco*, 320 So. 2d 354, 356 (La. Ct. App. 1975).

3. Is negligent storage of a firearm recognized in Louisiana?

A question commonly asked by gun owners is "if someone steals my gun, am I liable if they shoot someone?" In other words, if I store my gun and a criminal or another less-than-responsible person gets the gun, am I liable if they shoot someone? As of the date of this publication, the answer in Louisiana is no.

First, "[t]here is no duty to control, or warn against, the criminal actions of a third person so as to prevent him from causing physical injury to another, unless some special relationship exists to give rise to such a duty." *Brisco v. Fuller*, 623 So. 2d 196, 199 (La. Ct. App. 1993). Additionally, Louisiana places no "duty on gun owners to conceal or hide their weapons from a 'dangerous' person who might take them without the owner's permission." *Id.*

Thus, while no legal duty exists, it is still good practice and extraordinarily important to exercise care in the storage of your firearms.

B. Intentional discharge: a person intended to shoot

1. Negligence/gross negligence

Just because you intend to shoot someone, or otherwise "use" your gun, does not necessarily mean that the plaintiff will not assert negligence or gross negligence claims. In other words, you may have fully intended to pull the trigger, but the plaintiff may claim that you were negligent for any number of reasons; for example, you mistook the mailman for a burglar, or the criminal was retreating and you were negligent in using deadly force. The negligence and gross negligence claims, as defined above, can be brought even if you intended to pull the trigger.

2. Assault and battery

If a person has shot at or shot someone and they are sued, it may include a claim for assault and battery. This is an intentional act, not an accident or a claim based on a deviation from a standard of care. An assault under Louisiana law is:

"[W]hen an intentional threat of battery, or harmful or offensive contact, places one in reasonable apprehension of receiving an injury."

Gressett v. Southwest Airlines Company, 216 F. Supp. 3d 743, 750 (E.D. La. 2016).

EXAMPLE:

Bill is startled while driving. Martha is standing next to his passenger window at a light screaming that he cut her off in traffic, but taking no action to indicate she intends to harm Bill or do anything besides verbally lodge her complaints. In response, Bill fires a shot at Martha to make her go away, and hits her in the leg.

Bill has committed a civil assault. He intended to, and did, cause serious bodily injury to Martha with no legal justification. Therefore, a civil jury would likely find Bill liable and award damages to Martha.

EXAMPLE:

Bill is startled while driving. Martha is standing next to his passenger window at a light screaming that he cut her off in traffic, but taking no action to indicate she intends to harm Bill or do anything besides verbally lodge her complaints. In response, Bill points his gun at Martha and says, "You're dead!" He fires his gun, but misses.

Bill has committed a civil assault. He knowingly threatened Martha with imminent bodily injury with no legal justification.

3. False imprisonment: being sued for detaining people

What if a gun owner detains someone at gun point? If the person who was detained later decides to sue, it will likely include a claim for "false imprisonment." Louisiana recognizes a civil claim for false imprisonment. This claim can arise when someone detains persons waiting for police, *e.g.* homeowners detaining burglars, *etc.* However, it can also come up commonly in shoplifting cases (*see* Chapter 7). The elements of the tort of false imprisonment are: (1) detention of the person; and (2) the unlawfulness of such detention. *See* La. Rev. Stat. Ann. § 14:46.

EXAMPLE:

Emily fears she is about to be attacked in a grocery store parking lot by Randall. Randall follows her step-by-step through the parking lot and stops right next to Emily's car. Emily draws her .380 and tells Randall to "stay right there while I call the police." Randall complies, and Emily holds him at gunpoint until the police arrive. When the police arrive, they determine that Randall was an out-of-uniform store employee tasked with rounding up the grocery carts in the parking lot and was no threat to Emily.

If a jury determines that Emily acted without justification (*i.e.*, she was not reasonably in fear of death or bodily injury), Emily could be civilly liable for falsely imprisoning Randall and owe him damages, if any.

4. Wrongful death

If a person is in the unfortunate position that they have shot and killed another individual and a civil suit occurs because of the shooting, it likely will include a claim for wrongful death. In Louisiana, if a person dies due to the fault of another, a lawsuit may be brought to recover damages sustained as a result of the death. La. Civ. Code Ann. § art. 2315.2.

A wrongful death claim can be proven by establishing that one of the other claims described in this Chapter caused the death of another person. In other words, the fault needed to establish a wrongful death claim can be established by proving that the defendant was liable for a tort such as battery or negligence and that the tort caused the death of a person.

In accordance with Article 2315.2 of the Louisiana Civil Code, a wrongful death claim can be brought by:

1) "The surviving spouse and child or children of the deceased, or either the spouse or the child or children;
2) The surviving father and mother of the deceased, or either of them if he left no spouse or child surviving;
3) The surviving brothers and sisters of the deceased, or any of them, if he left no spouse, child, or parent surviving; or
4) The surviving grandfathers and grandmothers of the deceased, or any of them, if he left no spouse, child, parent, or sibling surviving."

III. WHAT CAN THE PLAINTIFF RECOVER?

If a person is sued in civil court and the plaintiff convinces a jury that the defendant was liable for damages, what and how much can a plaintiff get? There are scores of cases discussing the details of each category of damages that a plaintiff can recover in a civil lawsuit. The following is a brief description of two very important concepts: (1) "proximate cause," which is essential to recover damages in most circumstances, and (2) the basic types of damages that a plaintiff may typically seek in a gun case.

A. Proximate cause

One basic concept that is important to most civil claims, and is usually required to recover damages, is "proximate cause." Virtually every tort claim will require the plaintiff to prove that his damages were proximately caused by the defendant. Proximate cause is defined as cause that was a substantial factor in bringing about an event and without which the event would not have occurred. This concept has few bright-line tests.

For a gun owner, the most obvious cases of proximate cause are pulling the trigger on a firearm and hitting the person or thing you aimed at. The law will hold that your action proximately caused whatever physical damage the bullet did to persons or property. But, what about those circumstances where the use of the gun is so far removed from the damages claimed? This is where the doctrine of proximate cause will cut off liability. If the damage is too far removed from the act, then the act cannot be a proximate cause of that damage.

EXAMPLE:

Anthony is cleaning his AR-15 one night in his apartment and is negligent in his handling of the rifle. He has an accidental discharge and the bullet goes through the wall of his apartment and strikes his neighbor, Ray, in the leg. Ray, although in massive pain, received prompt medical care from his wife, Gail, and made a speedy recovery.

If Anthony is later sued by Ray and his wife Gail, Anthony's negligence undoubtedly "proximately caused" damages for things like Ray's medical bills, hospital stay, and perhaps even lost wages. But, what if Gail claims that because of her having to treat Ray's wounds that she missed a big job interview and lost out on a big raise in pay and that she wants Anthony to pay that as a component of damages? The law would hold that Gail likely could not recover damages for her lost raise in pay because the loss would not be "proximately caused" by the act being sued for. To put it another way, it is reasonably foreseeable that the negligent discharge of a firearm will cause medical bills, *etc,* for someone struck by a bullet. Therefore, this is recoverable. However, the law would say that the loss of a possible job opportunity for the wife who treated the person who was actually shot is not a reasonably foreseeable consequence of negligently discharging a firearm and, therefore, was not proximately caused by the act of negligence. In that case, there will be no recovery for the plaintiff, Gail. Proximate cause must be established in every case and may appear to be arbitrary legal line drawing, because it is.

B. What types of damages can a plaintiff recover?

The following is merely a brief snapshot of the types of damages recoverable in a firearms case. To recover any of the damages below, the plaintiff must first prove one of the claims above by a preponderance of the evidence. For example, if the jury determines a defendant was not negligent, a plaintiff cannot recover his or her medical costs, no matter how severe the plaintiff's injuries. Some of the damages a plaintiff can try to recover include:

- Lost Wages
- Medical Costs
- Disability
- Pain & Suffering (Physical, Mental & Emotional)
- Funeral and Burial Costs
- Disfigurement
- Loss of Companionship

- Loss of Household Services
- Lost Future Wages
- Future Medical Costs
- Punitive or exemplary damages (Note: punitive damages are only available in certain cases where statute allows. These cases typically do not include personal injury cases)

IV. HOW GOOD ARE LOUISIANA CIVIL IMMUNITY LAWS FOR GUN OWNERS?

A. No immunity from lawsuits

There is a common misunderstanding that there exists a law that if you are legally justified in using your gun that you can't be sued. This is just not the case. First, if a person has the filing fee, anyone can sue anyone else in the State of Louisiana. There is no one stopping anyone else from filing a lawsuit. Winning a lawsuit is a different issue entirely. If someone files the lawsuit, no matter how frivolous, it still must be dealt with, and it still must be shown to the court that this or that defense bars this lawsuit. This process can take significant time, money, and legal energy even for the most loser of cases. In short, lawyers get paid and even if you beat the "rap," you still have to take the civil "ride." So, if there is no immunity to lawsuits for gun owners, what protection is there?

B. Immunity for certain claims

If gun owners find themselves included in a civil suit after a justified use of force, the following will be important:

IMMUNITY FROM DAMAGES

***DUPLECHAIN V. TURNER*, 444 SO. 2D 1322, 1325 (LA. CT. APP. 1984)**

"[C]onduct which would otherwise be a tortious battery may be justified as self-defense, or in defense of others. When justified, there is no civil liability."

EXAMPLE:

John is the victim of a home invasion. He fires several shots at the intruder. The intruder is hit and hurt.

John likely has no civil liability for the resulting injury to the intruder because he will likely be found justified in shooting the intruder in his home.

C. Justification

All of the justifications under Subpart C of the Louisiana Criminal Code can also be asserted as affirmative defenses in a civil action. This means, for example, if you shoot someone in defense of yourself, others, or your property and are sued as a result, you may assert the applicable sections of the Criminal Code as a defense to the civil claims. If the judge or jury agrees that you acted in self-defense, or properly used force to defend others or property, the plaintiff will be barred from recovery. *See* Chapters 4 through 7.

D. Statute of limitations for civil claims

The statute of limitations is a doctrine in Louisiana (and almost every other jurisdiction) that requires civil claims to be brought within a certain period of time after the incident. Note: In Louisiana, this is referred to as a "prescriptive period," although other states use the term "statute of limitations." If the claim is not brought within the prescriptive period, it is barred. There are a number of issues relating to when the statute of limitations starts to run in many cases, but for the most part, limitations will start to run immediately after a shooting incident. The statute of limitations can vary from claim to claim, most, however, are between one and four years. In Louisiana, the limitations period most likely to apply to gun cases is going to be one year. Assault and battery, negligence, and false imprisonment claims are delictual claims, which involve the intentional or negligent breach of the duty of care, and have one-year limitation periods. *See* La. Civ. Code Ann. § art. 3492. A survival action for wrongful death also has a statute of limitation period of one year. *See* La. Civ. Code Ann. § art. 2315.1.

What does this mean for gun owners? If you "use" your gun, the plaintiff usually must bring a civil suit against you within a year of the incident in almost all cases or else the claim will be barred.

E. Superseding or intervening criminal conduct

In deciding the cause-in-fact element of a negligence claim under Louisiana law, a substantial factor test, whether the negligence was a substantial factor in causing the injury, is applied as an alternative to the but-for (but for the negligence, the injury would not have occurred) test when there are concurrent causes of an accident. Concurrent causes are those that "nevertheless would have occurred [even] in the absence of one of the causes." *Nagle v. Gusman*, 61 F. Supp. 3d 609, 622 (E.D. La. 2014).

"Typically, an intervening cause raises a question of concurrent cause[.]" *Guillie v. Comprehensive Addiction Programs, Inc.*, 98-2605 (La. App. 4 Cir. 4/21/99); 735 So. 2d 775, 778. If it is determined that an intervening cause is a superseding intervening cause, the defendant is not civilly liable. *Id.* It is the plaintiff's burden to prove an intervening act was not the cause of his injuries. *Id.*

EXAMPLE:

Justin allows his nephew, Randall to use his handgun for protection. Justin knows Randall has been in trouble with the law repeatedly and has been accused of armed robbery. While Randall has the handgun, his apartment is burglarized, and the gun is stolen and used in a crime spree. During the crime spree, Melanie is shot and injured.

Melanie would not be able to recover from Justin, even though Justin may have been negligent in giving his gun to Randall, because the criminal act of burglarizing Randall's apartment and subsequent crime spree were superseding causes that broke the link between Justin's actions and the resulting injuries.

F. Comparative fault

Louisiana has a doctrine called comparative negligence. Under Louisiana Civil Code Article 2323(A), "[i]n any action for damages where a person suffers injury, death, or loss, the degree or percentage of fault of all persons causing or contributing to the injury, death, or loss shall be determined, regardless of whether the person is a party to the action or a nonparty, and regardless of the person's insolvency, ability to pay, immunity by statute . . . or that the other person's identity is not known or reasonably ascertainable."

"If a person suffers injury, death, or loss as the result partly of his own negligence and partly as a result of the fault of another . . .the amount of damages recoverable shall be reduced in proportion to the degree or percentage of negligence attributable to the [suffering] person[.]" La. Civ. Code § art. 2323(A).

EXAMPLE:

Richard is a young adult trick-or-treater. He uses a fake gun as a part of his costume and knocks loudly on Nancy's door at 11:30 p.m. on October 31. Nancy, having forgotten about Halloween, is frightened by the knock, the fake gun, and the late hour of Richard's arrival. She fires through the door, injuring Richard.

In the civil suit that follows by Richard against Nancy, the jury will be permitted to consider whether Richard's negligence, if any, contributed to cause the resulting injuries. The jury could determine that Richard was 0% at fault, 100% at fault, or anything in between. By way of example only, if the jury awarded Richard $100,000 in damages, but found he was 30% at fault, and Nancy 70%, Richard would only be able to recover $70,000 of his damages.

V. WILL INSURANCE COVER IT IF I SHOOT SOMEONE?

A. Homeowners' insurance

With few exceptions, almost every homeowner's insurance policy excludes coverage for intentional acts. The act of using your firearm in self-defense is almost always an intentional act. You intended to stop the threat. Plaintiffs' attorneys will very likely assert a negligence claim against a homeowner in an attempt to fall within the coverage, but at the end of the day, if the only evidence is that you intentionally shot the plaintiff because you intended to stop a threat, it is likely that any policy with an intentional act exclusion will not provide coverage for any damages awarded.

B. Auto insurance

Scores of cases around the country exist where the parties allege that a gun incident is covered by automobile insurance merely because the use of the firearm occurs in the automobile or involves an automobile. Almost universally, courts have held that these incidents are not covered merely because the discharge occurs in a car or involves a car.

EXAMPLE:

Justin is cleaning his 9mm handgun in the car. It accidentally discharges, causing his passenger, Edwin, severe injuries.

This event will almost certainly not be covered by auto insurance.

EXAMPLE:

Justin discharges his 9mm handgun in the car at Edwin during an attempted carjacking, causing Edwin severe injuries and also hitting a bystander.

This event will almost certainly not be covered by auto insurance.

The term "use" with regard to a vehicle liability policy is a "broad, catch-all [word] designed to include all proper uses of the vehicle not falling within the terms of 'maintenance' or 'ownership'[.]" *Cantrelle v. State Farm Gen. Ins. Co.*, 618 So. 2d 997, 1001 (La. Ct. App. 1993). "In order for conduct to arise out of the use of the vehicle, the automobile must be essential to the theory of liability. The specific duty breached . . . must flow from use of the vehicle." *Id.* If the specific duty that was breached existed independently of the vehicle, liability does not arise out of use. *Id.*

VI. WHAT CIVIL LIABILITY DOES A PERSON FACE IF THEIR CHILDREN ACCESS THEIR FIREARMS?

A. Parents are not responsible for minor children's actions merely because they are parents

As a general rule, minors are civilly liable for their own torts (that is, their wrongful actions such as negligence, gross negligence, assault, *etc.*). The mere fact of paternity or maternity does not make a parent liable to third parties for the torts of his or her minor children. Under this general rule, parents are not responsible for their minor children's tortious actions when the minor child commits a tort and the parent had no direct relationship to the child's action, such as providing a firearm in a negligent manner, failing to supervise the child, or allowing the child to engage in behavior the parent knows is dangerous or risky.

B. Parents who fail to "parent" may become responsible for minor children's actions

Under Louisiana law, parents are responsible for the damage caused by their minor child who resides with them or who has been placed by them under the care of other persons. *See* La. Civ. Code Ann. § art. 2318. Parents are not, however, responsible for the damage caused by their minor child who has been emancipated by marriage, by judgment of full emancipation, or by judgment of limited emancipation that expressly relieves the parents of liability for such damages. *Id.*

Another issue related to one's minor children is the negligent storage of firearms and whether the storage of a gun could result in civil liability, even though it is not a crime under Louisiana law. The Louisiana Court of Appeals for the Second Circuit has ruled that "[a]n adult who leaves [a loaded gun] where it is accessible to minor children [remember, a "minor" with regards to firearms is under 18 years of age] may be held accountable for the harm caused to third persons as a result of the children's misconduct with the weapon." *Brisco v. Fuller*, 623 So. 2d 196, 197 (La. Ct. App. 1993).

➢ CHAPTER THIRTEEN ≺

BEYOND FIREARMS: KNIVES, CLUBS, AND TASERS

I. INTRODUCTION

Included in Louisiana's firearms laws are prohibitions and laws regulating the possession and use of "other instrumentalities." This includes any object that is not a firearm, but could be used as a weapon. This Chapter will briefly discuss the laws governing these other weapons, including weapons that are absolutely illegal under the law, weapons that are illegal to carry, and exceptions to the laws prohibiting the carrying of illegal weapons.

II. PROHIBITED WEAPONS

A. What weapons are prohibited under Louisiana law?

The law on prohibited weapons is found in Title 40, Chapter 9 of the Louisiana Revised Statutes Annotated entitled "Weapons."

1. Machine guns

Other than peace officers, guards, military personnel, and machine guns kept as war relics, Louisiana law prohibits the sale, keeping, offering for sale, loaning or giving away, purchase, possession, carrying, or transportation of any machine gun. La. Rev. Stat. Ann. § 40:1752. However, refer to other Chapters in this book discussing this subject in greater depth, as Louisianans can and do order machine guns in spite of this prohibition.

2. Switchblades and spring knives

Under Louisiana law, "[t]he manufacture, ownership, possession, custody or use of any switchblade knife, spring knife or other knife or similar instrument having a blade which may be automatically unfolded or extended from a handle by . . . a button, switch, latch or similar [instrument] located on the handle" constitutes the illegal carrying of a weapon. La. Rev. Stat. Ann. § 14:95(A)(4)(a).

It is also important to note that Louisiana law also makes it illegal, without explicitly listing specific weapons to be included, to conceal on one's person any firearm "or other instrumentality customarily used or intended for probable use as a dangerous weapon[.]" La. Rev. Stat. Ann. § 14:95(A)(1). Additionally, Louisiana makes it illegal to own, possess, have custody of, or use any tools, dynamite, nitroglycerine, explosives, or other instrumentality customarily used by thieves or burglars with the intent to commit a crime. *See* La. Rev. Stat. Ann. § 14:95(A)(3).

3. Local knife ordinances may be more restrictive than the general state law

Unlike firearms, there is no preemption by state law of local knife ordinances. This means that local municipalities, government agencies, and other regulatory bodies are free to enact laws, ordinances, and rules that are more restrictive than Louisiana law. As a result, there are divisions in the local knife laws enacted by parishes, cities, and towns throughout Louisiana. Examples of some of the ordinances are as follows:

Lake Charles

- Prohibits the "manufacture, ownership, possession, custody or use of any switchblade knife, spring knife or other knife or similar instrument having a blade which may be automatically unfolded or extended from a handle by the manipulation of a button, switch, latch, or similar contrivance."
- Prohibits the "possession, custody or use of a switchblade knife, spring knife, or other knife, or similar instrument having a blade which may be automatically unfolded or extended from a handle by the manipulation of a button, switch, latch or similar contrivance, or any knife with a blade in excess of four inches, in an establishment where alcoholic beverages are sold."
- Prohibits the "possession, custody or use of a switchblade knife, spring knife, or other knife, or similar instrument having a blade which may be automatically unfolded or extended from a handle by the manipulation of a button, switch, latch or similar contrivance, or any instrument with a blade in excess of two inches, in the Lake Charles City Council Chambers."

Lake Charles, Louisiana-Code of Ordinances. Article I, §§ 13-28(a)(4), 13-28.1(a)(2), and 13-28.2(a)(2).

Monroe

- Prohibits the "manufacture, ownership, possession, custody or use of any switchblade knife, spring knife or other knife or similar instrument having a blade which may be automatically unfolded or extended from a handle by the manipulation of a button, switch latch or similar contrivance."
- Does not allow one to draw, display, present, or exhibit a bowie knife or other dangerous weapon with the intent to commit a crime or intimidate another person within the corporate limits of the city.

Monroe, Louisiana-Code of Ordinances. Article X, §§ 12-201(4) and 12-203.

New Orleans

- Prohibits the knowing sale, manufacture, purchase, possession, or carrying of any blackjack, sandclub, metal knuckles, switchblade, spring knife, iron buckle, zip gun, or shotgun.
- Prohibits the possession, on one's person or in his vehicle, of any weapon (including firearms, knives, hatchets, axes, slingshots, blackjacks, metal knuckles, mace, iron buckles, baseball bats, ax handles, chains, crowbars, hammers, or other clubs or bludgeons or any other instrumentality, customarily used or intended for probable use as a dangerous weapon) while participating in or attending a demonstration being held at a public place.

New Orleans, Louisiana-Code of Ordinances. Article VI, §§ 54-339 and 54-342(c)(3).

Shreveport

- Prohibits the "manufacture, ownership, possession, custody or use of any switchblade knife, spring knife or other knife or similar instrument having a blade which may be automatically unfolded or extended from a handle by the manipulation of a button, switch, latch or similar contrivance[.]"
- Prohibits the intentional possession or use of any dangerous weapons by any person on a school campus during regular school hours or on a school bus.
- Prohibits the knowing or intentional possession of firearms or other instrumentalities intended for probable use as a dangerous weapon in court facilities, in the building or buildings designated as the city hall, any city hall annex or annexes, or other public buildings, structures, or facilities owned by, occupied by, used by, or under the control of the city.

Shreveport, Louisiana-Code of Ordinances. Article II, Division 5, §§ 50-135.1(4)-(5) and 50-135.2(a).

III. TASERS

There is no Louisiana statutory law governing the carrying or use of tasers. As such, it is perfectly legal for persons to purchase, sell, carry, and use tasers under Louisiana law. Of course, the use of tasers is not without controversy. Most frequently, tasers are used by law enforcement officers as a method of subduing a suspect without the use of a firearm.

Louisiana law does not provide a definition for a "taser" or "stun gun," but in the context of police use, calls them "electronic control devises." Louisiana considers tasers as "arms" protected by the Second Amendment of the US Constitution and Article 1, Section 11 of the Louisiana Constitution, citing a case from the United States Supreme Court ruling that even if modern devises such as tasers could not have been contemplated by Congress in 1789, they are still protected by the right to bear arms. *Caetano v. Massachusetts*, 136 S.Ct. 1027 (2016).

Handheld "Stun Gun"

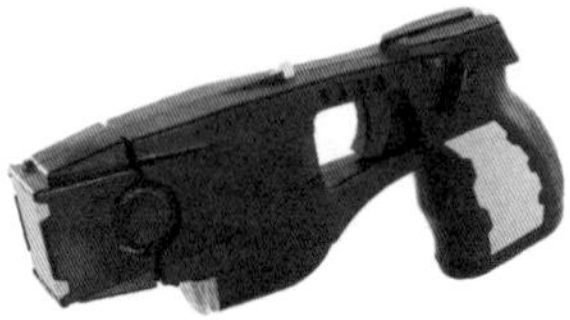

Cartridge Taser

For that reason, it is important to be aware that the use of a taser will subject a person to the same standards of self-defense as outlined in Chapters 4 through 6 of this book, in that a person will likely need to be justified in using either force or deadly force before the use of a taser will also be justified. Because the law does not clearly classify or define a taser in any way, and because there are no cases on this subject addressing it, how a prosecutor, judge, or jury will view a person's use of a taser as being either mere force or deadly force is unknown. Although a taser is not designed to kill, you should be aware that under certain circumstances, and when used in a manner other than designed (such as prolonged use), a taser may play a part in a person's cause of death.

➤ CHAPTER FOURTEEN ≺

SILENCERS, SHORT-BARRELED WEAPONS, AND MACHINE GUNS: THE NATIONAL FIREARMS ACT

Can an individual in Louisiana legally own a silencer or suppressor, short-barreled shotgun, short-barreled rifle, machine gun, or "destructive device?" Yes, if all NFA regulations are satisfied. This Chapter deals with the laws regarding the possession and use of firearms that are subject to the provisions of the National Firearms Act (NFA) codified in 26 U.S.C. Chapter 53, specifically, silencers, short-barreled firearms, machine guns, and firearms that are otherwise illegal. These firearms are illegal to purchase or possess without possessing the proper paperwork and a "tax stamp." In this Chapter, we will discuss the purpose behind the NFA, what firearms are regulated by the Act, as well as the process and procedure for legally possessing weapons that are subject to the Act's provisions.

I. WHAT IS THE NATIONAL FIREARMS ACT?

The National Firearms Act was enacted in 1934 in response to gangster crimes. Prior to the Act's passage, any person could go to the local hardware store and purchase a Thompson Submachine Gun or shorten the barrel on their rifle or shotgun. President Roosevelt pushed for the passage of the NFA in an attempt to diminish a gangster's ability to possess and carry dangerous and/or easily concealable firearms, such as machine guns and short-barreled rifles and shotguns.

The NFA is a firearm regulation requiring registration and tax

The NFA requires both the registration of and tax on the manufacture and transfer of certain firearms. The law created a tax of $200 on the transfer of the following firearms: short-barreled shotguns, short-barreled rifles, machine guns, silencers, and destructive devices. The tax is only $5 for firearms that are classified as "Any Other Weapons" or AOWs. Back in 1934, a $200 tax was the approximate equivalent to about $3,500 today!

Five years after the NFA's passage, the Supreme Court held in *United States v. Miller* that the right to bear arms can be subject to federal regulation. Miller brought suit against the government stating that the NFA infringed upon his Constitutional right to bear arms under the Second Amendment. While the Court agreed that the Constitution does guarantee a right to bear arms, it held that the right does not extend to every firearm. *See United States v. Miller*, 307 U.S. 174 (1939).

II. WHAT FIREARMS DOES THE NFA REGULATE?

A. Short-barreled rifles and shotguns

In order to be legal, short-barreled shotguns and rifles must be registered, and a tax paid on the firearm. What is a short-barreled shotgun? Under federal law, short-barreled shotguns have one or more barrels less than 18 inches in length and the overall length of the shotgun is less than 26 inches. What is a short-barreled rifle? It is any rifle with one or more barrels less than 16 inches in length, and the overall length of the rifle is less than 26 inches. *See* 27 C.F.R. § 478.11.

Short-barreled shotguns and rifles may be purchased from an FFL that deals in NFA items. Also, short-barreled firearms are very popular for individuals to build and/or modify on their own. This is legal if the person has properly registered the firearm to be modified into a short-barreled firearm with the ATF and paid the tax before it is modified. Once approved, a person may alter or produce a short-barreled firearm and must engrave legally required information on the receiver of the firearm, such as manufacturer, location, *etc*. See discussion later in this Chapter for detailed requirements.

B. Machine guns

Machine guns are illegal under federal and state law. However, if the requirements of the NFA are satisfied, machine guns may be legally owned by individuals. First, what is a machine gun? Federal law defines a machine gun as "[a]ny weapon which shoots, is designed to shoot, or can be readily restored to shoot, automatically more than one shot, without manual reloading, by a single function of the trigger. The term shall also include the frame or receiver of any such weapon, any part designed and intended solely and exclusively, or combination of parts designed and intended, for use in converting a weapon into a machine gun, and any combination of parts from which a machine gun can be assembled if such parts are in the possession or under the control of a person." 27 C.F.R. § 478.11. As a result of this definition, the individual metal components that make up a whole machine gun, such as a full-auto sear, individually meet the federal definition of machine gun. The parts for the machine gun do not have to be assembled.

Similarly, under Louisiana law, a machine gun is defined as a "firearm of any caliber, commonly known as machine rifles, machine guns, and sub-machine guns, capable of automatically discharging more than eight cartridges successively without reloading, in which the ammunition is fed to the gun from or by means of clips, disks, belts, or some other separable mechanical device." La. Rev. Stat. Ann. § 40:1751. In other words, if more than eight bullets come out of a firearm with only one pull of the trigger, the firearm is a machine gun.

No new manufacturing of machine guns for private ownership

Because of a federal law that effectively disallows private ownership (not military, police department, *etc.*) of any machine gun manufactured after May 19, 1986, machine guns available for private ownership are limited to the legally registered machine guns that existed prior to May 19, 1986. Thus, the private market is very limited and prices, as a result, are very high.

C. Firearm suppressors

What is a suppressor? It is just a muffler for a firearm and is legal if all NFA requirements are met. In legal terms, a firearm suppressor is defined in 27 C.F.R. § 478.11 as "[a]ny device for silencing, muffling, or diminishing the report of a portable firearm, including any combination of parts, designed or redesigned, and intended for use in assembling or fabricating a firearm silencer or firearm muffler, and any part intended only for use in such assembly or fabrication." Under Louisiana law, a "muffler" or "silencer" is defined as "any device for silencing or diminishing the report of any portable weapon such as a rifle, carbine, pistol, revolver, machine gun, submachine gun, shotgun, fowling piece, or other device from which a shot, bullet, or projectile may be discharged by an explosive[.]" La. Rev. Stat. Ann. § 40:1781(7).

Firearm suppressors are very practical instruments. They are great for hunting and recreational shooting not only because it suppresses gunshots in a way so as to not alarm other animals being hunted nearby, but also because it lessens the impact on the shooter's ears. However, firearms owners should be carefully aware that the definition of a suppressor is very broad. Suppressors do not need to be items manufactured specifically for use as a suppressor. There are some ordinary, every-day items that could be easily converted into a suppressor, such as a water bottle or an automotive oil filter. Possession of otherwise legal items when used or modified to be used as a suppressor is illegal.

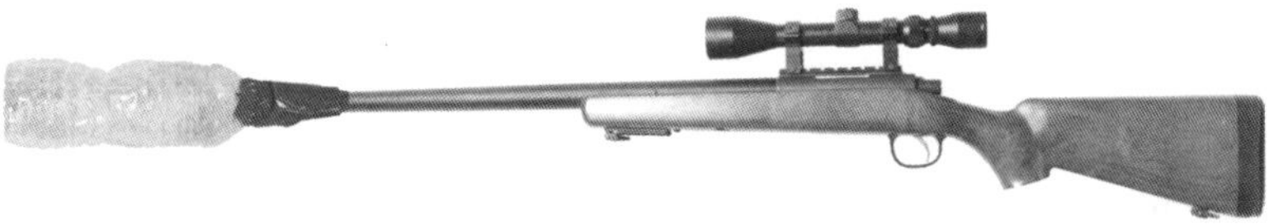

D. Destructive devices

The term "destructive device" is a legal term given to certain firearms, objects, and munitions that are illegal under the NFA. The "destructive devices" as defined in the statute are effectively broken down into three categories: explosive devices, large caliber weapons, and parts easily convertible into a destructive device.

DESTRUCTIVE DEVICES – PART A
27 C.F.R. § 478.11

"Any explosive, incendiary, or poison gas (1) bomb, (2) grenade, (3) rocket having a propellant charge of more than 4 ounces, (4) missile having an explosive or incendiary charge of more than one-quarter ounce, (5) mine, or (6) device similar to any of the devices described in the preceding paragraphs of this definition[.]"

DESTRUCTIVE DEVICES – PART B
27 C.F.R. § 478.11

"[A]ny type of weapon (other than a shotgun or shotgun shell which the Director finds is generally recognized as particularly suitable for sporting purposes) by whatever name known which will, or which may be readily converted to, expel a projectile by the action of an explosive or other propellant, and which has any barrel with a bore of more than one-half inch in diameter[.]"

DESTRUCTIVE DEVICES - PART C
27 C.F.R. § 478.11

"[A]ny combination of parts either designed or intended for use in converting any device into any destructive device described in [part] (a) or (b) of this section and from which a destructive device may be readily assembled."

The first portion of the definition of a destructive device deals with explosive, incendiary, and poison gas munitions. The definition specifies that any explosive, incendiary, or poison gas bomb, grenade, mine or similar device is a destructive device. In addition, the definition includes a rocket having a propellant charge of more than four ounces and a missile (projectile) having an explosive or incendiary charge of more than one-quarter ounce. These topics and the regulations thereof are beyond the scope of this book's discussion.

The second section of the definition addresses large caliber weapons and states that any type of weapon that has a bore diameter of more than one-half inch is a destructive device with the exception of shotguns (and shotgun shells) that are suitable for sporting purposes. Thus, any caliber in a rifle or handgun more than .5 inches or fifty caliber is classified as a destructive device. Shotguns are exempt from this prohibition on size unless the ATF rules it is not for "sporting purposes." How do you know if a shotgun is suitable for sporting purposes? The ATF keeps a list, and has issued rulings classifying specific shotguns as destructive devices because they are not considered to be particularly "suitable for sporting purposes" including the USAS-12, Striker-12, Streetsweeper, and

37/38mm Beanbags. The ATF does not provide any specific definition of what constitutes being "suitable for sporting purposes," nor does it specify the methodology in which it determines what makes a particular shotgun suitable for sporting purposes. Ultimately, one will have to check with the ATF lists to see whether a particular shotgun with a larger bore-diameter is classified as a destructive device or not.

Finally, a destructive device does not need to be a completed and assembled product to fall under the federal definition and regulation under the NFA. Much like machine guns, if a person possesses parts that can be readily assembled into a destructive device, then whether or not the device has actually been constructed is irrelevant—by law it's already a destructive device.

Although these firearms, munitions, and devices are prohibited by the law on its face pursuant to the National Firearms Act, a person may nevertheless receive permission to possess them so long as they possess the correct legal authorization.

E. "Any Other Weapons" or AOWs

The AOW category under the NFA pertains to firearms and weapons that may not fit the traditional definition of some of the firearms discussed elsewhere in this book due to the way in which they are manufactured or modified. Under federal law, an AOW is "any weapon or device capable of being concealed on the person from which a shot can be discharged through the energy of an explosive, a pistol or revolver having a barrel with a smooth bore designed or redesigned to fire a fixed shotgun shell, weapons with combination shotgun and rifle barrels 12 inches or more, less than 18 inches in length, from which only a single discharge can be made from either barrel without manual reloading, and shall include any such weapon which may be readily restored to fire. Such term shall not include a pistol or a revolver having a rifled bore, or rifled bores, or weapons designed, made, or intended to be fired from the shoulder and not capable of firing fixed ammunition." 26 U.S.C. § 5845(e).

1. Concealable weapons and devices

Weapons which are capable of being concealed from which one shot can be discharged are AOWs. This includes such weapons as a pen gun, knife gun, or umbrella gun.

Pen Gun

Knife Gun

Umbrella Gun

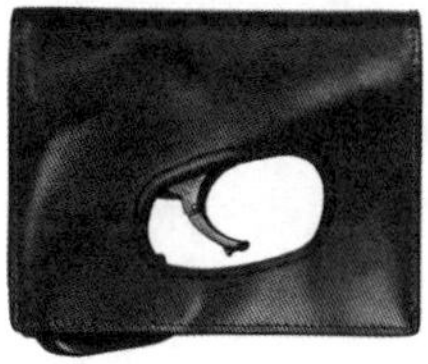

Wallet Gun

2. Pistols and revolvers having a smooth-bore barrel for firing shotgun shells

Pistols and revolvers that have a smooth bore (no rifling) that are designed to shoot shotgun ammunition are defined as an AOW. The ATF cites firearms such as the H&R Handy Gun or the Ithaca Auto & Burglar Gun as firearms which fall under the AOW category. Note: handguns with partially rifled barrels, such as The Judge, do not fall under this category due to the rifling of the barrel.

H&R Handy Gun

Ithaca Auto & Burglar Gun

3. Weapons with barrels 12 inches or longer and lengths 18 inches or shorter

The definition of Any Other Weapon also includes any weapon which has a shotgun or rifle barrel of 12 inches or more, but is 18 inches or less in overall length from which only a single discharge can be made from either barrel without manual reloading. The ATF identifies the "Marble Game Getter" as the firearm most commonly associated with this definition (excluding the model with an 18" barrel and folding shoulder stock).

4. Pistols and revolvers with vertical handgrips

If a pistol is modified with a vertical grip on the front, it will now be legally classified as an AOW and require registration and a paid tax. Note, vertical grips are readily available and are legal to own as long as they are not placed on a handgun. The definition of a handgun is a weapon which is intended to be fired by one hand; the addition of the vertical foregrip makes it so the weapon now is intended to be used with two hands to fire. This modification changes the weapon from a handgun to what is known as an "AOW" and is now a prohibited weapon without the proper documentation.

F. Antique firearms

Firearms that are defined by the NFA as "antique firearms" are not regulated by the NFA. The NFA definition of antique firearm is found in 26 U.S.C. § 5845(g) as "any firearm not designed or redesigned for using rim fire or conventional center fire ignition with fixed ammunition and manufactured in or before 1898 (including any matchlock, flintlock, percussion cap, or similar type of ignition system or replica thereof, whether actually manufactured before or after the year 1898) and also any firearm using fixed ammunition manufactured in or before 1898, for which ammunition is no longer manufactured in the United States and is not readily available in the ordinary channels of commercial trade." Under this statute and for NFA purposes, the only firearms that are antiques are firearms which were both actually manufactured in or before 1898 and ones for which fixed ammunition is no longer manufactured in the United States and is not readily available in the ordinary channels of commercial trade.

PRACTICAL LEGAL TIP

Some of the items regulated by the NFA simply don't make as much sense as the other things it regulates. Suppressors are really nothing more than mufflers for your firearm–they aren't really firearms themselves (notwithstanding the legal definition). Thinking about the utility of the suppressor, if the firearm was invented today, you can be sure that not only would the government not prohibit them, OSHA would probably require them for safety purposes!

With this in mind, the ATF states in its NFA guidebook, "it is important to note that a specific type of fixed ammunition that has been out of production for many years may again become available due to increasing interest in older firearms. Therefore, the classification of a specific NFA firearm as an antique can change if ammunition for the weapon becomes readily available in the ordinary channels of commercial trade."

G. NFA curio firearms and relics

Under federal law, curios or relics are defined in 27 C.F.R. § 478.11 as "[f]irearms which are of special interest to collectors by reason of some quality other than is associated with firearms intended for sporting use or as offensive or defensive weapons." Persons that collect curios or relics may do so with a special collector's license, although one is not required. The impact of an NFA item being classified as a curio or relic, however, is that it allows the item to be transferred interstate to persons possessing a collector's license. The collector's license does not allow the individual to deal in curios or relics, nor does it allow the collector to obtain other firearms interstate as those transactions still require an FFL.

To be classified as a curio or relic, federal law states that the firearm must fall into one of the following three categories:

a) "Firearms which were manufactured at least 50 years prior to the current date, but not including replicas thereof;
b) Firearms which are certified by the curator of a municipal, State, or Federal museum which exhibits firearms to be curios or relics of museum interest; and
c) Any other firearms which derive a substantial part of their monetary value from the fact that they are novel, rare, bizarre, or because of their association with some historical figure, period, or event."

27 C.F.R. § 478.11.

The ATF maintains a list of firearms that are classified as curios or relics.

H. How can some after-market gun parts make your firearm illegal?

A number of companies manufacture and sell gun products or parts that alter the appearance or utility of a firearm (*i.e.* shoulder stocks, forward hand grips, *etc.*). However, some of these after-market products can actually change the firearm you possess from one type of a weapon to another type of weapon for legal purposes whether you realize it or not. As a result, many individuals make the modifications to their firearms thinking that because there was no special process for purchasing the accessory, any modification would be in compliance with the law. Unfortunately, this is not always the case. Consider the example of short-barreled uppers for AR-15s: selling, buying, or possessing AR-15 "uppers" with barrels less than 16 inches is legal. However, it is illegal to put the upper on a receiver of an AR-15 because this would be the act of manufacturing a short-barreled rifle and is legally prohibited. This is equally true of vertical forward grips on a handgun. Vertical foregrips are legal to buy or possess, however, if you actually install one on a handgun, you have manufactured an AOW, and it is illegal, unless registered and a tax paid. Note: there are other types of braces that are permissible in their proper application and illegal in any application or adaptation that would alter the classification of the weapon. For example, the Sig Arm Brace is legal to attach to an AR Pistol when used as an arm brace, but illegal when used as a shoulder stock.

III. PROCESS AND PROCEDURE FOR OBTAINING NFA FIREARMS

A. Who can own and possess an NFA firearm?

Any person may own and possess an NFA firearm as long as they are legally not disqualified to own or possess firearms and live in a state that allows possession of NFA items. *See* Chapters 2 and 3. The ATF also allows for a non-person legal entity to own these items, such as corporations, partnerships, and trusts, *etc*.

PRACTICAL LEGAL TIP

Even if you don't own a machine gun today, that doesn't mean you won't be the intended owner of one later. A person could always leave you their NFA items in a will. If this happens, you must file the appropriate paperwork with the ATF as soon as possible, or at least before probate is closed.

B. What are the usual steps for buying or manufacturing NFA items?

Whether a person is buying or making (manufacturing) an NFA firearm, there are several steps in the process. The transfer or manufacture of an NFA firearm requires the filing of an appropriate form with the ATF, payment of any federally-mandated tax, approval of the transfer or making by the ATF, and registration of the firearm to the transferee or maker. Only after these steps have occurred may a buyer legally take possession of the NFA item, or may a person legally assemble or manufacture the NFA item. In this section, we will walk through the process, step-by-step, of: (1) purchasing an NFA item that already exists; and (2) manufacturing an NFA firearm.

Steps for buying an existing NFA item (for example, a suppressor):

1. select and purchase the item (suppressor) from a transferor who is usually an FFL dealer who is authorized to sell NFA weapons;
2. assemble appropriate paperwork: ATF Form 4 (*See* Appendix C), fingerprints on an FBI Form FD-258, a passport size photograph, and a payment for the tax of $200;
   a. if the buyer is an individual they must notify the Chief Law Enforcement Officer of their city or county of residence by delivering the CLEO copy of ATF Form 4;
   b. if the buyer is a corporation or trust, each "responsible person" of the corporation or trust must complete an ATF Form 5320.23 (*See* Appendix C), including fingerprints and a passport photograph, and must notify the Chief Law Enforcement Officer of their city or county of residence by delivering to them the CLEO copy of ATF Form 5320.23;
3. submit paperwork, fingerprints, and tax to the ATF form review and approval;

4. ATF sends approval (tax stamp affixed to Form 4) to the transferor; and then
5. transferor notifies the buyer to pick up the suppressor.

Steps for manufacturing an NFA item (such as a short-barreled rifle):

1. select the item to manufacture or modify, *i.e.*, short-barreled AR-15;
2. assemble appropriate paperwork: ATF Form 1 (*See* Appendix C), fingerprints on an FBI Form FD-258, a passport size photograph, and a payment for the tax ($200):
   a. if the maker is an individual they must notify the Chief Law Enforcement Officer of the city or county of their residence by delivering the CLEO copy of ATF Form 1;
   b. if the maker is a corporation or trust, each "responsible person" of the corporation or trust must complete an ATF Form 5320.23 (*See* Appendix C), including fingerprints and a passport photograph, and must notify the Chief Law Enforcement Officer of their city or county of residence by delivering to them the CLEO copy of ATF Form 5320.23;
3. the "Applicant" submits paperwork and tax to the ATF for review and approval;
4. ATF sends approval (tax stamp affixed to Form 1); and then
5. the short-barreled AR-15 may be legally assembled, *i.e.*, put upper with a barrel length of less than 16 inches on a lower receiver, *etc*. The item must now be engraved and identified.

When purchasing an NFA firearm from a dealer, the dealer is required to have the purchaser fill out ATF Form 4473 when the purchaser goes to pick up the item from the dealer.

C. How must an NFA item be engraved and identified if I make it myself?

Once you receive ATF approval to manufacture your own NFA item (such as the short-barreled AR-15 in the previous section), federal law requires that you engrave, cast, stamp, or otherwise conspicuously place or cause to be engraved, cast, stamped, or placed on the frame, receiver, or barrel of the NFA item the following information:

1. the item's serial number;
2. the item's model (if so designated);
3. caliber or gauge;
4. the name of the owner whether individual, corporation, or trust; and
5. the city and state where the item was made.

This information must be placed on the item with a minimum depth of .003 inch and in a print size no smaller than 1/16 inch. *See* 27 CFR § 479.102.

D. Which way should I own my NFA item? Paperwork requirements for individuals, trusts, or business entities to own NFA items

Form 4 and Form 1 are the appropriate paperwork that must be assembled and submitted to the ATF under the NFA and varies depending on whether an individual, or a legal entity such as a trust, corporation, or partnership is purchasing or manufacturing the NFA item. The paperwork generally starts either with an ATF Form 4 used for purchasing an existing item, or an ATF Form 1 which is used if a person wishes to manufacture a new NFA item. All relevant portions of the forms must be completed. Both Form 4 and Form 1 have a requirement that a Chief Law Enforcement

Officer for the city or county where the applicant lives must be given their copy of the ATF Form.

Who is a Chief Law Enforcement Officer who must be notified? For the purposes of ATF Form 4 or Form 1, and the responsible person questionnaire, ATF Form 5320.23, the Chief Law Enforcement Officer is considered to be the chief law enforcement officer who has jurisdiction where the transferor, the applicant, and any "responsible persons" are located. These persons include "the Chief of Police; the Sheriff; the Head of the State Police; or a State or local district attorney or prosecutor."

Photograph and fingerprints are required for individual applicants and "responsible persons." If an individual is purchasing or manufacturing an NFA item, the applicant must submit an appropriate photograph and their fingerprints. An entity such as a trust or corporation must designate "responsible persons" who are allowed to have access to use and possess an NFA weapon. As of July 13, 2016, corporations and trusts must submit the appropriate documents showing its existence, such as the trust or corporate formation documents, the ATF responsible person questionnaire, fingerprints, and passport photographs of these persons.

Responsible persons of trusts, partnerships, associations, companies, or corporations, are defined as "any individual who possesses, directly or indirectly, the power or authority to direct the management and policies of the trust or entity to receive, possess, ship, transport, deliver, transfer or otherwise dispose of a firearm for, or on behalf of, the trust or legal entity." *See* ATF Form 1, Instructions. Further, with regard to NFA trusts, responsible persons are defined in the following way: "those persons with the power or authority to direct the management and policies of the trust includes any person who has the capability to exercise such power and possesses, directly or indirectly the power or authority under any trust instrument, or under State law, to receive, possess, ship, transport, deliver, transfer, or otherwise dispose of a firearm for, or on behalf of the trust." The ATF Form 5320.23 provides examples of responsible persons, including, "settlors/grantors, trustees, partners, members, officers, directors, board members, or owners." Persons who are not "responsible persons" are "the beneficiary of a trust, if the beneficiary does not have the capability to exercise the enumerated powers or authorities."

E. Why are trusts so popular to own NFA items?

There are three major reasons trusts are very popular to own NFA items: paperwork, control, and ease of ownership. A trust is a legal entity that can hold property.

A major reason for having a trust own an NFA item is that it makes owning and using the NFA item easier if more than one person wishes to use the item. If an individual owns the item, then only the individual can ever possess it. On the other hand, if the item is owned by a trust, all trustees, including co-trustees, are able to possess and use the items contained in the trust. Therefore, co-trustees may be added or removed as necessary.

Further, unlike other entities such as corporations, LLCs, *etc*., a trust requires no filings with a government to create, which saves expenses. Further, these expense savings continue because there are no continuing government fees or compliance requirements. Thus, trusts are one of the best ways currently to own an NFA item.

F. The Tax Stamp

Once the ATF has an applicant's materials in hand, they will be reviewed and checked by NFA researchers and an examiner. The application will then either be approved or denied. A denial will be accompanied by an explanation of why the application was denied and how to remedy it, if possible. If the application is approved, the examiner will affix a tax stamp on one of the submitted Form 1 or Form 4 and send the newly-stamped form to the applicant.

This tax stamp on the appropriate form is a person's evidence of compliance with the NFA's requirements and is a very important document. A copy should always be kept with the NFA item.

G. What documents should I have with me when I am in actual possession of my suppressor, short-barreled firearm, or other NFA item?

If you have an NFA item, it is a good idea to have the proper documentation with you to prove that you legally possess the item. As of 2015 the law states it is a crime to be in possession of an unregistered NFA item which means the police officer will need reasonable suspicion of your failure to register in order to detain you to determine the status of your item. Reasonable suspicion is a very low standard to meet. It is good advice that if you are in possession of your suppressor, short-barreled firearm, destructive device, or if you are lucky enough, your machine gun—have your paperwork showing you are legal, or it may be a long day with law enforcement. To show you are legal, always keep a copy of your ATF Form 4 or Form 1 (whichever is applicable) with the tax stamp affixed for every NFA item in your possession, personal identification, and if the item is held in a trust or corporation, a copy of the trust or articles of incorporation, and the authorization for your possession. Care should be given to make sure these documents name the individual so as to show legal ownership, *i.e.*, trust and/or amendments showing the person is a co-trustee or an officer of the corporation.

Practically, individuals should not carry around the original documents as they could be destroyed by wear and tear, rain, or be misplaced, effectively destroying the required evidence of compliance. Photocopies of the stamp and any other pertinent documents are generally enough to satisfy inquisitive law enforcement officials. The more technologically advanced may take pictures on their phone or other mobile device, or even upload them to a cloud database. Keep in mind that if the phone dies or the cloud cannot be reached, and you have no way to access the documents, your proof is gone and you may have a very bad day ahead of you! We recommend keeping photocopies of the ATF Form with the tax stamp affixed and appropriate documents with the NFA weapon to avoid any problems with technology.

➤ APPENDICES ➤

APPENDIX A
Selected Louisiana Statutes

LOUISIANA CRIMINAL CODE SUBPART C: CULPABILITY

LOUISIANA REVISED STATUTE § 14:18
JUSTIFICATION; GENERAL PROVISIONS

The fact that an offender's conduct is justifiable, although otherwise criminal, shall constitute a defense to prosecution for any crime based on that conduct. This defense of justification can be claimed under the following circumstances:

(1) When the offender's conduct is an apparently authorized and reasonable fulfillment of any duties of public office; or
(2) When the offender's conduct is a reasonable accomplishment of an arrest which is lawful under the Code of Criminal Procedure; or
(3) When for any reason the offender's conduct is authorized by law; or

(4) When the offender's conduct is reasonable discipline of minors by their parents, tutors or teachers; or
(5) When the crime consists of a failure to perform an affirmative duty and the failure to perform is caused by physical impossibility; or
(6) When any crime, except murder, is committed through the compulsion of threats by another of death or great bodily harm, and the offender reasonably believes the person making the threats is present and would immediately carry out the threats if the crime were not committed; or
(7) When the offender's conduct is in defense of persons or of property under any of the circumstances described in Articles 19 through 22.

LOUISIANA REVISED STATUTE § 14:19
USE OF FORCE IN SELF DEFENSE

A.

(1) The use of force or violence upon the person of another is justifiable under either of the following circumstances:
  (a) When committed for the purpose of preventing a forcible offense against the person or a forcible offense or trespass against property in a person's lawful possession, provided that the force or violence used must be reasonable and apparently necessary to prevent such offense.
  (b)
    (i) When committed by a person lawfully inside a dwelling, a place of business, or a motor vehicle as defined in R.S. 32:1(40) when the conflict began, against a person who is attempting to make an unlawful entry into the dwelling, place of business, or motor vehicle, or who has made an

unlawful entry into the dwelling, place of business, or motor vehicle, and the person using the force or violence reasonably believes that the use of force or violence is necessary to prevent the entry or to compel the intruder to leave the dwelling, place of business, or motor vehicle.

(ii) The provisions of this Paragraph shall not apply when the person using the force or violence is engaged, at the time of the use of force or violence in the acquisition of, the distribution of, or possession of, with intent to distribute a controlled dangerous substance in violation of the provisions of the Uniform Controlled Dangerous Substances Law.

(2) The provisions of Paragraph (1) of this Section shall not apply where the force or violence results in a homicide.

B. For the purposes of this Section, there shall be a presumption that a person lawfully inside a dwelling, place of business, or motor vehicle held a reasonable belief that the use of force or violence was necessary to prevent unlawful entry thereto, or to compel an unlawful intruder to leave the premises or motor vehicle, if both of the following occur:

(1) The person against whom the force or violence was used was in the process of unlawfully and forcibly entering or had unlawfully and forcibly entered the dwelling, place of business, or motor vehicle.

(2) The person who used force or violence knew or had reason to believe that an unlawful and forcible entry was occurring or had occurred.

C. A person who is not engaged in unlawful activity and who is in a place where he or she has a right to be shall have no duty to retreat before using force or violence as provided for in this Section and may stand his or her ground and meet force with force.

D. No finder of fact shall be permitted to consider the possibility of retreat as a factor in determining whether or not the person who used force or violence in defense of his person or property had a reasonable belief that force or violence was reasonable and apparently necessary to prevent a forcible offense or to prevent the unlawful entry.

LOUISIANA REVISED STATUTE § 14:20
JUSTIFIABLE HOMICIDE

A. A homicide is justifiable:

(1) When committed in self-defense by one who reasonably believes that he is in imminent danger of losing his life or receiving great bodily harm and that the killing is necessary to save himself from that danger.

(2) When committed for the purpose of preventing a violent or forcible felony involving danger to life or of great bodily harm by one who reasonably believes that such an offense is about to be committed and that such action is necessary for its prevention. The circumstances must be sufficient to excite the fear of a reasonable person that there would be serious danger to his own life or person if he attempted to prevent the felony without the killing.

(3) When committed against a person whom one reasonably believes to be likely to use any unlawful force against a person present in a dwelling or a place of business, or when committed against a person whom one reasonably believes is attempting to use any unlawful force against a person present in a motor

vehicle as defined in R.S. 32:1(40), while committing or attempting to commit a burglary or robbery of such dwelling, business, or motor vehicle.

(4)

(a) When committed by a person lawfully inside a dwelling, a place of business, or a motor vehicle as defined in R.S. 32:1(40) when the conflict began, against a person who is attempting to make an unlawful entry into the dwelling, place of business, or motor vehicle, or who has made an unlawful entry into the dwelling, place of business, or motor vehicle, and the person committing the homicide reasonably believes that the use of deadly force is necessary to prevent the entry or to compel the intruder to leave the dwelling, place of business, or motor vehicle.

(b) The provisions of this Paragraph shall not apply when the person committing the homicide is engaged, at the time of the homicide, in the acquisition of, the distribution of, or possession of, with intent to distribute a controlled dangerous substance in violation of the provisions of the Uniform Controlled Dangerous Substances Law.

B. For the purposes of this Section, there shall be a presumption that a person lawfully inside a dwelling, place of business, or motor vehicle held a reasonable belief that the use of deadly force was necessary to prevent unlawful entry thereto, or to compel an unlawful intruder to leave the dwelling, place of business, or motor vehicle when the conflict began, if both of the following occur:

(1) The person against whom deadly force was used was in the process of unlawfully and forcibly entering or had unlawfully and forcibly entered the dwelling, place of business, or motor vehicle.

(2) The person who used deadly force knew or had reason to believe that an unlawful and forcible entry was occurring or had occurred.

C. A person who is not engaged in unlawful activity and who is in a place where he or she has a right to be shall have no duty to retreat before using deadly force as provided for in this Section, and may stand his or her ground and meet force with force.

D. No finder of fact shall be permitted to consider the possibility of retreat as a factor in determining whether or not the person who used deadly force had a reasonable belief that deadly force was reasonable and apparently necessary to prevent a violent or forcible felony involving life or great bodily harm or to prevent the unlawful entry.

LOUISIANA REVISED STATUTE § 14:21
AGGRESSOR CANNOT CLAIM SELF DEFENSE

A person who is the aggressor or who brings on a difficulty cannot claim the right of self-defense unless he withdraws from the conflict in good faith and in such a manner that his adversary knows or should know that he desires to withdraw and discontinue the conflict.

LOUISIANA REVISED STATUTE § 14:22
DEFENSE OF OTHERS

It is justifiable to use force or violence or to kill in the defense of another person when it is reasonably apparent that the person attacked could have justifiably used such means himself, and when it is reasonably believed that such intervention is necessary to protect the other person.

LOUISIANA CRIMINAL CODE PART III: OFFENSES AGAINST PROPERTY

LOUISIANA REVISED STATUTE § 14:55
AGGRAVATED CRIMINAL DAMAGE TO PROPERTY

A. Aggravated criminal damage to property is the intentional damaging of any structure, watercraft, or movable, wherein it is foreseeable that human life might be endangered, by any means other than fire or explosion.

LOUISIANA REVISED STATUTE § 14:56
SIMPLE CRIMINAL DAMAGE TO PROPERTY

A. (1) Simple criminal damage to property is the intentional damaging of any property of another, without the consent of the owner, and except as provided in R.S. 14:55, by any means other than fire or explosion.

(2) The provisions of this Section shall include the intentional damaging of a dwelling, house, apartment, or other structure used in whole or in part as a home, residence, or place of abode by a person who leased or rented the property.

LOUISIANA REVISED STATUTE § 14:59
CRIMINAL MISCHIEF

A. Criminal mischief is the intentional performance of any of the following acts:

---

(1) Tampering with any property of another, without the consent of the owner, with the intent to interfere with the free enjoyment of any rights of anyone thereto, or with the intent to deprive anyone entitled thereto of the full use of the property.
(2) Giving of any false alarm of fire or notice which would reasonably result in emergency response.
(3) Driving of any tack, nail, spike or metal over one and one-half inch in length into any tree located on lands belonging to another, without the consent of the owner, or without the later removal of the object from the tree.
(4) The felling, topping, or pruning of trees or shrubs within the right-of-way of a state highway, without prior written approval of the chief engineer of the Department of Transportation and Development or his designated representative, provided prior written approval is not required for agents or employees of public utility companies in situations of emergency where the person or property of others is endangered.
(5) Giving of any false report or complaint to a sheriff, or his deputies, or to any officer of the law relative to the commission of, or an attempt to commit, a crime.
(6) Throwing any stone or any other missile in any street, avenue, alley, road, highway, open space, public square, or enclosure, or throwing any stone, missile, or other object from any place into any street, avenue, road, highway, alley, open space, public square, enclosure, or at any train, railway car, or locomotive.
(7) Taking temporary possession of any part or parts of a place of business, or remaining in a place of business after the person in charge of such business or portion of such business has directed such person to leave the premises and to desist from the temporary possession of any part or parts of such business.
(8) The communication to any person for the purpose of disrupting

any public utility water service, when the communication causes any officer, employee, or agent of the service reasonably to be placed in sustained fear for his or another person's safety, or causes the evacuation of a water service building, or causes any discontinuance of any water services.

(9) The discharging of any firearm at a train, locomotive, or railway car.

LOUISIANA REVISED STATUTE § 14:60

AGGRAVATED BURGLARY

A. Aggravated burglary is the unauthorized entering of any inhabited dwelling, or of any structure, water craft, or movable where a person is present, with the intent to commit a felony or any theft therein, under any of the following circumstances:

(1) If the offender is armed with a dangerous weapon.

(2) If, after entering, the offender arms himself with a dangerous weapon.

(3) If the offender commits a battery upon any person while in such place, or in entering or leaving such place.

LOUISIANA REVISED STATUTE § 14:62

SIMPLE BURGLARY

A. Simple burglary is the unauthorized entering of any dwelling, vehicle, watercraft, or other structure, movable or immovable, or any cemetery, with the intent to commit a felony or any theft therein, other than as set forth in R.S. 14:60.

LOUISIANA REVISED STATUTE § 14:62.8

HOME INVASION

A. Home invasion is the unauthorized entering of any inhabited dwelling, or other structure belonging to another and used in whole or in part as a home or place of abode by a person, where a person is present, with the intent to use force or violence upon the person of another or to vandalize, deface, or damage the property of another.

LOUISIANA REVISED STATUTE § 14:63

CRIMINAL TRESPASS.

A. No person shall enter any structure, watercraft, or movable owned by another without express, legal, or implied authorization.

B.

(1) No person shall enter upon immovable property owned by another without express, legal, or implied authorization.

(2) For purposes of this Subsection, the phrase "enter upon immovable property" as used in this Subsection, in addition to its common meaning, signification, and connotation, shall include the operation of an unmanned aircraft system as defined by R.S. 14:337 in the air space over immovable property owned by another with the intent to conduct surveillance of the property or of any individual lawfully on the property.

(3) The provisions of Paragraph (1) of this Subsection shall not apply to any person operating an unmanned aircraft system in compliance with federal law or Federal Aviation Administration regulations or authorization.

C.

(1) No person shall remain in or upon property, movable or immovable, owned by another without express, legal, or implied authorization.

(2) For purposes of this Subsection, the phrase "remain in or upon property" as used in this Subsection, in addition to its common meaning, signification, and connotation, shall include the operation of an unmanned aircraft system as defined by R.S. 14:337 in the air space over immovable property owned by another with the intent to conduct surveillance of the property or of any individual lawfully on the property.

(3) The provisions of Paragraph (1) of this Subsection shall not apply to any person operating an unmanned aircraft system in compliance with federal law or Federal Aviation Administration regulations or authorization.

D. It shall be an affirmative defense to a prosecution for a violation of Subsection A, B, or C of this Section, that the accused had express, legal, or implied authority to be in the movable or on the immovable property.

E. The following persons may enter or remain upon the structure, watercraft, movable or immovable property, of another:

(1) A duly commissioned law enforcement officer in the performance of his duties.

(2) Any firefighter, whether or not a member of a volunteer or other fire department, and any employee or agent of the Louisiana Department of Agriculture and Forestry engaged in locating and suppressing a fire.

(3) Emergency medical personnel engaged in the rendering of medical assistance to an individual.

(4) Any federal, state or local government employee, public utility employee or agent engaged in suppressing or dealing with an emergency that presents an imminent danger to human safety or health or to the environment.
(5) Any federal, state or local government employee, public utility employee or agent in the performance of his duties when otherwise authorized by law to enter or remain on immovable or movable property.
(6) Any person authorized by a court of law to enter or remain on immovable property.
(7) Any person exercising the mere right of passage to an enclosed estate, as otherwise provided by law.

F. The following persons may enter or remain upon immovable property of another, unless specifically forbidden to do so by the owner or other person with authority, either orally or in writing:
(1) A professional land surveyor or his authorized personnel, engaged in the "practice of land surveying", as defined in R.S. 37:682.
(2) A person, affiliate, employee, agent or contractor of any business which is regulated by the Louisiana Public Service Commission or by a local franchising authority or the Federal Communication Commission under the Cable Reregulation Act of 1992 or of a municipal or public utility, while acting in the course and scope of his employment or agency relating to the operation, repair, or maintenance of a facility, servitude or any property located on the immovable property which belongs to such a business.
(3) Any person making a delivery, soliciting, selling any product or service, conducting a survey or poll, a real estate licensee or other person who has a legitimate reason for making a delivery,

conducting business or communicating with the owner, lessee, custodian or a resident of the immovable property, and who, immediately upon entry, seeks to make the delivery, to conduct business or to conduct the communication.

(4) An employee of the owner, lessee or custodian of the immovable property while performing his duties, functions and responsibilities in the course and scope of his employment.

(5) The owner of domestic livestock or his employees or agents while in the process of retrieving his domestic livestock that have escaped from an area fenced to retain such domestic livestock.

(6) The owner of a domestic animal while in the sole process of merely retrieving his domestic animal from immovable property and not having a firearm or other weapon on his person.

(7) Any candidate for political office or any person working on behalf of a candidate for a political office.

(8) The owner or occupant of a watercraft or vessel traveling in salt water engaged in any lawful purpose for the purpose of retrieval of his property or for obtaining assistance in an emergency situation.

LOUISIANA CRIMINAL CODE: ILLEGAL CARRYING AND DISCHARGE OF WEAPONS

LOUISIANA REVISED STATUTE § 14:94 ILLEGAL USE OF WEAPONS OR DANGEROUS INSTRUMENTALITIES

A. Illegal use of weapons or dangerous instrumentalities is the intentional or criminally negligent discharging of any firearm, or the throwing, placing, or other use of any article, liquid, or substance, where it is foreseeable that it may result in death or great bodily harm to a human being.

LOUISIANA REVISED STATUTE § 14:95
ILLEGAL CARRYING OF WEAPONS

A. Illegal carrying of weapons is:

(1) The intentional concealment of any firearm, or other instrumentality customarily used or intended for probable use as a dangerous weapon, on one's person; or

(2) The ownership, possession, custody or use of any firearm, or other instrumentality customarily used as a dangerous weapon, at any time by an enemy alien; or

(3) The ownership, possession, custody or use of any tools, or dynamite, or nitroglycerine, or explosives, or other instrumentality customarily used by thieves or burglars at any time by any person with the intent to commit a crime; or

(4)

(a) The manufacture, ownership, possession, custody or use of any switchblade knife, spring knife or other knife or similar instrument having a blade which may be automatically unfolded or extended from a handle by the manipulation of a button, switch, latch or similar contrivance located on the handle.

(b) The provisions of this Paragraph shall not apply to the following:

(i) Any knife that may be opened with one hand by manual pressure applied to the blade or any projection of the blade.

(ii) Any knife that may be opened by means of inertia produced by the hand, wrist, or other movement, provided the knife has either a detent or other structure that provides resistance that shall be overcome in opening or initiating the opening movement of the blade or a bias or spring load toward the closed position.

(5)

(a) The intentional possession or use by any person of a dangerous weapon on a school campus during regular school hours or on a school bus. "School" means any elementary, secondary, high school, or vo-tech school in this state and "campus" means all facilities and property within the boundary of the school property. "School bus" means any motor bus being used to transport children to and from school or in connection with school activities.

(b) The provisions of this Paragraph shall not apply to:

(i) A peace officer as defined by R.S. 14:30(B) in the performance of his official duties.

(ii) A school official or employee acting during the normal course of his employment or a student acting under the direction of such school official or employee.

(iii) Any person having the written permission of the principal or school board and engaged in competition or in marksmanship or safety instruction.

LOUISIANA REVISED STATUTE § 14:95.1

POSSESSION OF FIREARM OR CARRYING OF A CONCEALED WEAPON BY A PERSON CONVICTED OF CERTAIN FELONIES

A. It is unlawful for any person who has been convicted of a crime of violence as defined in R.S. 14:2(B) which is a felony or simple burglary, burglary of a pharmacy, burglary of an inhabited dwelling, unauthorized entry of an inhabited dwelling, felony illegal use of weapons or dangerous instrumentalities, manufacture or possession of a delayed action incendiary device, manufacture or possession of a bomb, or possession of a firearm while in the possession of or during the sale or distribution of a controlled dangerous substance, or any violation of the Uniform Controlled Dangerous Substances Law1 which is a felony, or any crime which is defined as a sex offense in R.S. 15:541, or any crime defined as an attempt to commit one of the above-enumerated offenses under the laws of this state, or who has been convicted under the laws of any other state or of the United States or of any foreign government or country of a crime which, if committed in this state, would be one of the above-enumerated crimes, to possess a firearm or carry a concealed weapon.

LOUISIANA REVISED STATUTE § 14:95.1.1
ILLEGALLY SUPPLYING A FELON WITH A FIREARM

A. Illegally supplying a felon with a firearm is the intentional giving, selling, donating, providing, lending, delivering, or otherwise transferring a firearm to any person known by the offender to be a person convicted of a felony and prohibited from possessing a firearm as provided for in R.S. 14:95.1.

LOUISIANA REVISED STATUTE § 14:95.1.2
ILLEGALLY SUPPLYING A FELON WITH AMMUNITION

A. Illegally supplying a felon with ammunition is the intentional giving, selling, donating, providing, lending, delivering, or otherwise transferring ammunition to any person known by the offender to be a person convicted of a felony and prohibited from possessing a firearm as provided for in R.S. 14:95.1.

B. For the purposes of this Section, the following words shall have the following meanings:

(1) "Ammunition" means any projectiles with their fuses, propelling charges, or primers fired from any firearm.

(2) "Firearm" means any pistol, revolver, rifle, shotgun, machine gun, submachine gun, or assault rifle, which is designed to fire or is capable of firing fixed cartridge ammunition or from which a shot or projectile is discharged by an explosive.

LOUISIANA REVISED STATUTE § 14:95.1.3
FRAUDULENT AMMUNITION AND FIREARM PURCHASE

A. It is unlawful for any person:

(1) To knowingly solicit, persuade, encourage, or entice a licensed dealer or private seller of firearms or ammunition to sell a firearm or ammunition under circumstances which the person knows would violate the laws of this state or of the United States.

(2) To provide to a licensed dealer or private seller of firearms or ammunition what the person knows to be materially false information with intent to deceive the dealer or seller about the legality of a sale of a firearm or ammunition.

(3) To willfully procure another person to engage in conduct prohibited by this Section.

B. For purposes of this Section:

(1) "Ammunition" means any cartridge, shell, or projectile designed for use in a firearm.

(2) "Licensed dealer" means a person who is licensed pursuant to 18 U.S.C. § 923 to engage in the business of dealing in firearms or ammunition.

---

(3) "Materially false information" means information that portrays an illegal transaction as legal or a legal transaction as illegal.

(4) "Private seller" means a person who sells or offers for sale any firearm or ammunition.

C. The provisions of this Section shall not apply to a law enforcement officer acting in his official capacity or to a person acting at the direction of such law enforcement officer.

LOUISIANA REVISED STATUTE § 14:95.2
CARRYING OF A FIREARM OR DANGEROUS WEAPON BY A STUDENT OR NONSTUDENT ON SCHOOL PROPERTY, AT SCHOOL-SPONSORED FUNCTIONS, OR IN A FIREARM FREE ZONE

A. Carrying a firearm, or dangerous weapon as defined in R.S. 14:2, by a student or nonstudent on school property, at a school sponsored function, or in a firearm-free zone is unlawful and shall be defined as possession of any firearm or dangerous weapon, on one's person, at any time while on a school campus, on school transportation, or at any school sponsored function in a specific designated area including but not limited to athletic competitions, dances, parties, or any extracurricular activities, or within one thousand feet of any school campus.

B. For purposes of this Section, the following words have the following meanings:

(1) "Campus" means all facilities and property within the boundary of the school property.

(2) "Nonstudent" means any person not registered and enrolled in that school or a suspended student who does not have permission to be on the school campus.

(3) "School" means any elementary, secondary, high school, vocational-technical school, college, or university in this state.

(4) "School bus" means any motor bus being used to transport children to and from school or in connection with school activities.

C. The provisions of this Section shall not apply to:

(1) A federal law enforcement officer or a Louisiana-commissioned state or local Post Certified law enforcement officer who is authorized to carry a firearm.

(2) A school official or employee acting during the normal course of his employment or a student acting under the direction of such school official or employee.

(3) Any person having the written permission of the principal or as provided in R.S. 17:3361.1.

(4) The possession of a firearm occurring within one thousand feet of school property and entirely on private property, or entirely within a private residence, or in accordance with a concealed handgun permit issued pursuant to R.S. 40:1379.1 or 1379.3.

(5) Any constitutionally protected activity which cannot be regulated by the state, such as a firearm contained entirely within a motor vehicle.

(6) Any student carrying a firearm to or from a class, in which he is duly enrolled, that requires the use of the firearm in the class.

(7) A student enrolled or participating in an activity requiring the use of a firearm including but not limited to any ROTC function under the authorization of a university.

(8) A student who possesses a firearm in his dormitory room or while going to or from his vehicle or any other person with permission of the administration.

LOUISIANA REVISED STATUTE § 14:95.5
POSSESSION OF FIREARM ON PREMISES OF ALCOHOL BEVERAGE OUTLET

A. No person shall intentionally possess a firearm while on the premises of an alcoholic beverage outlet.

B. "Alcoholic beverage outlet" as used herein means any commercial establishment in which alcoholic beverages of either high or low alcoholic content are sold in individual servings for consumption on the premises, whether or not such sales are a primary or incidental purpose of the business of the establishment.

C.

(1) The provisions of this Section shall not apply to the owner or lessee of an alcoholic beverage outlet, an employee of such owner or lessee, or to a law enforcement officer or other person vested with law enforcement authority or listed in R.S. 14:95(G) or (H).

(2) The provisions of this Section shall not apply to a person possessing a firearm in accordance with a concealed handgun permit issued pursuant to R.S. 40:1379.1 or 1379.3 on the premises of an alcoholic beverage outlet which has been issued a Class A-Restaurant permit, as defined in Part II of Chapter 1 or Part II of Chapter 2 of Title 26 of the Louisiana Revised Statutes of 1950.

(3) The provisions of this Section shall not be construed to limit the ability of a sheriff or chief law enforcement officer to establish policies within his department or office regarding the carrying of a concealed handgun on the premises of an alcoholic beverage outlet by any law enforcement officer under his authority.

LOUISIANA REVISED STATUTE § 14:95.6

FIREARM FREE ZONE; NOTICE; SIGNS; CRIME; PENALTIES

A. A "firearm-free zone" is an area inclusive of any school campus and within one thousand feet of any such school campus, and within a school bus, wherein the possession of firearms is prohibited, except as specifically set forth in Subsection B of this Section and R.S. 14:95.2(C).

B. The provisions of this Section shall not apply to:

(1) A federal, state, or local law enforcement building.

(2) A military base.

(3) A commercial establishment which is permitted by law to have firearms or armed security.

(4) Private premises where a firearm is kept pursuant to law.

(5) Any constitutionally protected activity within the firearm-free zone, such as a firearm contained entirely within a motor vehicle.

C. For purposes of this Section:

(1) "School" means any public or private elementary, secondary, high school, or vocational-technical school, college, or university in this state.

(2) "School campus" means all facilities and property within the boundary of the school property.

(3) "School bus" means any motor bus being used to transport children to and from school or in connection with school activities.

D. The local governing authority which has jurisdiction over zoning matters in which each firearm-free zone is located shall publish a map clearly indicating the boundaries of each firearm-free zone in accordance with the specifications in Subsection A. The firearm-free zone map shall be made an official public document and placed with the clerk of court for the parish or parishes in which the firearm-free zone is located.

E.

(1) The state superintendent of education, with the approval of the State Board of Elementary and Secondary Education, and the commissioner of higher education, with the approval of the Board of Regents, shall develop a method by which to mark firearm-free zones, including the use of signs or other markings suitable to the situation. Signs or other markings shall be located in a visible manner on or near each school and on and in each school bus indicating that such area is a firearm-free zone and that such zone extends to one thousand feet from the boundary of school property. The state Department of Education shall assist each approved school with the posting of notice as required in this Subsection.

(2) Signs or other markings, in addition to the method developed pursuant to Paragraph (1) of this Subsection, shall provide notice that armed law enforcement officers are permitted within the firearm-free zone by including in the signs or other markings the language "Law Enforcement Weapons Permitted" or language substantially similar thereto.

F.

(1) It is unlawful for any person to cover, remove, deface, alter, or destroy any sign or other marking identifying a firearm-free zone as provided in this Section.

(2) Whoever violates the provisions of this Subsection shall be fined not more than one thousand dollars or imprisoned for not more than six months, or both.

LOUISIANA REVISED STATUTE § 14:95.8

ILLEGAL POSSESSION OF A HANDGUN BY A JUVENILE

A. It is unlawful for any person who has not attained the age of seventeen years knowingly to possess any handgun on his person. Any person possessing any handgun in violation of this Section commits the offense of illegal possession of a handgun by a juvenile.

B.

(1) On a first conviction, the offender shall be fined not more than one hundred dollars and imprisoned for not less than ninety days and not more than six months.

(2) On a second conviction, the offender shall be fined not more than five hundred dollars and imprisoned with or without hard labor for not more than two years.

(3) On a third or subsequent conviction, the offender shall be fined not more than one thousand dollars and imprisoned at hard labor for not more than five years.

(4) A juvenile adjudicated delinquent under this Section, having been previously found guilty or adjudicated delinquent for any crime of violence as defined by R.S. 14:2(B), or attempt or conspiracy to commit any such offense, shall upon a first or subsequent conviction be fined not less than five hundred dollars and not more than one thousand dollars and shall be imprisoned with or without hard labor for not less than six months and not more than five years. At least ninety days shall be served without benefit of probation, parole, or suspension of sentence.

C. The provisions of this Section shall not apply to any person under the age of seventeen years who is:

(1) Attending a hunter's safety course or a firearms safety course.

(2) Engaging in practice in the use of a firearm or target shooting at an established range.
(3) Hunting or trapping pursuant to a valid license issued to him pursuant to the laws of this state.
(4) Traveling to or from any activity described in Paragraph (1), (2), or (3) of this Subsection while in possession of an unloaded gun.
(5) On real property with the permission of his parent or legal guardian and with the permission of the owner or lessee of the property.
(6) At such person's residence and who, with the permission of such person's parent or legal guardian, possesses a handgun.
(7) Possessing a handgun with the written permission of such person's parent or legal guardian; provided that such person carries on his person a copy of such written permission.

D. For the purposes of this Section "handgun" means a firearm as defined in R.S. 14:37.2, provided however, that the barrel length shall not exceed twelve inches.

LOUISIANA REVISED STATUTE § 14:95.10
POSSESSION OF A FIREARM OR CARRYING OF A CONCEALED WEAPON BY A PERSON CONVICTED OF DOMESTIC ABUSE BATTERY

A. It is unlawful for any person who has been convicted of the crime of domestic abuse battery, R.S. 14:35.3, to possess a firearm or carry a concealed weapon.

LOUISIANA REVISED STATUTES TITLE 40: PUBLIC HEALTH AND SAFETY

LOUISIANA REVISED STATUTE § 40:1379.3
STATEWIDE PERMITS FOR CONCEALED HANDGUNS; APPLICATION PROCEDURES; DEFINITIONS

A.

(1) Notwithstanding any other provision of law to the contrary, the deputy secretary of public safety services of the Department of Public Safety and Corrections shall issue a concealed handgun permit to any Louisiana resident who qualifies for a permit under the provisions of this Section and may promulgate rules and adopt regulations regarding concealed handgun permits in accordance with the Administrative Procedure Act. The permit shall contain a permit number, expiration date, photograph, and the name, address, and date of birth of the permittee.

(2) Any information in any application for a concealed handgun permit or any information provided in connection with the application submitted to the deputy secretary of public safety services of the Department of Public Safety and Corrections under the provisions of this Section shall be held confidential and shall not be subject to any public records request nor shall the information be considered as a public record pursuant to R.S. 44:1 et seq. The Department of Public Safety and Corrections shall not release any list of persons who applied for or received a permit for a concealed handgun pursuant to this Section. However, nothing contained herein shall limit or impede the free flow of information between law enforcement agencies, prohibit the department from releasing information necessary to perform the background investigation, or provide statistical information which does not identify individual applicants or permittees.

(3)

(a) Absent a valid court order requiring the release of information, or unless an applicant or a recipient of a concealed handgun permit is charged with a felony offense involving the use of a handgun, it shall be unlawful for any employee of the Department of Public Safety and Corrections or any law enforcement officer to intentionally release or disseminate for publication any information contained in an application for a concealed handgun permit or any information regarding the identity of any person who applied for or received a concealed handgun permit issued pursuant to this Section. A person who violates the provisions of this Subparagraph shall be fined not more than five hundred dollars, imprisoned for not more than six months, or both.

(b)

(i) It shall be unlawful for any person other than an employee of the Department of Public Safety and Corrections or a law enforcement officer to intentionally release, disseminate, or make public in any manner any information contained in an application for a concealed handgun permit or any information regarding the identity of any person who applied for or received a concealed handgun permit issued pursuant to this Section. Any person who violates the provisions of this Subparagraph shall be fined ten thousand dollars and may be imprisoned for not more than six months.

(ii) The provisions of this Subparagraph shall not apply to the release of information under any of the following circumstances:

(aa) A valid court order requires the release of the information.

(bb) The information released identifies a concealed handgun permit holder or applicant who is charged with a felony offense involving the use of a handgun.

(cc) The information regarding a concealed handgun permit applicant or holder is released pursuant to the express approval for the release of such information by that permit applicant or holder.

(dd) The information regarding a concealed handgun permit holder or applicant has been made public by that concealed handgun permit holder or applicant.

B.

(1) A concealed handgun permit shall be issued only to a Louisiana resident who qualifies for a permit under the provisions of this Section. A concealed handgun permit issued pursuant to the provisions of this Section shall grant authority to a Louisiana resident to carry a concealed handgun on his person.

(2) A Louisiana resident shall be required to possess a valid concealed handgun permit issued by the state of Louisiana pursuant to the provisions of this Section in order to carry a concealed handgun in the state of Louisiana.

C. To qualify for a concealed handgun permit, a Louisiana resident shall:

(1)

(a) Make sworn application to the deputy secretary of public safety services of the Department of Public Safety and Corrections. The providing of false or misleading information on the application or any documents submitted with the application shall be grounds for the denial or revocation of a concealed handgun permit. The application shall reflect training in pistols, revolvers, or both. Any permittee under this Section shall notify the department of any address or name change within thirty days of the change. Failure to timely notify the department of a name or address change may result in suspension of the permit for up to thirty days.

(b) In the case of an applicant who is not a United States citizen, the applicant shall provide any alien or admission number issued by the United States Bureau of Immigration and Customs Enforcement and any basis, if applicable, for an exception to the prohibitions of 18 U.S.C. 922(g)(5)(B).

(2) Agree in writing to hold harmless and indemnify the department, the state, or any peace officer for any and all liability arising out of the issuance or use of the concealed handgun permit.

(3) Be a resident of the state.

(4) Be twenty-one years of age or older.

(5) Not suffer from a mental or physical infirmity due to disease, illness, or intellectual disability which prevents the safe handling of a handgun.

(6) Not be ineligible to possess a firearm by virtue of having been convicted of a felony. A conviction for a felony offense which has been expunged prior to August 1, 2014, pursuant to the provisions of R.S. 44:9 or on or after August 1, 2014, pursuant to Title XXXIV of the Code of Criminal Procedure shall not be considered a conviction for the purposes of this Paragraph if ten years have elapsed since the completion of the resident's probation, parole, or suspended sentence. However, the provisions of this Paragraph shall not apply to a conviction for a crime of violence as defined in R.S. 14:2(B) even if that conviction has been expunged. A conviction for which a person has been pardoned by the governor shall not be considered a

conviction for purposes of this Paragraph, unless that pardon expressly provides that the person may not ship, transport, possess, or receive firearms.

(7) Not have been committed, either voluntarily or involuntarily, for the abuse of a controlled dangerous substance, as defined by R.S. 40:961 and 964, or been found guilty of, or entered a plea of guilty or nolo contendere to a misdemeanor under the laws of this state or similar laws of any other state relating to a controlled dangerous substance within a five-year period immediately preceding the date on which the application is submitted, or be presently charged under indictment or a bill of information for such an offense.

(8) Not chronically and habitually use alcoholic beverages to the extent that his normal faculties are impaired. It shall be presumed that an applicant or permittee chronically and habitually uses alcoholic beverages to the extent that his normal faculties are impaired if the applicant has been found guilty of, or entered a plea of guilty or nolo contendere to operating a vehicle while intoxicated, or has been admitted, either voluntarily or involuntarily, for treatment as an alcoholic, within the five-year period immediately preceding the date on which the application is submitted, or at any time after the application has been submitted.

(9) Not have entered a plea of guilty or nolo contendere to or been found guilty of a crime of violence as defined in R.S. 14:2 at the misdemeanor level, unless five years have elapsed since completion of sentence or any other conditions set by the court have been fulfilled, or unless the conviction was set aside and the prosecution dismissed, prior to the date on which the application is submitted.

(10) Not have been convicted of, have entered a plea of guilty or nolo contendere to, or not be charged under indictment or a bill of information for any crime of violence or any crime punishable by imprisonment for a term of one year or greater. However, a person who has been convicted of a violation of 18 U.S.C. 491(a) shall be permitted to qualify for a concealed handgun permit if fifteen or more years has elapsed between the date of application and the successful completion or service of any sentence, deferred adjudication, or period of probation or parole. A conviction for a felony offense which has been expunged prior to August 1, 2014, pursuant to the provisions of R.S. 44:9 or on or after August 1, 2014, pursuant to Title XXXIV of the Code of Criminal Procedure shall not be considered a conviction for the purposes of this Paragraph if ten years have elapsed since the completion of the resident's probation, parole, or suspended sentence. However, the provisions of this Paragraph shall not apply to a conviction for a crime of violence as defined in R.S. 14:2(B) even if that conviction has been expunged. A conviction for which a person has been pardoned by the governor shall not be considered a conviction for purposes of this Paragraph, unless that pardon expressly provides that the person may not ship, transport, possess, or receive firearms.

(11) Not be a fugitive from justice.

(12) Not be an unlawful user of, or addicted to, marijuana, depressants, stimulants, or narcotic drugs.

(13) Not have been adjudicated to be mentally deficient or been committed to a mental institution, unless the resident's right to possess a firearm has been restored pursuant to R.S. 28:57.

(14) Not be an illegal alien in the United States.

(15) Not have been discharged from the Armed Forces of the

United States with a discharge characterized as "Under Other than Honorable Conditions", a "Bad Conduct Discharge", or a "Dishonorable Discharge". In the case of Commissioned Officers and Warrant Officers of the United States Armed Forces, the punishment of "Dismissal" rendered subject to a verdict of "guilty" at a trial by military court-martial is deemed to be disqualifying under this Paragraph. For the purposes of this Paragraph, the United States Coast Guard is considered an armed force.

(16) Not have a history of engaging in violent behavior. There shall be a rebuttable presumption that an applicant has a history of engaging in violent behavior upon proof that, within a ten-year period immediately preceding the date of the application, the applicant has been arrested or charged on three or more occasions for any crime of violence as defined in R.S. 14:2(B), or has been arrested or charged on two or more occasions for any crime of violence that may be punished by death.

(17) Not be ineligible to possess or receive a firearm under 18 U.S.C. 922(g) or (n).

(18) Not have had a permit denied within one year prior to the most recent application.

(19) Not have had a permit revoked within four years prior to the most recent application.

D.

(1) In addition to the requirements of Subsection C of this Section, an applicant shall demonstrate competence with a handgun by any one of the following:

(a) Completion of any National Rifle Association handguns safety or training course conducted by a National Rifle Association certified instructor within the preceding twelve months.

(b) Completion of any Department of Public Safety and Corrections approved firearms safety or training course or class available to the general public offered by a law enforcement agency, college, or private or public institution or organization or firearms training school within the preceding twelve months.

(c) Completion of any law enforcement firearms safety or training course or class approved by the Department of Public Safety and Corrections and offered for correctional officers, investigators, special deputies, or any division or subdivision of law enforcement or security enforcement within the preceding twelve months.

(d) Possession of a current valid license to carry a concealed weapon issued by a parish law enforcement officer.

(e) Completion of any firearms training or safety course or class approved by the Department of Public Safety and Corrections within the preceding twelve months.

(f) Completion of a law enforcement training academy program certified by the Council on Peace Officer Standards and Training. However, any person retired from full-time service as a Louisiana peace officer need only demonstrate that he was properly certified by the Council on Peace Officer Standards and Training at the time of retirement.

(g) Completion of small arms training within the preceding sixty months while serving with the armed forces of the United States as evidenced by any of the following:

(i) For personnel released or retired from active duty, possession of an "Honorable Discharge" or "General Discharge Under Honorable Conditions" as evidenced by a Department of Defense Form 214 (DD-214).

(ii) For personnel on active duty or serving in one of the

National Guard or reserve components of the Armed Forces, possession of certification of completion of basic training with service record evidence of having successfully completed small arms training and qualification.

(h) The National Rifle Association's personal protection course.

(i) For personnel released or retired from active duty or the National Guard or reserve components of the Armed Forces for more than sixty months, possession of proof indicating combat service and an "Honorable Discharge" or "General Discharge Under Honorable Conditions" as evidenced by a Department of Defense Form 214 (DD-214) and completion of the following:

(i) A three-hour course of instruction on the use of deadly force and conflict resolution which shall include a review of R.S. 14:18 through 22 and which may include a review of any other laws relating to the use of deadly force within the preceding sixty months.

(ii) A one-hour course of instruction on child access prevention within the preceding sixty months.

(2) Instructors for any class, training, or course of instruction authorized by this Subsection, except for small arms training in military service as provided in Subparagraph (1)(g) of this Subsection, shall be certified by the Council on Peace Officer Standards and Training as a firearms instructor or by the National Rifle Association as an instructor for Basic Pistol Shooting, Personal Protection in the Home, or Personal Protection Outside the Home. Any safety or training course or class as described in this Subsection, except for basic

handguntraining in military service provided in Subparagraph (1)(g) of this Subsection, shall include instruction in child access prevention.

(3) Any live range fire training required to demonstrate competency as authorized by the provisions of this Subsection may use live ammunition or fixed-case marking projectiles capable of being fired from a handgun.

E.

(1) A photocopy of a certificate of completion of any of the courses or classes, or an affidavit from the instructor, school, club, organization, or group that conducted or taught said course or class attesting to the completion of the course or class by the applicant, or a copy of any document which shows completion of the course or class or confirms participation in firearms competition or honorable discharge shall constitute evidence of qualification pursuant to Subsection D of this Section.

(2) It shall be illegal to intentionally present false, fraudulent, altered, or counterfeit documents to prove training in handguns in order to obtain a concealed handgun permit. Whoever intentionally presents false, fraudulent, altered, or counterfeit documents to prove training in handguns in order to obtain a concealed handgun permit shall be fined not more than one thousand dollars or imprisoned for not more than six months, or both. In addition, no person convicted of a violation of this Subsection shall be eligible to obtain a permit.

F.

(1) The deputy secretary shall revoke the permit if at any time during the permit period the permittee fails to satisfy any one of the qualification requirements provided for in Subsection C of this Section.

(2) The deputy secretary shall revoke the permit for a violation of Subsection I of this Section or R.S. 40:1382.

G. Neither the state, the deputy secretary of public safety services, nor any applicable permitting process employee of the Department of Public Safety and Corrections shall be liable for acts committed by the permittee, unless the deputy secretary or applicable permitting process employee had actual knowledge at the time the permit was issued that the permittee was disqualified by law from carrying a concealed handgun.

H.

(1) The deputy secretary of public safety services of the Department of Public Safety and Corrections shall, within two working days of the initial application, notify the chief of police of the municipality and the chief law enforcement officer of the parish in which the applicant is domiciled of such application. Those officers shall have ten days to forward to the deputy secretary any information relating to the applicant's legal qualification to receive a permit.

(2) The deputy secretary of public safety services of the Department of Public Safety and Corrections shall issue timely and without delay the concealed handgun permit to all qualified applicants, which permit shall be for a term of five years, at a cost of twenty-five dollars per year, and which shall be valid in all parishes statewide. The division may promulgate rules for the purpose of providing for permits and fees for fewer than five years to the applicants requesting a shorter time period. Fees may be reduced proportionately for terms of fewer than five years. The permit shall be retained by the permittee who shall immediately produce it upon the request of any law enforcement officer.

(3) Anyone who violates the provisions of this Subsection shall be fined not more than one hundred dollars.

I.

(1) No individual to whom a concealed handgun permit is issued may carry and conceal such handgun while under the influence of alcohol or a controlled dangerous substance. While a permittee is under the influence of alcohol or a controlled dangerous substance, an otherwise lawful permit is considered automatically suspended and is not valid. A permittee shall be considered under the influence as evidenced by a blood alcohol reading of .05 percent or greater by weight of alcohol in the blood, or when a blood test or urine test shows any confirmed presence of a controlled dangerous substance as defined in R.S. 40:961 and 964.

(2) A permittee armed with a handgun in accordance with this Section shall notify any police officer who approaches the permittee in an official manner or with an identified official purpose that he has a weapon on his person, submit to a pat down, and allow the officer to temporarily disarm him. Whenever a law enforcement officer is made aware that an individual is carrying a concealed handgun and the law enforcement officer has reasonable grounds to believe that the individual is under the influence of either alcohol or a controlled dangerous substance, the law enforcement officer may take temporary possession of the handgun and request submission of the individual to a department certified chemical test for determination of the chemical status of the individual. Whenever a law enforcement officer is made aware that an individual is behaving in a criminally negligent manner as defined under the provisions of this Section, or is negligent in

the carrying of a concealed handgun as provided for in R.S. 40:1382, the law enforcement officer may seize the handgun, until adjudication by a judge, if the individual is issued a summons or arrested under the provisions of R.S. 40:1382. Failure by the permittee to comply with the provisions of this Paragraph shall result in a six-month automatic suspension of the permit.

(3) The permit to carry a concealed weapon shall be revoked by the deputy secretary when the permittee is carrying and concealing a handgun under any of the following circumstances:

  (a) The blood alcohol reading of a permittee is .05 percent or greater by weight of alcohol in the blood.

  (b) A permittee's blood test or urine test shows the confirmed presence of a controlled dangerous substance as defined in R.S. 40:961 and 964.

  (c) A permittee refuses to submit to a department-certified chemical test when requested to do so by a law enforcement officer pursuant to Paragraph (2) of this Subsection.

  (d) An individual is found guilty of negligent carrying of a concealed handgun as provided for in R.S. 40:1382.

(4) The person tested may have a physician or a qualified technician, chemist, registered nurse, or other qualified person of his own choosing administer a chemical test or tests in addition to any administered at the direction of a law enforcement officer, and he shall be given the opportunity to telephone and request the qualified person to administer such test.

(5) Whenever a peace officer determines that grounds under this Subsection exist for the revocation of a concealed handgun permit, he shall prepare an affidavit, on a form provided by the Department of Public Safety and Corrections, indicating the reasons for the revocation and all other information regarding

the revocation available to the officer. A copy of the peace officer's report relating to the incident shall be attached to the affidavit when submitted to the department.

J. For the purposes of this Section, the following terms shall have the meanings ascribed herein:

(1) "Crime of violence" means a crime as defined in R.S. 14:2(B).

(2) "Criminal negligence" means there exists such disregard of the interest of others that the license holder's conduct amounts to a gross deviation below the standard of care expected to be maintained by a reasonably careful man under like circumstances.

(3) "Handgun" means a type of firearm commonly referred to as a pistol or revolver originally designed to be fired by the use of a single hand and which is designed to fire or is capable of firing fixed cartridge ammunition. The term "handgun" shall not include shotguns or rifles that have been altered by having their stocks or barrels cut or shortened.

(4) "Resident" means a person who is legally domiciled in Louisiana. An individual shall prove legal domicile by providing a copy of a valid Louisiana driver's license or an official Louisiana identification card. Notwithstanding anything in this Section to the contrary, a person who maintains a dwelling in this state but is residing elsewhere as a member of the United States military or as a student is still considered to be a resident for the purposes of this Section.

K. The department shall execute a thorough background investigation, including a criminal history check, of every applicant for the purpose of verifying the qualifications of the applicant pursuant to the requirements of this Section. For purposes of this

Subsection, a background check shall be defined as a computer check of available on-line state records, and, if warranted, the fingerprints may be forwarded to the Federal Bureau of Investigation for a national criminal history record check. In addition, the department shall submit an inquiry on every applicant to the National Instant Criminal Background Check System of the Federal Bureau of Investigation.

L. Anyone who carries and conceals a handgun in violation of any provision of this Section, unless authorized to do so by another provision of the law, shall be fined not more than five hundred dollars, or imprisoned for not more than six months, or both.

M. No concealed handgun permit shall be valid or entitle any permittee to carry a concealed weapon in any facility, building, location, zone, or area in which firearms are banned by state or federal law.

N. No concealed handgun may be carried into and no concealed handgun permit issued pursuant to this Section shall authorize or entitle a permittee to carry a concealed handgun in any of the following:

(1) A law enforcement office, station, or building.
(2) A detention facility, prison, or jail.
(3) A courthouse or courtroom, provided that a judge may carry such a weapon in his own courtroom.
(4) A polling place.
(5) A meeting place of the governing authority of a political subdivision.
(6) The state capitol building.
(7) Any portion of an airport facility where the carrying of firearms

is prohibited under federal law, except that no person shall be prohibited from carrying any legal firearm into the terminal, if the firearm is encased for shipment, for the purpose of checking such firearm as lawful baggage.

(8) Any church, synagogue, mosque, or other similar place of worship, eligible for qualification as a tax-exempt organization under 26 U.S.C. 501, except as provided for in Subsection U of this Section.

(9) A parade or demonstration for which a permit is issued by a governmental entity.

(10) Any portion of the permitted area of an establishment that has been granted a Class A-General retail permit, as defined in Part II of Chapter 1 or Part II of Chapter 2 of Title 26 of the Louisiana Revised Statutes of 1950, to sell alcoholic beverages for consumption on the premises.

(11) Any school, school campus, or school bus as defined in R.S. 14:95.6.

O. The provisions of Subsection N of this Section shall not limit the right of a property owner, lessee, or other lawful custodian to prohibit or restrict access of those persons possessing a concealed handgun pursuant to a permit issued under this Section. No individual to whom a concealed handgun permit is issued may carry such concealed handgun into the private residence of another without first receiving the consent of that person.

P. Within three months of April 19, 1996, the Department of Public Safety and Corrections shall promulgate rules and regulations in accordance with the Administrative Procedure Act to provide an appeal process in the event that an applicant is denied issuance of a permit. The department may also promulgate educational requirements for renewal of concealed handgun permits.

Q. The provisions of this Section shall not apply to commissioned law enforcement officers.

R.

(1) Each permittee, within fifteen days of a misdemeanor or a felony arrest, other than a minor traffic violation, in this state or any other state, shall notify the deputy secretary of public safety services by certified mail. The deputy secretary may suspend, for up to ninety days, the permit of any permittee who fails to meet the notification requirements of this Section.

(2) The Department of Public Safety and Corrections shall submit a report by March thirty-first of each year to the Senate Committee on Judiciary C and the House Committee on the Administration of Criminal Justice relative to concealed handgun permits. The report shall include information on the number of licenses issued, denied, revoked, or suspended and the reasons for such denial, revocation, or suspension to be categorized by age, sex, race, and zip code of the applicant or licensee. The report shall include data concerning any known accidents or deaths involving permittees.

S. Notwithstanding any other provision of law to the contrary, the department may develop, print, and distribute an informational newsletter relative to concealed handgun permittees, safety training, and related matters.

T.

(1) Possession of a current and valid concealed handgun permit issued pursuant to this Section shall constitute sufficient evidence of the background check required pursuant to 18 U.S.C. 922(t) provided that the appropriate waiver has been

granted by the Bureau of Alcohol, Tobacco, Firearms and Explosives. A person whose permit has been suspended or revoked by the department and who uses that permit to purchase a firearm from a licensed dealer knowing that the permit has been suspended or revoked shall be fined not more than five hundred dollars or imprisoned for not more than six months, or both.

(2) A current and valid concealed handgun permit issued by another state to an individual having attained the age of twenty-one years shall be deemed to be valid for the out-of-state permit holder to carry a concealed weapon within this state if a current and valid concealed handgun permit issued by Louisiana is valid in those states.

(3) An out-of-state permit holder carrying a concealed handgun pursuant to this Paragraph is bound by the laws of this state regarding carrying a concealed handgun pursuant to a permit issued in accordance with this Section.

(4) A concealed handgun permit issued by another state is invalid in the state of Louisiana for the purpose of authorizing a Louisiana resident to carry a concealed handgun in the state of Louisiana.

(5) The deputy secretary for public safety services shall also have the authority to enter into reciprocity agreements with other states so that full-time active peace officers commissioned in another state shall have the same authority as a person issued a concealed handgun permit pursuant to this Section to carry a concealed handgun while in this state, regardless of whether or not they are in the official discharge of their duties, and full-time active law enforcement officers commissioned in this state shall have the authority to carry a concealed handgun in those states whether or not they are in the official discharge of

their duties. An out-of-state law enforcement officer carrying a concealed handgun pursuant to this Paragraph is bound by the laws of this state regarding carrying a concealed handgun pursuant to a permit issued in accordance with this Section.

U.

(1) The entity which owns the business or has authority over the administration of a church, synagogue, or mosque shall have the authority to authorize any person issued a valid concealed handgun permit as authorized by the provisions of this Section to carry a concealed handgun in the church, synagogue, or mosque.

(2) The provisions of this Subsection shall not be construed to limit or prohibit any church, synagogue, or mosque from employing armed security guards who are either certified law enforcement officers or who are authorized to carry concealed handguns pursuant to the provisions of this Section.

(3) If the church, synagogue, or mosque authorizes the carrying of concealed handguns as authorized by the provisions of this Subsection, the pastor, priest, minister, or other authority of the church, synagogue, or mosque shall inform the congregation of the authorization.

(4) The provisions of this Section shall not be construed to authorize the carrying of a concealed handgun in a church, synagogue, or mosque located on the property of any school or school property, which would otherwise be prohibited by the provisions of R.S. 14:95.2.

(5) Any church, synagogue, or mosque authorizing the carrying of concealed handguns pursuant to the provisions of this Subsection shall require an additional eight hour tactical training for those persons wishing to carry concealed handguns

in the church, synagogue, or mosque. The training shall be conducted annually.

V.

(1) Notwithstanding any other provision of law to the contrary, a Louisiana resident who meets the provisions of this Section may be issued a lifetime concealed handgun permit. The term for the lifetime concealed handgun permit shall be for the life of the permit holder.

(2) A person issued a lifetime concealed handgun permit shall be required to meet the qualifications and competency requirements for the issuance of a concealed handgun permit pursuant to the provisions of Subsections C and D of this Section.

(3) A person issued a lifetime concealed handgun permit shall have a continuing obligation to comply with the provisions of this Section and any other rules or provisions of law regarding the carrying of concealed handguns.

(4)

(a) A lifetime concealed handgun permit holder shall provide the division with proof of completion of educational training every five years. The educational training shall include all of the following:

(i) Instruction on handgun nomenclature and safe handling procedures for a revolver and a semiautomatic pistol.

(ii) Instruction on ammunition knowledge and fundamentals of pistol shooting.

(iii) Instruction on handgun shooting positions.

(iv) Instruction on the use of deadly force and conflict resolution which shall include a review of R.S. 14:18 through 22 and which may include a review of any other laws relating to use of deadly force.

(v) Instruction on child access prevention.

(vi) Actual live range fire and proper handgun cleaning procedures:

(aa) Live range fire shall include twelve rounds each at six feet, ten feet, and fifteen feet for a total of thirty-six rounds.

(bb) Each applicant or permittee must perform at least one safe reload of the handgun at each distance.

(cc) Each applicant or permittee must score one hundred percent hits within the silhouette portion of a N.R.A. B-27 type silhouette target with at least thirty-six rounds.

(b) Failure to submit proof of completion of the educational training pursuant to the provisions of this Paragraph shall result in the suspension of the lifetime concealed handgun permit until such time as the lifetime concealed handgun permit holder submits proof of the educational training required in the provisions of this Paragraph.

(5) The deputy secretary of the department shall revoke the lifetime concealed handgun permit if the permittee fails to satisfy the qualifications and requirements of Subsection C of this Section or violates the provisions of Subsection I of this Section.

(6) A lifetime concealed handgun permit shall be suspended if the holder of that permit becomes a resident of another state. The lifetime concealed handgun permit shall be reactivated upon reestablishment of residency in Louisiana if the applicant otherwise meets the requirements of this Section and upon successful completion of a criminal history records check.

(7) An applicant for a lifetime concealed handgun permit shall pay the yearly fee provided for in Paragraph (H)(2) of this Section but shall prepay that fee for a total of twenty years at

the time the application is made. If the applicant is sixty-five years of age or older, he shall pay the yearly fee provided for in Paragraph (H)(2) of this Section but shall prepay that fee for a total of ten years at the time the application is made.

W.

(1) Notwithstanding any provision of law to the contrary, an active duty member or reserve member of the armed forces of the United States shall pay one half of the annual fee provided for in Paragraph (H)(2) of this Section for a five-year permit, or if applying for a lifetime concealed handgun permit, he shall prepay that fee for a total of ten years at the time the application for the lifetime concealed handgun permit is made.

(2) A veteran of the armed forces of the United States shall be exempt from all fees associated with the five-year permit or lifetime concealed carry permit.

(3) For the purposes of this Subsection, "veteran" shall mean any honorably discharged veteran of the armed forces of the United States including reserve components of the armed forces, the Army National Guard, the Air National Guard, the United States Public Health Service Commissioned Corps, and any other category of persons designated by the president in time of war or emergency.

LOUISIANA REVISED STATUTE § 40:1752

HANDLING OF MACHINE GUNS UNLAWFUL; EXCEPTIONS

No person shall sell, keep or offer for sale, loan or give away, purchase, possess, carry, or transport any machine gun within this state, except that:

(1) All duly appointed peace officers may purchase, possess, carry, and transport machine guns.

(2) This Part does not apply to the Army, Navy, or Marine Corps of the United States, the National Guard, and organizations authorized by law to purchase or receive machine guns from the United States or from this state. The members of such Corps, National Guard, and organizations may possess, carry, and transport machine guns while on duty.

(3) Persons possessing war relics may purchase and possess machine guns which are relics of any war in which the United States was involved, may exhibit and carry the machine guns in the parades of any military organization, and may sell, offer to sell, loan, or give the machine guns to other persons possessing war relics.

(4) Guards or messengers employed by common carriers, banks, and trust companies, and pay-roll guards or messengers may possess and carry machine guns while actually employed in and about the shipment, transportation, or delivery, or in the guarding of any money, treasure, bullion, bonds, or other thing of value. Their employers may purchase or receive machine guns and keep them in their possession when the guns are not being used by their guards or messengers.

(5) Manufacturers and merchants may sell, keep or offer for sale, loan or give away, purchase, possess, and transport machine guns in the same manner as other merchandise except as otherwise provided in this Part. Common carriers may possess and transport unloaded machine guns as other merchandise.

APPENDIX B
Federal Law

18 USCS § 922. UNLAWFUL ACTS

(a) It shall be unlawful–

(1) for any person–

(A) except a licensed importer, licensed manufacturer, or licensed dealer, to engage in the business of importing, manufacturing, or dealing in firearms, or in the course of such business to ship, transport, or receive any firearm in interstate or foreign commerce; or

(B) except a licensed importer or licensed manufacturer, to engage in the business of importing or manufacturing ammunition, or in the course of such business, to ship, transport, or receive any ammunition in interstate or foreign commerce;

(2) for any importer, manufacturer, dealer, or collector licensed under the provisions of this chapter to ship or transport in interstate or foreign commerce any firearm to any person other than a licensed importer, licensed manufacturer, licensed dealer, or licensed collector, except that–

   (A) this paragraph and subsection (b)(3) shall not be held to preclude a licensed importer, licensed manufacturer, licensed dealer, or licensed collector from returning a firearm or replacement firearm of the same kind and type to a person from whom it was received; and this paragraph shall not be held to preclude an individual from mailing a firearm owned in compliance with Federal, State, and local law to a licensed importer, licensed manufacturer, licensed dealer, or licensed collector;

   (B) this paragraph shall not be held to preclude a licensed importer, licensed manufacturer, or licensed dealer from depositing a firearm for conveyance in the mails to any officer, employee, agent, or watchman who, pursuant to the provisions of section 1715 of this title, is eligible to receive through the mails pistols, revolvers, and other firearms capable of being concealed on the person, for use in connection with his official duty; and

   (C) nothing in this paragraph shall be construed as applying in any manner in the District of Columbia, the Commonwealth of Puerto Rico, or any possession of the United States differently than it would apply if the District of Columbia, the Commonwealth of Puerto Rico, or the possession were in fact a State of the United States;

(3) for any person, other than a licensed importer, licensed manufacturer, licensed dealer, or licensed collector to transport into or receive in the State where he resides (or if the person is a corporation or other business entity, the State where it maintains a place of business) any firearm purchased or otherwise obtained by such person outside that State, except that this paragraph (A) shall not preclude any person who lawfully acquires a firearm by bequest or intestate succession in a State other than his State of residence from transporting the firearm into or receiving it in that State, if it is lawful for such person to purchase or possess such firearm in that State, (B) shall not apply to the transportation or receipt of a firearm obtained in conformity with subsection (b)(3) of this section, and (C) shall not apply to the transportation of any firearm acquired in any State prior to the effective date of this chapter;

(4) for any person, other than a licensed importer, licensed manufacturer, licensed dealer, or licensed collector, to transport in interstate or foreign commerce any destructive device, machinegun (as defined in section 5845 of the Internal Revenue Code of 1986), short-barreled shotgun, or short-barreled rifle, except as specifically authorized by the Attorney General consistent with public safety and necessity;

(5) for any person (other than a licensed importer, licensed

manufacturer, licensed dealer, or licensed collector) to transfer, sell, trade, give, transport, or deliver any firearm to any person (other than a licensed importer, licensed manufacturer, licensed dealer, or licensed collector) who the transferor knows or has reasonable cause to believe does not reside in (or if the person is a corporation or other business entity, does not maintain a place of business in) the State in which the transferor resides; except that this paragraph shall not apply to (A) the transfer, transportation, or delivery of a firearm made to carry out a bequest of a firearm to, or an acquisition by intestate succession of a firearm by, a person who is permitted to acquire or possess a firearm under the laws of the State of his residence, and (B) the loan or rental of a firearm to any person for temporary use for lawful sporting purposes;

(6) for any person in connection with the acquisition or attempted acquisition of any firearm or ammunition from a licensed importer, licensed manufacturer, licensed dealer, or licensed collector, knowingly to make any false or fictitious oral or written statement or to furnish or exhibit any false, fictitious, or misrepresented identification, intended or likely to deceive such importer, manufacturer, dealer, or collector with respect to any fact material to the lawfulness of the sale or other disposition of such firearm or ammunition under the provisions of this chapter;

(7) for any person to manufacture or import armor piercing ammunition, unless–

(A) the manufacture of such ammunition is for the use of the United States, any department or agency of the United States, any State, or any department, agency, or political subdivision of a State;

(B) the manufacture of such ammunition is for the purpose of exportation; or

(C) the manufacture or importation of such ammunition is for the purpose of testing or experimentation and has been authorized by the Attorney General;

(8) for any manufacturer or importer to sell or deliver armor piercing ammunition, unless such sale or delivery–

(A) is for the use of the United States, any department or agency of the United States, any State, or any department, agency, or political subdivision of a State;

(B) is for thc purposc of cxportation; or

(C) is for the purpose of testing or experimentation and has been authorized by the Attorney General; and

(9) or any person, other than a licensed importer, licensed manufacturer, licensed dealer, or licensed collector, who does not reside in any State to receive any firearms unless such receipt is for lawful sporting purposes.

(b) It shall be unlawful for any licensed importer, licensed manufacturer, licensed dealer, or licensed collector to sell or deliver–

(1) any firearm or ammunition to any individual who the licensee knows or has reasonable cause to believe is less than eighteen years of age, and, if the firearm, or ammunition is other than a shotgun or rifle, or ammunition for a shotgun or rifle, to any individual who the licensee knows or has reasonable cause to believe is less than twenty-one years of age;

(2) any firearm to any person in any State where the purchase or possession by such person of such firearm would be in violation of any State law or any published ordinance applicable at the place of sale, delivery or other disposition, unless the licensee knows or has reasonable cause to believe that the purchase or possession would not be in violation of such State law or such published ordinance;

(3) any firearm to any person who the licensee knows or has reasonable cause to believe does not reside in (or if the person is a corporation or other business entity, does not maintain a place of business in) the State in which the licensee's place of business is located, except that this paragraph (A) shall not apply to the sale or delivery of any rifle or shotgun to a resident of a State other than a State in which the licensee's place of business is located if the transferee meets in person with the transferor to accomplish the transfer, and the sale, delivery, and receipt fully comply with the legal conditions of sale in both such States (and any licensed manufacturer, importer or dealer shall be presumed, for purposes of this subparagraph, in the absence of evidence to the contrary, to have had actual knowledge of the State laws and published ordinances of both States), and (B) shall not apply to the loan or rental of a firearm to any person for temporary use for lawful sporting purposes;

(4) to any person any destructive device, machinegun (as defined in section 5845 of the Internal Revenue Code of 1986), short-barreled shotgun, or short-barreled rifle, except as specifically authorized by the Attorney

General consistent with public safety and necessity; and

(5) any firearm or armor-piercing ammunition to any person unless the licensee notes in his records, required to be kept pursuant to section 923 of this chapter, the name, age, and place of residence of such person if the person is an individual, or the identity and principal and local places of business of such person if the person is a corporation or other business entity.

Paragraphs (1), (2), (3), and (4) of this subsection shall not apply to transactions between licensed importers, licensed manufacturers, licensed dealers, and licensed collectors. Paragraph (4) of this subsection shall not apply to a sale or delivery to any research organization designated by the Attorney General.

(c) In any case not otherwise prohibited by this chapter, a licensed importer, licensed manufacturer, or licensed dealer may sell a firearm to a person who does not appear in person at the licensee's business premises (other than another licensed importer, manufacturer, or dealer) only if

(1) the transferee submits to the transferor a sworn statement in the following form:

"Subject to penalties provided by law, I swear that, in the case of any firearm other than a shotgun or a rifle, I am twenty-one years or more of age, or that, in the case of a shotgun or a rifle, I am eighteen years or more of age; that I am not prohibited by the provisions of chapter 44 of Title 18, United States Code, from receiving a firearm in interstate or foreign commerce; and that my receipt of this firearm will not be in violation of any statute of the State and published ordinance applicable to the locality in which I reside. Further, the true title, name, and address of the principal law enforcement officer of the locality to which the firearm will be delivered is ______________________________

____

Signature ______________________ Date _________."

and containing blank spaces for the attachment of a true copy of any permit or other information required pursuant to such statute or published ordinance;

(2) the transferor has, prior to the shipment or delivery of the firearm, forwarded by registered or certified mail (return receipt requested) a copy of the sworn statement, together with a description of the firearm, in a form prescribed by the Attorney General, to the chief law enforcement officer of the transferee's place of residence, and has received a return receipt evidencing delivery of the statement or has had the statement returned due to the refusal of the named addressee to accept such letter in accordance with United States Post Office Department regulations; and

(3) the transferor has delayed shipment or delivery for a period of at least seven days following receipt of the notification of the acceptance or refusal of delivery of the statement.

A copy of the sworn statement and a copy of the notification to the local law enforcement officer, together with evidence of receipt or rejection of that notification shall be retained by the licensee as a part of the records required to be kept under section 923(g).

(d) It shall be unlawful for any person to sell or otherwise dispose of any firearm or ammunition to any person knowing or having reasonable cause to believe that such person–

(1) is under indictment for, or has been convicted in any

court of, a crime punishable by imprisonment for a term exceeding one year;

(2) is a fugitive from justice;

(3) is an unlawful user of or addicted to any controlled substance (as defined in section 102 of the Controlled Substances Act (21 U.S.C. 802));

(4) has been adjudicated as a mentally defective or has been committed to any mental institution;

(5) who, being an alien–

  (A) is illegally or unlawfully in the United States; or

  (B) except as provided in subsection (y)(2), has been admitted to the United States under a nonimmigrant visa (as that term is defined in section 101(a)(26) of the Immigration and Nationality Act (8 U.S.C. 1101(a)(26)));

(6) who has been discharged from the Armed Forces under dishonorable conditions;

(7) who, having been a citizen of the United States, has renounced their citizenship;

(8) is subject to a court order that restrains such person from harassing, stalking, or threatening an intimate partner of such person or child of such intimate partner or person, or engaging in other conduct that would place an intimate partner in reasonable fear of bodily injury to the partner or child, except that this paragraph shall only apply to a court order that–

  (A) was issued after a hearing of which such person

received actual notice, and at which such person had the opportunity to participate; and

(B)

(i) includes a finding that such person represents a credible threat to the physical safety of such intimate partner or child; or

(ii) by its terms explicitly prohibits the use, attempted use, or threatened use of physical force against such intimate partner or child that would reasonably be expected to cause bodily injury.

(9) has been convicted in any court of a misdemeanor crime of domestic violence.

This subsection shall not apply with respect to the sale or disposition of a firearm or ammunition to a licensed importer, licensed manufacturer, licensed dealer, or licensed collector who pursuant to subsection (b) of section 925 of this chapter is not precluded from dealing in firearms or ammunition, or to a person who has been granted relief from disabilities pursuant to subsection (c) of section 925 of this chapter.

(e) It shall be unlawful for any person knowingly to deliver or cause to be delivered to any common or contract carrier for transportation or shipment in interstate or foreign commerce, to persons other than licensed importers, licensed manufacturers, licensed dealers, or licensed collectors, any package or other container in which there is any firearm or ammunition without written notice to the carrier that such firearm or ammunition is being transported or shipped; except that any passenger who owns or legally possesses a firearm or ammunition being transported aboard any common or contract carrier for movement with the passenger in interstate or foreign commerce may deliver said firearm or ammunition into the custody of the pilot, captain, conductor or operator of such common or contract carrier for the duration of the trip without violating any of the provisions of this chapter. No common or contract carrier shall require or cause any label, tag, or other written notice to be placed on the outside of any package, luggage, or other container that such package, luggage, or other container contains a firearm.

(f)

(1) It shall be unlawful for any common or contract carrier to transport or deliver in interstate or foreign commerce any firearm or ammunition with knowledge or reasonable cause to believe that the shipment, transportation, or receipt thereof would be in violation of the provisions of this chapter.

(2) It shall be unlawful for any common or contract carrier to deliver in interstate or foreign commerce any firearm without obtaining written acknowledgement of receipt from the recipient of the package or other container in which there is a firearm.

(g) It shall be unlawful for any person–

(1) who has been convicted in any court of, a crime punishable by imprisonment for a term exceeding one year;

(2) who is a fugitive from justice;

(3) who is an unlawful user of or addicted to any controlled substance (as defined in section 102 of the Controlled Substances Act (21 U.S.C. 802));

(4) who has been adjudicated as a mental defective or who

has been committed to a mental institution;

(5) who, being an alien–

(A) is illegally or unlawfully in the United States; or

(B) except as provided in subsection (y)(2), has been admitted to the United States under a nonimmigrant visa (as that term is defined in section 101(a)(26) of the Immigration and Nationality Act (8 U.S.C. 1101(a)(26)));

(6) who has been discharged from the Armed Forces under dishonorable conditions;

(7) who, having been a citizen of the United States, has renounced his citizenship;

(8) who is subject to a court order that–

(A) was issued after a hearing of which such person received actual notice, and at which such person had an opportunity to participate;

(B) restrains such person from harassing, stalking, or threatening an intimate partner of such person or child of such intimate partner or person, or engaging in other conduct that would place an intimate partner in reasonable fear of bodily injury to the partner or child; and

(C)

(i) includes a finding that such person represents a credible threat to the physical safety of such intimate partner or child; or

(ii) by its terms explicitly prohibits the use, attempted use, or threatened use of physical force against such intimate partner or child that would reasonably be expected to cause bodily injury; or

(9) who has been convicted in any court of a misdemeanor crime of domestic violence, to ship or transport in interstate or foreign commerce, or possess in or affecting commerce, any firearm or ammunition; or to receive any firearm or ammunition which has been shipped or transported in interstate or foreign commerce.

(h) It shall be unlawful for any individual, who to that individual's knowledge and while being employed for any person described in any paragraph of subsection (g) of this section, in the course of such employment–

(1) to receive, possess, or transport any firearm or ammunition in or affecting interstate or foreign commerce; or

(2) to receive any firearm or ammunition which has been shipped or transported in interstate or foreign commerce.

(i) It shall be unlawful for any person to transport or ship in interstate or foreign commerce, any stolen firearm or stolen ammunition, knowing or having reasonable cause to believe that the firearm or ammunition was stolen.

(j) It shall be unlawful for any person to receive, possess, conceal, store, barter, sell, or dispose of any stolen firearm or stolen ammunition, or pledge or accept as security for a loan any stolen firearm or stolen ammunition, which is moving as, which is a part of, which constitutes, or which has been shipped or transported in, interstate or foreign commerce, either before or after it was stolen, knowing or having reasonable cause to believe that the firearm or ammunition was stolen.

(k) It shall be unlawful for any person knowingly to transport, ship, or receive, in interstate or foreign commerce, any firearm which has had the importer's or manufacturer's serial number removed, obliterated, or altered or to possess or receive any firearm which has had the importer's or manufacturer's serial number removed, obliterated, or altered and has, at any time, been shipped or transported in interstate or foreign commerce.

(l) Except as provided in section 925(d) of this chapter, it shall be unlawful for any person knowingly to import or bring into the United States or any possession thereof any firearm or ammunition; and it shall be unlawful for any person knowingly to receive any firearm or ammunition which has been imported or brought into the United States or any possession thereof in violation of the provisions of this chapter.

(m) It shall be unlawful for any licensed importer, licensed manufacturer, licensed dealer, or licensed collector knowingly to make any false entry in, to fail to make appropriate entry in, or to fail to properly maintain, any record which he is required to keep pursuant to section 923 of this chapter or regulations promulgated thereunder.

(n) It shall be unlawful for any person who is under indictment for a crime punishable by imprisonment for a term exceeding one year to ship or transport in interstate or foreign commerce any firearm or ammunition or receive any firearm or ammunition which has been shipped or transported in interstate or foreign commerce.

(o)

(1) Except as provided in paragraph (2), it shall be unlawful for any person to transfer or possess a machinegun.

(2) This subsection does not apply with respect to–

(A) a transfer to or by, or possession by or under the authority of, the United States or any department or agency thereof or a State, or a department, agency, or political subdivision thereof; or

(B) any lawful transfer or lawful possession of a

machinegun that was lawfully possessed before the date this subsection takes effect.

(p)

(1) It shall be unlawful for any person to manufacture, import, sell, ship, deliver, possess, transfer, or receive any firearm–

(A) that, after removal of grips, stocks, and magazines, is not as detectable as the Security Exemplar, by walk-through metal detectors calibrated and operated to detect the Security Exemplar; or

(B) any major component of which, when subjected to inspection by the types of x-ray machines commonly used at airports, does not generate an image that accurately depicts the shape of the component. Barium sulfate or other compounds may be used in the fabrication of the component.

(2) For purposes of this subsection–

(A) the term "firearm" does not include the frame or receiver of any such weapon;

(B) the term "major component" means, with respect to a firearm, the barrel, the slide or cylinder, or the frame or receiver of the firearm; and

(C) the term "Security Exemplar" means an object, to be fabricated at the direction of the Attorney General, that is–

(i) constructed of, during the 12-month period beginning on the date of the enactment of this subsection, 3.7 ounces of material type 17–4 PH stainless steel in a shape resembling a handgun; and

(ii) suitable for testing and calibrating metal detectors:

Provided, however, That at the close of such 12-month period, and at appropriate times thereafter the Attorney General shall promulgate regulations to permit the manufacture, importation, sale, shipment, delivery, possession, transfer, or receipt of firearms previously prohibited under this subparagraph that are as detectable as a "Security Exemplar" which contains 3.7 ounces of material type 17–4 PH stainless steel, in a shape resembling a handgun, or such lesser amount as is detectable in view of advances in state-of-the-art developments in weapons detection technology.

(3) Under such rules and regulations as the Attorney General shall prescribe, this subsection shall not apply to the manufacture, possession, transfer, receipt, shipment, or delivery of a firearm by a licensed manufacturer or any person acting pursuant to a contract with a licensed manufacturer, for the purpose of examining and testing such firearm to determine whether paragraph (1) applies to such firearm. The Attorney General shall ensure that rules and regulations adopted pursuant to this paragraph do not impair the manufacture of prototype firearms or the development of new technology.

(4) The Attorney General shall permit the conditional importation of a firearm by a licensed importer or licensed manufacturer, for examination and testing to determine whether or not the unconditional importation of such firearm would violate this subsection.

(5) This subsection shall not apply to any firearm which–

(A) has been certified by the Secretary of Defense

or the Director of Central Intelligence, after consultation with the Attorney General and the Administrator of the Federal Aviation Administration, as necessary for military or intelligence applications; and

(B) is manufactured for and sold exclusively to military or intelligence agencies of the United States.

(6) This subsection shall not apply with respect to any firearm manufactured in, imported into, or possessed in the United States before the date of the enactment of the Undetectable Firearms Act of 1988.

(q)

(1) The Congress finds and declares that–

(A) crime, particularly crime involving drugs and guns, is a pervasive, nationwide problem;

(B) crime at the local level is exacerbated by the interstate movement of drugs, guns, and criminal gangs;

(C) firearms and ammunition move easily in interstate commerce and have been found in increasing numbers in and around schools, as documented in numerous hearings in both the Committee on the Judiciary 3 the House of Representatives and the Committee on the Judiciary of the Senate;

(D) in fact, even before the sale of a firearm, the gun, its component parts, ammunition, and the raw materials from which they are made have considerably moved in interstate commerce;

(E) while criminals freely move from State to

State, ordinary citizens and foreign visitors may fear to travel to or through certain parts of the country due to concern about violent crime and gun violence, and parents may decline to send their children to school for the same reason;

(F) the occurrence of violent crime in school zones has resulted in a decline in the quality of education in our country;

(G) this decline in the quality of education has an adverse impact on interstate commerce and the foreign commerce of the United States;

(H) States, localities, and school systems find it almost impossible to handle gun-related crime by themselves-even States, localities, and school systems that have made strong efforts to prevent, detect, and punish gun-related crime find their efforts unavailing due in part to the failure or inability of other States or localities to take strong measures; and

(I) the Congress has the power, under the interstate commerce clause and other provisions of the Constitution, to enact measures to ensure the integrity and safety of the Nation's schools by enactment of this subsection.

(2)

(A) It shall be unlawful for any individual knowingly to possess a firearm that has moved in or that otherwise affects interstate or foreign commerce at a place that the individual knows, or has reasonable cause to believe, is a school zone.

(B) Subparagraph (A) does not apply to the possession of a firearm–

(i) on private property not part of school grounds;

(ii) if the individual possessing the firearm is licensed to do so by the State in which the school zone is located or a political subdivision of the State, and the law of the State or political subdivision requires that, before an individual obtains such a license, the law enforcement authorities of the State or political subdivision verify that the individual is qualified under law to receive the license;

(iii) that is–

(I) not loaded; and

(II) in a locked container, or a locked firearms rack that is on a motor vehicle;

(iv) by an individual for use in a program approved by a school in the school zone;

(v) by an individual in accordance with a contract entered into between a school in the school zone and the individual or an employer of the individual;

(vi) by a law enforcement officer acting in his or her official capacity; or

(vii) that is unloaded and is possessed by an individual while traversing school premises for the purpose of gaining access to public or private lands open to hunting, if the entry on school premises is authorized by school authorities.

(3)

(A) Except as provided in subparagraph (B), it shall be unlawful for any person, knowingly or with reckless disregard for the safety of another, to discharge or attempt to discharge a firearm that has moved in or that otherwise affects interstate or foreign commerce at a place that the person knows is a school zone.

(B) Subparagraph (A) does not apply to the discharge of a firearm–

(i) on private property not part of school grounds;

(ii) as part of a program approved by a school in the school zone, by an individual who is participating in the program;

(iii) by an individual in accordance with a contract entered into between a school in a school zone and the individual or an employer of the individual; or

(iv) by a law enforcement officer acting in his or her official capacity.

(4) Nothing in this subsection shall be construed as preempting or preventing a State or local government from enacting a statute establishing gun free school zones as provided in this subsection.

(r) It shall be unlawful for any person to assemble from imported parts any semiautomatic rifle or any shotgun which is identical to any rifle or shotgun prohibited from importation under section 925(d)(3) of this chapter as not being particularly suitable for or readily adaptable to sporting purposes except that this subsection shall not apply to–

(1) the assembly of any such rifle or shotgun for sale or distribution by a licensed manufacturer to the United

States or any department or agency thereof or to any State or any department, agency, or political subdivision thereof; or

(2) the assembly of any such rifle or shotgun for the purposes of testing or experimentation authorized by the Attorney General.

(s)

(1) Beginning on the date that is 90 days after the date of enactment of this subsection and ending on the day before the date that is 60 months after such date of enactment, it shall be unlawful for any licensed importer, licensed manufacturer, or licensed dealer to sell, deliver, or transfer a handgun (other than the return of a handgun to the person from whom it was received) to an individual who is not licensed under section 923, unless–

(A) after the most recent proposal of such transfer by the transferee–

(i) the transferor has–

(I) received from the transferee a statement of the transferee containing the information described in paragraph (3);

(II) verified the identity of the transferee by examining the identification document presented;

(III) within 1 day after the transferee furnishes the statement, provided notice of the contents of the statement to the chief law enforcement officer of the place of residence of the transferee; and

(IV) within 1 day after the transferee furnishes the statement, transmitted a copy of the statement to the chief law enforcement officer of the place of residence of the transferee; and

(ii)

(I) 5 business days (meaning days on which State offices are open) have elapsed from the date the transferor furnished notice of the contents of the statement to the chief law enforcement officer, during which period the transferor has not received information from the chief law enforcement officer that receipt or possession of the handgun by the transferee would be in violation of Federal, State, or local law; or

(II) the transferor has received notice from the chief law enforcement officer that the officer has no information indicating that receipt or possession of the handgun by the transferee would violate Federal, State, or local law;

(B) the transferee has presented to the transferor a written statement, issued by the chief law enforcement officer of the place of residence of the transferee during the 10-day period ending on the date of the most recent proposal of such transfer by the transferee, stating that the transferee requires access to a handgun because of a threat to the life of the transferee or of any member of the household of the transferee;

(C)

(i) the transferee has presented to the transferor a permit that–

(I) allows the transferee to possess or acquire a handgun; and

(II) was issued not more than 5 years earlier by the State in which the transfer is to take place; and

(ii) the law of the State provides that such a permit is to be issued only after an authorized government official has verified that the information available to such official does not indicate that possession of a handgun by the transferee would be in violation of the law;

(D) the law of the State requires that, before any licensed importer, licensed manufacturer, or licensed dealer completes the transfer of a handgun to an individual who is not licensed under section 923, an authorized government official verify that the information available to such official does not indicate that possession of a handgun by the transferee would be in violation of law;

(E) the Attorney General has approved the transfer under section 5812 of the Internal Revenue Code of 1986; or

(F) on application of the transferor, the Attorney General has certified that compliance with subparagraph (A)(i)(III) is impracticable because–

(i) the ratio of the number of law enforcement officers of the State in which the transfer is to occur to the number of square miles of land area of the State does not exceed 0.0025;

(ii) the business premises of the transferor at which the transfer is to occur are extremely remote in relation to the chief law enforcement officer; and

(iii) there is an absence of telecommunications facilities in the geographical area in which the business premises are located.

(2) A chief law enforcement officer to whom a transferor has provided notice pursuant to paragraph (1)(A)(i)(III) shall make a reasonable effort to ascertain within 5 business days whether receipt or possession would be in violation of the law, including research in whatever State and local recordkeeping systems are available and in a national system designated by the Attorney General.

(3) The statement referred to in paragraph (1)(A)(i)(I) shall contain only–

(A) the name, address, and date of birth appearing on a valid identification document (as defined in section 1028(d)(1) 4) of the transferee containing a photograph of the transferee and a description of the identification used;

(B) a statement that the transferee–

(i) is not under indictment for, and has not been convicted in any court of, a crime punishable by imprisonment for a term exceeding 1 year, and has not been convicted in any court of a misdemeanor crime of domestic violence;

(ii) is not a fugitive from justice;

(iii) is not an unlawful user of or addicted to any controlled substance (as defined in section 102 of the Controlled Substances Act);

(iv) has not been adjudicated as a mental defective or been committed to a mental institution;

(v) is not an alien who–

(I) is illegally or unlawfully in the United States; or

(II) subject to subsection (y)(2), has been admitted to the United States under a nonimmigrant visa (as that term is defined in section 101(a)(26) of the Immigration and Nationality Act (8 U.S.C. 1101(a)(26)));

(vi) has not been discharged from the Armed Forces under dishonorable conditions; and

(vii) is not a person who, having been a citizen of the United States, has renounced such citizenship;

(C) the date the statement is made; and

(D) notice that the transferee intends to obtain a handgun from the transferor.

(4) Any transferor of a handgun who, after such transfer, receives a report from a chief law enforcement officer containing information that receipt or possession of the handgun by the transferee violates Federal, State, or local law shall, within 1 business day after receipt of such request, communicate any information related to the transfer that the transferor has about the transfer and the transferee to–

(A) the chief law enforcement officer of the place of business of the transferor; and

(B) the chief law enforcement officer of the place of residence of the transferee.

(5) Any transferor who receives information, not otherwise available to the public, in a report under this subsection shall not disclose such information except to the transferee, to law enforcement authorities, or pursuant to the direction of a court of law.

(6)

(A) Any transferor who sells, delivers, or otherwise transfers a handgun to a transferee shall retain the copy of the statement of the transferee with respect to the handgun transaction, and shall retain evidence that the transferor has complied with subclauses (III) and (IV) of paragraph (1)(A)(i) with respect to the statement.

(B) Unless the chief law enforcement officer to whom a statement is transmitted under paragraph (1)(A)(i)(IV) determines that a transaction would violate Federal, State, or local law–

(i) the officer shall, within 20 business days after the date the transferee made the statement on the basis of which the notice was provided, destroy the statement, any record containing information derived from the statement, and any record created as a result of the notice required by paragraph (1)(A)(i)(III);

(ii) the information contained in the statement shall not be conveyed to any person except a person who has a need to know in order to carry out this subsection; and

(iii) the information contained in the statement shall not be used for any purpose other than to carry out this subsection.

(C) If a chief law enforcement officer determines that an individual is ineligible to receive a handgun and the individual requests the officer to provide the reason for such determination, the officer shall provide such reasons to the individual in writing within 20 business days after receipt of the request.

(7) A chief law enforcement officer or other person responsible for providing criminal history background information pursuant to this subsection shall not be liable in an action at law for damages–

(A) for failure to prevent the sale or transfer of a handgun to a person whose receipt or possession of the handgun is unlawful under this section; or

(B) for preventing such a sale or transfer to a person who may lawfully receive or possess a handgun.

(8) For purposes of this subsection, the term "chief law enforcement officer" means the chief of police, the sheriff, or an equivalent officer or the designee of any such individual.

(9) The Attorney General shall take necessary actions to ensure that the provisions of this subsection are published and disseminated to licensed dealers, law enforcement officials, and the public.

(t)

(1) Beginning on the date that is 30 days after the Attorney General notifies licensees under section 103(d) of the Brady Handgun Violence Prevention Act that the national instant criminal background check system is established, a licensed importer, licensed manufacturer, or licensed dealer shall not transfer a firearm to any other person who is not licensed under this chapter, unless–

(A) before the completion of the transfer, the licensee contacts the national instant criminal background check system established under section 103 of that Act;

(B)

(i) the system provides the licensee with a unique identification number; or

(ii) 3 business days (meaning a day on which State offices are open) have elapsed since the licensee contacted the system, and the system has not notified the licensee that the receipt of a firearm by such other person would violate subsection (g) or (n) of this section; and

(C) the transferor has verified the identity of the transferee by examining a valid identification document (as defined in section 1028(d) of this title) of the transferee containing a photograph of the transferee.

(2) If receipt of a firearm would not violate subsection (g) or (n) or State law, the system shall–

(A) assign a unique identification number to the transfer;

(B) provide the licensee with the number; and

(C) destroy all records of the system with respect to the call (other than the identifying number and the date the number was assigned) and all records of the system relating to the person or the transfer.

(3) Paragraph (1) shall not apply to a firearm transfer between a licensee and another person if–

(A)

(i) such other person has presented to the licensee a permit that–

(I) allows such other person to possess or acquire a firearm; and

(II) was issued not more than 5 years earlier by the State in which the transfer is to take place; and

(ii) the law of the State provides that such a permit is to be issued only after an authorized government official has verified that the information available to such official does not indicate that possession of a firearm by such other person would be in violation of law;

(B) the Attorney General has approved the transfer

under section 5812 of the Internal Revenue Code of 1986; or

(C) on application of the transferor, the Attorney General has certified that compliance with paragraph (1)(A) is impracticable because–

(i) the ratio of the number of law enforcement officers of the State in which the transfer is to occur to the number of square miles of land area of the State does not exceed 0.0025;

(ii) the business premises of the licensee at which the transfer is to occur are extremely remote in relation to the chief law enforcement officer (as defined in subsection (s)(8)); and

(iii) there is an absence of telecommunications facilities in the geographical area in which the business premises are located.

(4) If the national instant criminal background check system notifies the licensee that the information available to the system does not demonstrate that the receipt of a firearm by such other person would violate subsection (g) or (n) or State law, and the licensee transfers a firearm to such other person, the licensee shall include in the record of the transfer the unique identification number provided by the system with respect to the transfer.

(5) If the licensee knowingly transfers a firearm to such other person and knowingly fails to comply with paragraph (1) of this subsection with respect to the transfer and, at the time such other person most recently proposed the

transfer, the national instant criminal background check system was operating and information was available to the system demonstrating that receipt of a firearm by such other person would violate subsection (g) or (n) of this section or State law, the Attorney General may, after notice and opportunity for a hearing, suspend for not more than 6 months or revoke any license issued to the licensee under section 923, and may impose on the licensee a civil fine of not more than $5,000.

(6) Neither a local government nor an employee of the Federal Government or of any State or local government, responsible for providing information to the national instant criminal background check system shall be liable in an action at law for damages–

(A) for failure to prevent the sale or transfer of a firearm to a person whose receipt or possession of the firearm is unlawful under this section; or

(B) for preventing such a sale or transfer to a person who may lawfully receive or possess a firearm.

(u) It shall be unlawful for a person to steal or unlawfully take or carry away from the person or the premises of a person who is licensed to engage in the business of importing, manufacturing, or dealing in firearms, any firearm in the licensee's business inventory that has been shipped or transported in interstate or foreign commerce.

(v), (w) Repealed. Pub. L. 103–322, title XI, §110105(2), Sept. 13, 1994, 108 Stat. 2000 .

(x)

(1) It shall be unlawful for a person to sell, deliver, or otherwise transfer to a person who the transferor knows or has reasonable cause to believe is a juvenile–

(A) a handgun; or

(B) ammunition that is suitable for use only in a handgun.

(2) It shall be unlawful for any person who is a juvenile to knowingly possess–

(A) a handgun; or

(B) ammunition that is suitable for use only in a handgun.

(3) This subsection does not apply to–

(A) a temporary transfer of a handgun or ammunition to a juvenile or to the possession or use of a handgun or ammunition by a juvenile if the handgun and ammunition are possessed and used by the juvenile–

(i) in the course of employment, in the course of ranching or farming related to activities at the residence of the juvenile (or on property used for ranching or farming at which the juvenile, with the permission of the property owner or lessee, is performing activities related to the operation of the farm or ranch), target practice, hunting, or a course of instruction in the safe and lawful use of a handgun;

(ii) with the prior written consent of the juvenile's parent or guardian who is not prohibited by Federal, State, or local law from possessing a firearm, except–

(I) during transportation by the juvenile of an unloaded handgun in a locked container directly from the place of transfer to a place at which an activity described in clause (i) is to take place and transportation by the juvenile of that handgun, unloaded and in a locked container, directly from the place at which such an activity took place to the transferor; or

(II) with respect to ranching or farming activities as described in clause (i), a juvenile may possess and use a handgun or ammunition with the prior written approval of the juvenile's parent or legal guardian and at the direction of an adult who is not prohibited by Federal, State or local law from possessing a firearm;

(iii) the juvenile has the prior written consent in the juvenile's possession at all times when a handgun is in the possession of the juvenile; and

(iv) in accordance with State and local law;

(B) a juvenile who is a member of the Armed Forces of the United States or the National Guard who possesses or is armed with a handgun in the line of duty;

(C) a transfer by inheritance of title (but not possession) of a handgun or ammunition to a juvenile; or

(D) the possession of a handgun or ammunition by a juvenile taken in defense of the juvenile or other persons against an intruder into the residence of the juvenile or a residence in which the juvenile is an invited guest.

(4) A handgun or ammunition, the possession of which is transferred to a juvenile in circumstances in which the transferor is not in violation of this subsection shall not be subject to permanent confiscation by the Government if its possession by the juvenile subsequently becomes unlawful because of the conduct of the juvenile, but shall be returned to the lawful owner when such handgun or ammunition is no longer required by the Government for the purposes of investigation or prosecution.

(5) For purposes of this subsection, the term "juvenile" means a person who is less than 18 years of age.

(6)

(A) In a prosecution of a violation of this subsection, the court shall require the presence of a juvenile defendant's parent or legal guardian at all proceedings.

(B) The court may use the contempt power to enforce subparagraph (A).

(C) The court may excuse attendance of a parent or legal guardian of a juvenile defendant at a proceeding in a prosecution of a violation of this subsection for good cause shown.

(y) Provisions Relating to Aliens Admitted Under Nonimmigrant Visas.–

(1) Definitions.– In this subsection–

(A) the term "alien" has the same meaning as in section 101(a)(3) of the Immigration and Nationality Act (8 U.S.C. 1101(a)(3)); and

(B) the term "nonimmigrant visa" has the same meaning as in section 101(a)(26) of the Immigration and Nationality Act (8 U.S.C. 1101(a)(26)).

(2) Exceptions.–Subsections (d)(5)(B), (g)(5)(B), and (s)(3)(B)(v)(II) do not apply to any alien who has been lawfully admitted to the United States under a nonimmigrant visa, if that alien is–

(A) admitted to the United States for lawful hunting or sporting purposes or is in possession of a hunting license or permit lawfully issued in the United States;

(B) an official representative of a foreign government who is–

(i) accredited to the United States Government or the Government's mission to an international organization having its headquarters in the United States; or

(ii) en route to or from another country to which that alien is accredited;

(C) an official of a foreign government or a distinguished foreign visitor who has been so designated by the Department of State; or

(D) a foreign law enforcement officer of a friendly foreign government entering the United States on official law enforcement business.

(3) Waiver.–

(A) Conditions for waiver.–Any individual who has been admitted to the United States under a nonimmigrant visa may receive a waiver from the requirements of subsection (g)(5), if–

(i) the individual submits to the Attorney General a petition that meets the requirements of subparagraph (C); and

(ii) the Attorney General approves the petition.

(B) Petition.–Each petition under subparagraph (B) shall–

(i) demonstrate that the petitioner has resided in the United States for a continuous period of not less than 180 days before the date on which the petition is submitted under this paragraph; and

(ii) include a written statement from the embassy or consulate of the petitioner, authorizing the petitioner to acquire a firearm or ammunition and certifying that the alien would not, absent the application of subsection (g)(5)(B), otherwise be prohibited from such acquisition under subsection (g).

(C) Approval of petition.–The Attorney General shall approve a petition submitted in accordance with this paragraph, if the Attorney General determines that waiving the requirements of subsection (g)(5)(B) with respect to the petitioner–

(i) would be in the interests of justice; and

(ii) would not jeopardize the public safety.

(z) Secure Gun Storage or Safety Device.–

(1) In general.-Except as provided under paragraph (2), it shall be unlawful for any licensed importer, licensed manufacturer, or licensed dealer to sell, deliver, or transfer any handgun to any person other than any

person licensed under this chapter, unless the transferee is provided with a secure gun storage or safety device (as defined in section 921(a)(34)) for that handgun.

(2) Exceptions.–Paragraph (1) shall not apply to–

(A)

(i) the manufacture for, transfer to, or possession by, the United States, a department or agency of the United States, a State, or a department, agency, or political subdivision of a State, of a handgun; or

(ii) the transfer to, or possession by, a law enforcement officer employed by an entity referred to in clause (i) of a handgun for law enforcement purposes (whether on or off duty); or

(B) the transfer to, or possession by, a rail police officer directly employed by or contracted by a rail carrier and certified or commissioned as a police officer under the laws of a State of a handgun for purposes of law enforcement (whether on or off duty);

(C) the transfer to any person of a handgun listed as a curio or relic by the Secretary pursuant to section 921(a)(13); or

(D) the transfer to any person of a handgun for which a secure gun storage or safety device is temporarily unavailable for the reasons described in the exceptions stated in section 923(e), if the licensed manufacturer, licensed importer, or licensed dealer delivers to the transferee within 10 calendar days from the date of the delivery of the handgun to the transferee a secure gun storage or safety device for the handgun.

(3) Liability for use.–

(A) In general.–Notwithstanding any other provision of law, a person who has lawful possession and control of a handgun, and who uses a secure gun storage or safety device with the handgun, shall be entitled to immunity from a qualified civil liability action.

(B) Prospective actions.–A qualified civil liability action may not be brought in any Federal or State court.

(C) Defined term.–As used in this paragraph, the term "qualified civil liability action"–

(i) means a civil action brought by any person against a person described in subparagraph (A) for damages resulting from the criminal or unlawful misuse of the handgun by a third party, if–

(I) the handgun was accessed by another person who did not have the permission or authorization of the person having lawful possession and control of the handgun to have access to it; and

(II) at the time access was gained by the person not so authorized, the handgun had been made inoperable by use of a secure gun storage or safety device; and

(ii) shall not include an action brought against the person having lawful possession and control of the handgun for negligent entrustment or negligence per se.

➢ APPENDICES ➣

APPENDIX C
ATF Forms

ATF Form 1 Page 1

OMB No. 1140-0011 (06/30/2019)

U.S. Department of Justice
Bureau of Alcohol, Tobacco, Firearms and Explosives

Application to Make and Register a Firearm

ATF Control Number

To: National Firearms Act Division, Bureau of Alcohol, Tobacco, Firearms and Explosives, P.O. Box 5015, Portland, OR 97208-5015

(Submit in duplicate. Please do not staple documents. See instructions attached.)

As required by Sections 5821 (b), 5822, and 5841 of the National Firearms Act, Title 26 U.S.C., Chapter 53, the undersigned hereby submits application to make and register the firearm described below.

1. Type of Application *(check one)*

☐ a. Tax Paid. Submit your tax payment of $200 with the application. The tax may be paid by credit or debit card, check, or money order. Please complete item 17. Upon approval of the application, we will affix and cancel the required National Firearms Act Stamp. *(See instruction 2c and 3)*

☐ b. Tax Exempt because firearm is being made on behalf of the United States, or any department, independent establishment, or agency thereof.

☐ c. Tax Exempt because firearm is being made by or on behalf of any State or possession of the United States, or any political subdivision thereof, or any official police organization of such a government entity engaged in criminal investigations.

2. Application is made by: ☐ INDIVIDUAL ☐ TRUST or LEGAL ENTITY ☐ GOVERNMENT ENTITY

3a. Trade name *(If any)*

3b. Applicant's name and mailing address *(Type or print below) (see instruction 2d)*

3c. If P.O. Box is shown above, street address must be given here

3d. County

3e. Telephone Number

3f. E-mail address *(optional)*

4. Description of Firearm *(complete items a through k) (See instruction 2j)*

a. Name and Address of Original Manufacturer and/or Importer of Firearm *(if any)*

b. Type of Firearm to be made *(See definition 1c) If a destructive device, complete item 4j*

c. Caliber or Gauge *(Specify one)*

d. Model *(as marked on firearm)*

e. Barrel length:

f. Overall length:

g. Serial Number

h. Additional Description *(Indicate required maker's markings to include maker's name (as registered), city and state as each will appear on firearm)*

i. Specify Why You Intend To Make Firearm *(Use additional sheet if necessary)*

j. Type of destructive device (check one box): ☐ Firearm ☐ Explosives *(if the Explosives box is checked, complete item 5 and see instruction 2l)*

If an explosive type destructive device, identify the type of explosive(s):

k. Is this firearm being reactivated? ☐ Yes ☐ No *(See definition 1k)*

5. Applicant's Federal Firearms License *(If any)* or Explosives License or Permit Number *(Give complete 15-digit Number)*

6. Special *(Occupational)* Tax Status *(if applicable) (See definitions)*

a. Employer Identification Number

b. Class

Under Penalties of Perjury, I Declare that I have examined this application, including accompanying documents, and to the best of my knowledge and belief it is true, accurate and complete and the making and possession of the firearm described above would not constitute a violation of Title 18, U.S.C., Chapter 44, Title 26, U.S.C., Chapter 53; or any provisions of State or local law.

7. Signature of Applicant	8. Name and Title of Authorized Official	9. Date

The space below is for the use of the Bureau of Alcohol, Tobacco, Firearms and Explosives

By authority of the Director, Bureau of Alcohol, Tobacco, Firearms and Explosives, this application has been examined and the applicant's making and registration of the firearm described above is:

☐ Approved *(With the following conditions, if any)*

☐ Disapproved *(For the following reasons)*

Authorized ATF Official

Date

Previous Editions Are Obsolete

ATF Copy

ATF E-Form 1 (5320.1)
Revised November 2018

ATF Form 1 Page 2

MAKER'S CERTIFICATION ***(not completed by a GOVERNMENT ENTITY)***

10. Law Enforcement Notification ***(See instruction 2g)***

Each applicant is to provide notification of the proposed making and possession of the firearm described on this Form 1 by providing a copy of the completed form to the chief law enforcement officer in the agency identified below:

Agency or Department Name	Name and Title of Official

Address (Street address or P.O. Box, City, State and Zip Code) to which sent (mailed or delivered)

Information for the Chief Law Enforcement Officer

This form provides notification of the applicant's intent to make and register a National Firearms Act (NFA) firearm. No action on your part is required. However, should you have information that may disqualify this person from making or possessing a firearm, please contact the NFA Division at (304) 616-4500 or NFA@atf.gov. A "Yes" answer to items 11.a. through 11.h. or 13.b. or 13.c. could disqualify a person from acquiring or possessing a firearm. Also, ATF will not approve an application if the making or possession of the firearm is in violation of State or local law.

12. Photograph

Affix a 2" x 2" Photograph Here
No Stapling. Please Tape Sides of Photo to the Application.

1. Photo must have been taken within the last year.
2. Photo must have been taken in full face view without a hat or head covering that obscures the hair or hairline.
3. On back of photograph print full name, last 4 of SSN, and business address.

Maker's Questions *(complete only when the maker is an individual)*

A maker who is an individual must complete this Section.

11. Answer questions 11.a. through 11.h. Answer questions 13 and 14, if applicable. For any "Yes" answer the applicant shall provide details on a separate sheet. *(See instruction 7c and definitions)*

	Yes	No
a. Are you under indictment or information in any court for a felony, or any other crime, for which the judge could imprison you for more than one year? *(See definition 1n)*		
b. Have you ever been convicted in any court for a felony, or any other crime, for which the judge could have imprisoned you for more than one year, even if you received a shorter sentence including probation? *(See definition 1n)*		
c. Are you a fugitive from justice? *(See definition 1t)*		
d. Are you an unlawful user of, or addicted to, marijuana or any depressant, stimulant, narcotic drug, or any other controlled substance? **Warning: The use or possession of marijuana remains unlawful under Federal law regardless of whether it has been legalized or decriminalized for medicinal or recreational purposes in the state where you reside.**		
e. Have you ever been adjudicated as a mental defective **OR** have you ever been committed to a mental institution? *(See definition 1o and 1p)*		
f. Have you been discharged from the Armed Forces under **dishonorable** conditions?		
g. Are you subject to a court order restraining you from harassing, stalking, or threatening your child or an intimate partner or child of such partner? *(See definition 1q)*		
h. Have you ever been convicted in any court of a misdemeanor crime of domestic violence? *(See definition 1r)*		

13a. Country of Citizenship: *(Check/List more than one, if applicable. Nationals of the United States may check U.S.A.) (See definition 1s)*

☐ United States of America ☐ Other Country/Countries *(specify)*:

		Yes	No
b. Have you ever renounced your United States citizenship?			
c. Are you an alien illegally or unlawfully in the United States?			
d.1. Are you an alien who has been admitted to the United States under a nonimmigrant visa?			
d.2. If "yes", do you fall within any of the exceptions stated in the instructions? Attach the documentation to the application	☐ N/A		

14. If you are an alien, record your U.S.-Issued Alien or Admission number (AR#, USCIS#, or 194#):

CERTIFICATION: Under penalties imposed by 18 U.S.C. § 924 and 26 U.S.C. § 5861, I certify that, upon submission of this form to ATF, a completed copy of this form will be directed to the chief law enforcement officer (CLEO) shown in item 10, that the statements, as applicable, contained in this certification, and any attached documents in support thereof, are true and correct to the best of my knowledge and belief. NOTE: See instructions 2.d(2) and 2.d(3) for the items to be completed depending on the type of applicant.

Signature of Maker   Date

ATF Copy

ATF E-Form 1 (5320.1)
Revised November 2018

ATF Form 1 Page 3

15. Number of Responsible Persons *(see definitions)* associated with the applicant trust or legal entity ______

16. Provide the full name (printed or typed) below for each Responsible Person associated with the applicant trust or legal entity *(if there are more Responsible Persons than can be listed on the form, attach a separate sheet listing the additional Responsible Person(s)).* Please note that a completed Form 5320.23, National Firearms Act (NFA) Responsible Person Questionnaire, must be submitted with the Form 1 application for each Responsible Person.

Full Name	Full Name

17. Method of Payment *(Check one) (See instruction 2h) (if paying by credit/debit card, complete the sections below)*

☐ Check *(Enclosed)* ☐ Cashier's Check or Money Order *(Enclosed)* ☐ Visa ☐ Mastercard ☐ American Express ☐ Discover ☐ Diners Club

Credit/Debit Card Number *(No dashes)*	Name as Printed on the Credit/Debit Card	Expiration Date *(Month & year)*

Credit/Debit Card Billing Address:	Address:		
	City:	State:	Zip Code:
			Tax Amount: $

I Authorize ATF to Charge my Credit/Debit Card the Above Amount.

Signature of Cardholder ______ Date ______

Your credit/debit card will be charged the above stated amount upon receipt of your application. The charge will be reflected on your credit/debit card statement. In the event your application is NOT approved, the above amount will be credited to the credit/debit card noted above.

Important Information for Currently Registered Firearms

If you are the current registrant of the firearm described on this form, please note the following information.

Estate Procedures: For procedures regarding the transfer of firearms in an estate resulting from the death of the registrant identified in item 3b, the executor should contact the NFA Division, Bureau of ATF, 244 Needy Road, Martinsburg, WV 25405.

Interstate Movement: If the firearm identified in item 4 is a **machinegun**, **short-barreled rifle**, **short-barreled shotgun**, or **destructive device**, the registrant may be required by 18 U.S.C. § 922(a)(4) to obtain permission from ATF prior to any transportation in interstate or foreign commerce. ATF Form 5320.20 can be used to request this permission.

Change of Description or Address: The registrant shall notify the NFA Division, Bureau of Alcohol, Tobacco, Firearms and Explosives, 244 Needy Road, Martinsburg, WV 25405, in writing, of any change to the description of the firearm in item 4, or any change to the address of the registrant.

Restrictions on Possession: Any restriction *(see approval block on face of form)* on the possession of the firearm identified in item 4 continues with the further transfer of the firearm.

Persons Prohibited from Possessing Firearms: If the registrant becomes prohibited from possessing a firearm, please contact the NFA Division for procedures on how to dispose of the firearm.

Proof of Registration: A person possessing a firearm registered as required by the NFA shall retain proof of registration which shall be made available to any ATF officer upon request.

Paperwork Reduction Act Notice

This form is in accordance with the Paperwork Reduction Act of 1995. The information you provide is used to establish that the applicant's making and possession of the firearm would be in conformance with Federal, State, and local law. The data is used as proof of lawful registration of a firearm to the manufacturer. The furnishing of this information is mandatory *(26 U.S.C. § 5822).*

The estimated average burden associated with this collection of information is 4.0 hours per respondent or recordkeeper, depending on individual circumstances. Comments concerning the accuracy of this burden estimate and suggestion for reducing this burden should be addressed to Reports Management Officer, Information Technology Coordination Staff, Bureau of Alcohol, Tobacco, Firearms and Explosives, Washington, DC 20226.

An agency may not conduct or sponsor, and a person is not required to respond to, a collection of information unless it displays a currently valid OMB control number.

ATF Copy

ATF E-Form 1 (5320.1)
Revised November 2018

ATF Form 4 Page 1

OMB No. 1140-0014 (06/30/2019)

U.S. Department of Justice
Bureau of Alcohol, Tobacco, Firearms and Explosives

Application for Tax Paid Transfer and Registration of Firearm

ATF Control Number

SUBMIT in DUPLICATE to: **National Firearms Act Division**
Bureau of Alcohol, Tobacco, Firearms and Explosives, P.O. Box 5015, Portland, OR 97208-5015

1. Type of Transfer *(Check one)*

☐ $5 ☐ $200

Submit the appropriate tax payment with the application. The tax may be paid by credit or debit card, check, or money order. Please complete item 20. Upon approval of the application, we will affix and cancel the required National Firearms Act stamp. *(See instructions 2b, 2i and 3)*

2a. Transferee's Name and Address *(Include trade name, if any) (See instruction 2d)*

☐ INDIVIDUAL ☐ TRUST or LEGAL ENTITY

2b. County

3a. Transferor's Name and Address *(Include trade name, if any)* *(Executors: see instruction 2k)*

3b. e-mail address *(optional)*

3c. Transferor's Telephone *(Area Code and Number)*

3d. If Applicable: Decedent's Name, Address, and Date of Death

3e. Number, Street, City, State and Zip Code of Residence *(or Firearms Business Premises)* If Different from Item 3a.

The above-named and undersigned transferor hereby makes application as required by Section 5812 of the National Firearms Act to transfer and register the firearm described below to the transferee.

4. Description of Firearm *(Complete items a through h) (See instruction 2m)*

a. Name and Address of Maker Manufacturer and/or Importer of Firearm

b. Type of Firearm *(see definitions)*

c. Caliber or Gauge

d. Model

e. Of Barrel Length:

f. Overall Length:

g. Serial Number

h. Additional Description or Data Appearing on Firearm *(Attach additional sheet if necessary)*

5. Transferee's Federal Firearms License *(If any)*
(Give complete 15-digit number) (See instruction 2c)

First 6 digits	2 digits	2 digits	5 digits

6. Transferee's Special (Occupational) Tax Status *(If any)*

a. Employer Identification Number	b. Class

7. Transferor's Federal Firearms License *(If any)*

First 6 digits	2 digits	2 digits	5 digits

8. Transferor's Special (Occupational) Tax Status *(If any)*

a. Employer Identification Number	b. Class

Under Penalties of Perjury, I Declare that I have examined this application, and to the best of my knowledge and belief it is true, correct and complete, and that the transfer of the described firearm to the transferee and receipt and possession of it by the transferee are not prohibited by the provisions of Title 18, United States Code; Chap 44; Title 26, United States Code; Chap 53; or any provisions of State or local law.

9. Signature of Transferor *(Or authorized official)*

10. Name and Title of Authorized Official *(Print or type)*

11. Date

The Space Below is for the use of the Bureau of Alcohol, Tobacco, Firearms and Explosives

By Authority of The Director, This Application Has Been Examined, and the Transfer and Registration of the Firearm Described Herein and the Interstate Movement of that Firearm, When Applicable, to the Transferee are:

Stamp Denomination

☐ Approved *(With the following conditions, if any)*

☐ Disapproved *(For the following reasons)*

Signature of Authorized ATF Official

Date

Previous Editions Are Obsolete

ATF Copy

ATF E-Form 4 (5320.4)
Revised November 2018

ATF Form 4 Page 2

Transferee Certification

12. Law Enforcement Notification *(See instruction 2f)*

The transferee is to provide notification of the proposed acquisition and possession of the firearm described on this Form 4 by providing a copy of the completed form to the chief law enforcement officer in the agency identified below:

Agency or Department Name

Name and Title of Official

Address (Street address or P.O. Box, City, State and Zip Code) to which sent (mailed or delivered))

Information for the Chief Law Enforcement Officer

This form provides notification of the transferee's intent to acquire and possess a National Firearms Act (NFA) firearm. No action on your part is required. However, should you have information that may disqualify this person from acquiring or possessing a firearm, please contact the NFA Division at (304) 616-4500 or NFA@atf.gov. A "Yes" answer to items 14.a. through 14.h. or 16.b. or 16.c. could disqualify a person from acquiring or possessing a firearm. Also, ATF will not approve an application if the transfer or possession of the firearm is in violation of State or local law.

13. Transferee Necessity Statement *(See instruction 2e)*

I, ______________________________, have a reasonable necessity to possess the machinegun, short-barreled rifle,
(Name and Title of Transferee)
short-barreled shotgun, or destructive device described on this application for the following reason(s) ______________________________

and my possession of the device or weapon would be consistent with public safety (18 U.S.C. § 922(b) (4) and 27 CFR § 478.98).

Transferee Questions *(Complete Only When Transferee is An Individual)*

14. Answer questions 14.a. through 14.h. Answer questions 16 and 17, if applicable. For any "Yes" answer the transferee shall provide details on a separate sheet. *(See instruction 7b and definitions)*

	Yes	No
a. Are you under indictment or information in any court for a felony, or any other crime, for which the judge could imprison you for more than one year? *(See definition 1m)*		
b. Have you ever been convicted in any court for a felony, or any other crime, for which the judge could have imprisoned you for more than one year, even if you received a shorter sentence including probation? *(See definition 1m)*		
c. Are you a fugitive from justice? *(See definition 1s)*		
d. Are you an unlawful user of, or addicted to, marijuana or any depressant, stimulant, narcotic drug, or any other controlled substance? **Warning: The use or possession of marijuana remains unlawful under Federal law regardless of whether it has been legalized or decriminalized for medicinal or recreational purposes in the state where you reside.**		
e. Have you ever been adjudicated as a mental defective **OR** have you ever been committed to a mental institution? *(See definitions 1n and 1o)*		
f. Have you been discharged from the Armed Forces under **dishonorable** conditions?		
g. Are you subject to a court order restraining you from harassing, stalking, or threatening your child or an intimate partner or child of such partner? *(See definition 1p)*		
h. Have you ever been convicted in any court of a misdemeanor crime of domestic violence? *(See definition 1q)*		

15. Photograph

Affix a 2" x 2" Photograph here. No Stapling. Tape Sides of Photo to the Application.

1. Photo must have been taken within the last year.
2. Photo must have been taken in full face view without a hat or head covering that obscures the hair or hairline.
3. On back of photograph print full name, last 4 of SSN, and business address.

16a. Country of Citizenship: *(Check/List more than one, if applicable. Nationals of the United States may check U.S.A.) (See definition 1r)*

☐ United States of America ☐ Other Country/Countries *(specify)*: ______________________________

	Yes	No
b. Have you ever renounced your United States citizenship?		
c. Are you an alien illegally or unlawfully in the United States?		
d.1. Are you an alien who has been admitted to the United States under a nonimmigrant visa?		
d.2. If "yes", do you fall within any of the exceptions stated in the instructions? Attach the documentation to the application ☐ N/A		

17. If you are an alien, record your U.S.-Issued Alien or Admission number (AR#, USCIS#, or 194#): ______________________________

CERTIFICATION: Under penalties imposed by 18 U.S.C. § 924 and 26 U.S.C. § 5861, I certify that, upon submission of this form to ATF, a completed copy of this form will be directed to the chief law enforcement officer *(CLEO)* shown in item 12, that the statements, as applicable, contained in this certification, and any attached documents in support thereof, are true and correct to the best of my knowledge and belief. NOTE: See instructions 2.d(2) and 2.d(3) for the items to be completed depending on the type of transferee.

Signature of Transferee

Date

ATF Copy

ATF E-Form 4 (5320.4)
Revised November 2018

ATF Form 4 Page 3

18. Number of Responsible Persons *(see definitions)* associated with the transferee trust or legal entity________

19. Provide the full name (printed or typed) below for each Responsible Person associated with the applicant trust or legal entity (if there are more Responsible Persons than can be listed on the form, attach a separate sheet listing the additional Responsible Person(s)). Please note that a completed Form 5320.23, National Firearms Act (NFA) Responsible Person Questionnaire, must be submitted with the Form 4 application for each Responsible Person.

Full Name	Full Name

20. Method of Payment *(Check one) (See instruction 2i)* (if paying by credit/debit card, complete the section below)

☐ Check *(Enclosed)* ☐ Cashier's Check or Money Order *(Enclosed)* ☐ Visa ☐ Mastercard ☐ American Express ☐ Discover ☐ Diners Club

Credit/Debit Card Number *(No dashes)*	Name as Printed on the Credit/Debit Card	Expiration Date *(Month & year)*

Credit/Debit Card Billing Address:	Address:		
	City:	State:	Zip Code:

	Tax Amount: $

I Authorize ATF to Charge my Credit/Debit Card the Tax Amount.

Signature of Cardholder Date

Your credit/debit card will be charged the above stated amount upon receipt of the application. The charge will be reflected on your credit/debit card statement. In the event your application is NOT approved, the above amount will be credited to the credit/debit card noted above.

Important Information for Currently Registered Firearms

If you are the current registrant of the firearm described on this form, please note the following information.

Estate Procedures: For procedures regarding the transfer of firearms in an estate resulting from the death of the registrant identified in item 2a, the executor should contact the NFA Division, Bureau of Alcohol, Tobacco, Firearms and Explosives, 244 Needy Road, Martinsburg, WV 25405.

Change of Address: Unless currently licensed under the Gun Control Act, the registrant shall notify the NFA Division, Bureau of Alcohol, Tobacco, Firearms and Explosives, 244 Needy Road, Martinsburg, WV 25405, in writing, of any change to the address in item 2a.

Change of Description: The registrant shall notify the NFA Division, Bureau of Alcohol, Tobacco, Firearms and Explosives, 244 Needy Road, Martinsburg, WV 25405, in writing, of any change to the description of the firearm(s) in item 4.

Interstate Movement: If the firearm identified in item 4 is a **machinegun**, **short-barreled rifle**, **short-barreled shotgun**, or **destructive device**, the registrant may be required by 18 U.S.C. § 922(a)(4) to obtain permission from ATF prior to any transportation in interstate or foreign commerce. ATF Form 5320. 20 can be used to request this permission.

Restrictions on Possession: Any restriction *(see approval block on face of form)* on the possession of the firearm identified in item 4 continues with the further transfer of the firearm.

Persons Prohibited from Possessing Firearms: If the registrant becomes prohibited from possessing a firearm, please contact the NFA Division for procedures on how to dispose of the firearm.

Proof of Registration: A person possessing a firearm registered as required by the NFA shall retain proof of registration which shall be made available to any ATF officer upon request.

Paperwork Reduction Act Notice

This form meets the clearance requirements of the Paperwork Reduction Act of 1995. The information you provide is used in applying to transfer serviceable firearms taxpaid. Data is used to identify transferor, transferee, and firearm, and to ensure legality for transfer under Federal, State and local laws. The furnishing of this information is mandatory (26 U.S.C. § 5812).

The estimated average burden associated with this collection of information is 3.78 hours per respondent or recordkeeper, depending on individual circumstances. Comments concerning the accuracy of this burden estimate and suggestion for reducing this burden should be addressed to Reports Management Officer, Information Technology Coordination Staff, Bureau of Alcohol, Tobacco, Firearms and Explosives, Washington, DC 20226.

An agency may not conduct or sponsor, and a person is not required to respond to, a collection of information unless it displays a currently valid OMB control number.

ATF Copy

ATF E-Form 4 (5320.4)
Revised November 2018

ATF Form 4473 Page 1

OMB No. 1140-0020

U.S. Department of Justice
Bureau of Alcohol, Tobacco, Firearms and Explosives

Firearms Transaction Record

WARNING: You may not receive a firearm if prohibited by Federal or State law. The information you provide will be used to determine whether you are prohibited from receiving a firearm. Certain violations of the Gun Control Act, 18 U.S.C. 921 et. seq., are punishable by up to 10 years imprisonment and/or up to a $250,000 fine.

Read the Notices, Instructions, and Definitions on this form. Prepare in original only at the licensed premises *("licensed premises" includes business temporarily conducted from a qualifying gun show or event in the same State in which the licensed premises is located)* unless the transaction qualifies under 18 U.S.C. 922(c). All entries must be handwritten in ink. "PLEASE PRINT."

Transferor's/Seller's Transaction Serial Number *(If any)*

Section A - Must Be Completed Personally By Transferee/Buyer

1. Transferee's/Buyer's Full Name *(If legal name contains an initial only, record "IO" after the initial. If no middle initial or name, record "NMN".)*

Last Name *(Including suffix (e.g., Jr, Sr, II, III))*	First Name	Middle Name

2. Current State of Residence and Address (**U.S. Postal abbreviations are acceptable. Cannot be a post office box.**)

Number and Street Address	City	County	State	ZIP Code

3. Place of Birth U.S. City and State **-OR-**	Foreign Country	4. Height Ft. ____ In. ____	5. Weight *(Lbs.)*	6. Sex ☐ Male ☐ Female	7. Birth Date Month	Day	Year

8. Social Security Number *(Optional, but will help prevent misidentification)*

9. Unique Personal Identification Number *(UPIN)* if applicable *(See Instructions for Question 9.)*

10.a. Ethnicity
- ☐ Hispanic or Latino
- ☐ Not Hispanic or Latino

10.b. Race ***(In addition to ethnicity, select one or more race in 10.b. Both 10.a. and 10.b. must be answered.)***
- ☐ American Indian or Alaska Native
- ☐ Black or African American
- ☐ White
- ☐ Asian
- ☐ Native Hawaiian or Other Pacific Islander

11. Answer the following questions by checking or marking *"yes"* or *"no"* in the boxes to the right of the questions.	Yes	No
a. Are you the actual transferee/buyer of the firearm(s) listed on this form? **Warning: You are not the actual transferee/buyer if you are acquiring the firearm(s) on behalf of another person. If you are not the actual transferee/buyer, the licensee cannot transfer the firearm(s) to you.** *Exception: **If you are picking up a repaired firearm(s)** for another person, you are **not** required to answer 11.a. and may proceed to question 11.b. (See Instructions for Question 11.a.)*	☐	☐
b. Are you under indictment or information in any court for a **felony**, or any other crime for which the judge could imprison you for more than one year? *(See Instructions for Question 11.b.)*	☐	☐
c. Have you ever been convicted in any court of a **felony**, or any other crime for which the judge could have imprisoned you for more than one year, even if you received a shorter sentence including probation? *(See Instructions for Question 11.c.)*	☐	☐
d. Are you a fugitive from justice? *(See Instructions for Question 11.d.)*	☐	☐
e. Are you an unlawful user of, or addicted to, marijuana or any depressant, stimulant, narcotic drug, or any other controlled substance? **Warning: The use or possession of marijuana remains unlawful under Federal law regardless of whether it has been legalized or decriminalized for medicinal or recreational purposes in the state where you reside.**	☐	☐
f. Have you ever been adjudicated as a mental defective **OR** have you ever been committed to a mental institution? *(See Instructions for Question 11.f.)*	☐	☐
g. Have you been discharged from the Armed Forces under **dishonorable** conditions?	☐	☐
h. Are you subject to a court order restraining you from harassing, stalking, or threatening your child or an intimate partner or child of such partner? *(See Instructions for Question 11.h.)*	☐	☐
i. Have you ever been **convicted** in any court of a misdemeanor crime of domestic violence? *(See Instructions for Question 11.i.)*	☐	☐

12.a. Country of Citizenship: *(Check/List more than one, if applicable. Nationals of the United States may check U.S.A.)*

☐ United States of America *(U.S.A.)* ☐ Other Country/Countries *(Specify)*

	Yes	No
12.b. Have you ever renounced your United States citizenship?	☐	☐
12.c. Are you an alien **illegally** or **unlawfully** in the United States?	☐	☐
12.d.1. Are you an alien who has been admitted to the United States under a nonimmigrant visa? *(See Instructions for Question 12.d.)*	☐	☐
12.d.2. If "yes", do you fall within any of the exceptions stated in the instructions? ☐ N/A	☐	☐

13. If you are an alien, record your U.S.-Issued Alien or Admission number *(AR#, USCIS#, or I94#)*:

Previous Editions Are Obsolete

Transferee/Buyer Continue to Next Page
STAPLE IF PAGES BECOME SEPARATED

Page 1 of 6

ATF E-Form 4473 (5300.9)
Revised October 2016

I certify that my answers in Section A are true, correct, and complete. I have read and understand the Notices, Instructions, and Definitions on ATF Form 4473. I understand that answering "yes" to question 11.a. if I am not the actual transferee/buyer is a crime punishable as a felony under Federal law, and may also violate State and/or local law. I understand that a person who answers "yes" to any of the questions 11.b. through 11.i and/or 12.b. through 12.c. is prohibited from purchasing or receiving a firearm. I understand that a person who answers "yes" to question 12.d.1. is prohibited from receiving or possessing a firearm, unless the person answers "yes" to question 12.d.2. and provides the documentation required in 18.c. I also understand that making any false oral or written statement, or exhibiting any false or misrepresented identification with respect to this transaction, is a crime punishable as a felony under Federal law, and may also violate State and/or local law. I further understand that the repetitive purchase of firearms for the purpose of resale for livelihood and profit without a Federal firearms license is a violation of Federal law. ***(See Instructions for Question 14.)***

14. Transferee's/Buyer's Signature	15. Certification Date

Section B - Must Be Completed By Transferor/Seller

16. Type of firearm(s) to be transferred *(check or mark all that apply)*:

☐ Handgun ☐ Long Gun *(rifles or shotguns)* ☐ Other Firearm *(frame, receiver, etc. See Instructions for Question 16.)*

17. If transfer is at a qualifying gun show or event:

Name of Function: ____________________

City, State: ____________________

18.a. Identification *(e.g., Virginia Driver's license (VA DL) or other valid government-issued photo identification.) (See Instructions for Question 18.a.)*

Issuing Authority and Type of Identification	Number on Identification	Expiration Date of Identification *(if any)* Month	Day	Year

18.b. Supplemental Government Issued Documentation *(if identification document does not show current residence address) (See Instructions for Question 18.b.)*

18.c. Exception to the Nonimmigrant Alien Prohibition: If the transferee/buyer answered "YES" to 12.d.2. the transferor/seller must record the type of documentation showing the exception to the prohibition and attach a copy to this ATF Form 4473. *(See Instructions for Question 18.c.)*

Questions 19, 20, or 21 Must Be Completed Prior To The Transfer Of The Firearm(s) *(See Instructions for Questions 19, 20 and 21.)*

19.a. Date the transferee's/buyer's identifying information in Section A was transmitted to NICS or the appropriate State agency:

Month	Day	Year

19.b. The NICS or State transaction number *(if provided)* was:

19.c. The response initially (first) provided by NICS or the appropriate State agency was:

☐ Proceed ☐ Delayed

☐ Denied *[The firearm(s) may be transferred on*

☐ Cancelled ____________ *if State law permits (optional)]*

19.d. The following response(s) was/were later received from NICS or the appropriate State agency:

☐ Proceed ____________ *(date)* ☐ Overturned

☐ Denied ____________ *(date)*

☐ Cancelled ____________ *(date)*

☐ No response was provided within 3 business days.

19.e. *(Complete if applicable.)* After the firearm was transferred, the following response was received from NICS or the appropriate State agency on:

____________ *(date)*. ☐ Proceed ☐ Denied ☐ Cancelled

19.f. The name and Brady identification number of the NICS examiner. *(Optional)*

____________ *(name)* ____________ *(number)*

19.g. Name of FFL Employee Completing NICS check. *(Optional)*

20. ☐ No NICS check was required because a background check was completed during the NFA approval process on the individual who will receive the NFA firearm(s), as reflected on the approved NFA application. *(See Instructions for Question 20.)*

21. ☐ No NICS check was required because the transferee/buyer has a valid permit from the State where the transfer is to take place, which qualifies as an exemption to NICS. *(See Instructions for Question 21.)*

Issuing State and Permit Type	Date of Issuance *(if any)*	Expiration Date *(if any)*	Permit Number *(if any)*

Section C - Must Be Completed Personally By Transferee/Buyer

If the transfer of the firearm(s) takes place on a different day from the date that the transferee/buyer signed Section A, the transferee/buyer must complete Section C immediately prior to the transfer of the firearm(s). *(See Instructions for Question 22 and 23.)*

I certify that my answers to the questions in Section A of this form are still true, correct, and complete.

22. Transferee's/Buyer's Signature	23. Recertification Date

Transferor/Seller Continue to Next Page
STAPLE IF PAGES BECOME SEPARATED

Page 2 of 6

ATF E-Form 4473 (5300.9)
Revised October 2016

ATF Form 4473 Page 3

Section D - Must Be Completed By Transferor/Seller Even If The Firearm(s) is Not Transferred

	24. Manufacturer and Importer *(If any) (If the manufacturer and importer are different, the FFL must include both.)*	25. Model *(If Designated)*	26. Serial Number	27. Type *(See Instructions for Question 27.)*	28. Caliber or Gauge
1.					
2.					
3.					
4.					

REMINDER - By the Close of Business Complete ATF Form 3310.4 For Multiple Purchases of Handguns Within 5 Consecutive Business Days

29. Total Number of Firearms Transferred *(Please handwrite by printing e.g., zero, one, two, three, etc. **Do not use numerals.**)*	30. Check if any part of this transaction is a pawn redemption. ☐ Line Number(s) From Question 24 Above:
31. For Use by Licensee *(See Instructions for Question 31.)*	32. Check if this transaction is to facilitate a private party transfer. ☐ *(See Instructions for Question 32.)*

33. Trade/corporate name and address of transferor/seller and Federal Firearm License Number *(Must contain at least first three and last five digits of FFL Number X-XX-XXXXX.) (Hand stamp may be used.)*

The Person Transferring The Firearm(s) Must Complete Questions 34-37.
For Denied/Cancelled Transactions, the Person Who Completed Section B Must Complete Questions 34-36.

I certify that: (1) I have read and understand the Notices, Instructions, and Definitions on this ATF Form 4473; (2) the information recorded in Sections B and D is true, correct, and complete; and (3) this entire transaction record has been completed at my licensed business premises ("licensed premises" includes business temporarily conducted from a qualifying gun show or event in the same State in which the licensed premises is located) unless this transaction has met the requirements of 18 U.S.C. 922(c). Unless this transaction has been denied or cancelled, I further certify on the basis of — (1) the transferee's/buyer's responses in Section A (and Section C, if applicable); (2) my verification of the identification recorded in question 18 (and my re-verification at the time of transfer, *if Section C was completed*); and (3) State or local law applicable to the firearms business — it is my belief that it is not unlawful for me to sell, deliver, transport, or otherwise dispose of the firearm(s) listed on this form to the person identified in Section A.

34. Transferor's/Seller's Name ***(Please print)***	35. Transferor's/Seller's Signature	36. Transferor's/Seller's Title	37. Date Transferred

NOTICES, INSTRUCTIONS, AND DEFINITIONS

Purpose of the Form: The information and certification on this form are designed so that a person licensed under 18 U.S.C. 923 may determine if he/she may lawfully sell or deliver a firearm to the person identified in Section A, and to alert the transferee/buyer of certain restrictions on the receipt and possession of firearms. The transferor/seller of a firearm must determine the lawfulness of the transaction and maintain proper records of the transaction. Consequently, the transferor/seller must be familiar with the provisions of 18 U.S.C. 921-931 and the regulations in 27 CFR Parts 478 and 479. In determining the lawfulness of the sale or delivery of a rifle or shotgun to a resident of another State, the transferor/seller is presumed to know the applicable State laws and published ordinances in both the transferor's/seller's State and the transferee's/buyer's State. *(See ATF Publication 5300.5, State Laws and Published Ordinances.)*

Generally, ATF Form 4473 must be completed at the licensed business premises when a firearm is transferred over-the-counter. Federal law, 18 U.S.C. 922(c), allows a licensed importer, manufacturer, or dealer to sell a firearm to a nonlicensee who does not appear in person at the licensee's business premises only if the transferee/buyer meets certain requirements. These requirements are set forth in section 922(c), 27 CFR 478.96(b), and ATF Procedure 2013-2.

After the transferor/seller has completed the firearms transaction, he/she must make the completed, original ATF Form 4473 *(which includes the Notices, General Instructions, and Definitions)*, and any supporting documents, part of his/her permanent records. Such Forms 4473 must be retained for at least 20 years and after that period may be submitted to ATF. Filing may be chronological *(by date of disposition)*, alphabetical *(by name of purchaser)*, or numerical *(by transaction serial number)*, as long as all of the transferor's/seller's completed Forms 4473 are filed in the same manner.

FORMS 4473 FOR DENIED/CANCELLED TRANSFERS MUST BE RETAINED: If the transfer of a firearm is denied/cancelled by NICS, or if for any other reason the transfer is not completed after a NICS check is initiated, the licensee must retain the ATF Form 4473 in his/her records for at least 5 years. Forms 4473 with respect to which a sale, delivery, or transfer did not take place shall be separately retained in alphabetical *(by name of transferee)* or chronological *(by date of transferee's certification)* order.

If the transferor/seller or the transferee/buyer discovers that an ATF Form 4473 is incomplete or improperly completed after the firearm has been transferred, and the transferor/seller or the transferee/buyer wishes to correct the omission(s) or error(s), photocopy the inaccurate form and make any necessary additions or revisions to the photocopy. The transferor/seller should only make changes to Sections B and D. The transferee/buyer should only make changes to Section A and C. Whoever made the changes should initial and date the changes. The corrected photocopy should be attached to the original Form 4473 and retained as part of the transferor's/seller's permanent records.

Exportation of Firearms: The State or Commerce Departments may require a firearms exporter to obtain a license prior to export. **Warning:** Any person who exports a firearm without proper authorization may be fined not more than $1,000,000 and/or imprisoned for not more than 20 years. See 22 U.S.C. 2778(c).

Section A

The transferee/buyer must personally complete Section A of this form and certify *(sign)* that the answers are true, correct, and complete. However, if the transferee/buyer is unable to read and/or write, the answers *(other than the signature)* may be completed by another person, excluding the transferor/seller. Two persons *(other than the transferor/seller)* must then sign as witnesses to the transferee's/buyer's answers and signature/certification in question 14.

ATF Form 5320.23 Page 1

U.S. Department of Justice
Bureau of Alcohol, Tobacco, Firearms and Explosives

OMB No. 1140-0107 (06/30/2019)

National Firearms Act *(NFA)*
Responsible Person Questionnaire

Complete the form in duplicate. The ATF copy of the form, with fingerprints on Form FD-258 and photograph, will be submitted with the ATF Form 1, 4, or 5 (to the address shown on the specific form) and the other copy will be directed to the responsible person's chief law enforcement officer. *(See Instructions)*

1. Please check the appropriate box to indicate with which ATF form this questionnaire will be submitted.

☐ ATF Form 1 ☐ ATF Form 4 ☐ ATF Form 5

2. Name and Address of Applicant or Transferee *(as shown on the ATF Form 1, 4 or 5) (see instruction 2)*

3a. Name and Home Address of Responsible Person

3b. Telephone *(Area code and Number)*

3c. e-mail address *(optional)*

3d. Other names used *(including maiden name)*

4a. Type of Firearm *(see definition 5)*

3e. Photograph

Affix recent Photograph Here

(Approximately 2" x 2")
(See instruction 3b)

4b. Name and Address of Maker, Manufacturer and/or Importer of Firearm

4c. Firearm Model

4d. Caliber or Gauge

4e. Firearm Serial Number

5. Law Enforcement Notification *(See instruction 5)*

As a responsible person (see definition 4) of the trust or legal entity identified in Item 2 of this form, I am required to provide notification of the proposed making or acquisition and possession of the firearm described in item 4 of this form by providing a copy of the completed form to the chief law enforcement officer (CLEO) in the agency identified below:

Agency or Department Name

Name and Title of Official

Address (Street address or P.O. Box, City, State and Zip Code) to which sent (mailed or delivered)

Information for the Chief Law Enforcement Officer

This form provides notification of the maker or transferee's intent to make or acquire and possess a National Firearms Act (NFA) firearm. No action on your part is required. However, should you have information that may disqualify this person from making or possessing a firearm, please contact the NFA Branch at (304) 616-4500 or NFA@atf.gov. A "Yes" answer to items 6h or item 7b or 7c could disqualify a person from acquiring or possessing a firearm. Also, ATF may not approve an application if the transfer or possession of the firearm would be in violation of State or local law.

ATF Copy

ATF E-Form 5320.23
Revised May 2016

ATF Form 5320.23 Page 2

6. Answer questions 6.a through 6.h. Answer questions 7 and 8 if applicable. For any "Yes" answer the transferee shall provide details on a separate sheet. *(See definitions 8-12)*

	Yes	No
a. Are you under indictment or information in any court for a felony, or any other crime, for which the judge could imprison you for more than one year? *(See definition 8)*		
b. Have you ever been convicted in any court for a felony, or any other crime, for which the judge could have imprisoned you for more than one year, even if you received a shorter sentence including probation? *(See definition 8)*		
c. Are you a fugitive from justice? *(See definition 13)*		
d. Are you an unlawful user of, or addicted to, marijuana or any depressant, stimulant, narcotic drug, or any other controlled substance? **Warning: The use or possession of marijuana remains unlawful under Federal law regardless of whether is has been legalized or decriminalized for medicinal or recreational purposes in the state where you reside.**		
e. Have you ever been adjudicated as a mental defective **OR** have you ever been committed to a mental institution? *(See definitions 9 and 10)*		
f. Have you been discharged from the Armed Forces under **dishonorable** conditions?		
g. Are you subject to a court order restraining you from harassing, stalking, or threatening your child or an intimate partner or child of such partner? *(See definition 11)*		
h. Have you ever been convicted in any court of a misdemeanor crime of domestic violence? *(See definition 14)*		

7a. Country of Citizenship: *(Check/List more than one, if applicable. Nationals of the United States may check U.S.A.) (See definition 12)*

☐ United States of America ☐ Other Country/Countries (specify): ______________________

		Yes	No
b. Have you ever renounced your United States citizenship?			
c. Are you an alien illegally or unlawfully in the United States?			
d.1. Are you an alien who has been admitted to the United States under a nonimmigrant visa?			
d.2. If "yes", do you fall within any of the exceptions stated in the instructions? Attach the documentation to the questionnaire	☐ N/A		

8. If you are an alien, record your U.S. -Issued Alien or Admission number (AR#, USCIS#, or 194#): ______________________

CERTIFICATION: Under penalties imposed by 18 U.S.C. § 924 and 26 U.S.C. § 5861, I certify that, upon submission of this form to ATF, a completed copy of this form will be directed to the chief law enforcement officer (CLEO) shown in item 5, that the statements contained in this certification, and any attached documents in support thereof, are true and correct to the best of my knowledge and belief.

______________________ ______________________

Signature of Responsible Person Date

Instructions

1. Completion: Each responsible person (see definition 4) of a trust or legal entity seeking to make or acquire a National Firearms Act *(NFA)* firearm shall complete this form in duplicate. (see instruction 9)
   a. Each responsible person must submit his/her fingerprints and photograph with this form *(see below)*.
   b. Please note that this form is not required when the applicant on Form 1, 4 or 5 is an individual.
2. Item 2- Enter the name, trade name *(if any)* and address of the trust or legal entity identified on the Form 1 (items 3a and b); Form 4 *(item 2a)*; or Form 5 *(item 2a)*
3. Item 3- Responsible Person information
   a. Provide the information for the responsible person in items 3a through 3e.
   b. Item 3e - Photograph: The responsible person shall attach, in item 3e on the ATF copy of the form only, a 2-inch by 2-inch frontal view photograph taken within one year prior to the date of the filing of the form. Item 3e is obscured on the CLEO copy.
4. Firearm information
   a. Type of NFA firearm: see definition 5 and as identified in item 4b of Form 1, 4, or 5
   b. Name of maker, manufacturer and/or importer: as identified in item 4a of Form 1, 4, or 5
   c. Firearm Model: identified in item 4d of Form 1, 4, or 5
   d. Caliber or Gauge: identified in item 4c of Form 1, 4 or 5
   e. Firearm Serial Number: identified in item 4g of Form 1, 4 or 5. Item 4e is obscured on the CLEO copy.
5. Item 5- Law Enforcement Notification: Each responsible person must provide a notification on this form of the proposed making or acquisition of an NFA firearm to his/her chief law enforcement officer having jurisdiction where the responsible person is located. The chief law enforcement officer is considered to be the Chief of Police; the Sheriff; the Head of the State Police; or a State or local district attorney or prosecutor.
6. Complete items 6 through 8
7. Fingerprints: The responsible person shall submit, in duplicate with the ATF copy of this form, his or her fingerprints on FBI Form FD-258 and the fingerprints must be clear for accurate classification and taken by someone properly equipped to take them. No fingerprints are required with the copy of the form sent to the chief law enforcement officer.
8. State or Local Permit: If the State in which the responsible person resides requires the responsible person to have a State or Local permit or licensee, a copy of the permit or license must be submitted with this form.
9. Disposition: The ATF copy of the form, with the fingerprints and photograph, shall be submitted with the ATF Form 1, 4 or 5. The other copy shall be directed to the responsible person's chief law enforcement officer identified in item 5 of this form.
10. Sign and date the form. The signature must be original.

ATF Copy

ATF E-Form 5320.23
Revised May 2016

ATF Form 5320.23 Page 3

U.S. Department of Justice
Bureau of Alcohol, Tobacco, Firearms and Explosives

OMB No. 1140-0107 (06/30/2019)

National Firearms Act *(NFA)*
Responsible Person Questionnaire

Complete the form in duplicate. The ATF copy of the form, with fingerprints on Form FD-258 and photograph, will be submitted with the ATF Form 1, 4, or 5 (to the address shown on the specific form) and the other copy will be directed to the responsible person's chief law enforcement officer. *(See Instructions)*

1. Please check the appropriate box to indicate with which ATF form this questionnaire will be submitted.

☐ ATF Form 1 ☐ ATF Form 4 ☐ ATF Form 5

2. Name and Address of Applicant or Transferee *(as shown on the ATF Form 1, 4 or 5) (see instruction 2)*

3a. Name and Home Address of Responsible Person

3b. Telephone *(Area code and Number)*

3c. e-mail address *(optional)*

3d. Other names used *(including maiden name)*

4a. Type of Firearm *(see definition 5)*

4b. Name and Address of Maker, Manufacturer and/or Importer of Firearm

4c. Firearm Model

4d. Caliber or Gauge

5. Law Enforcement Notification *(See instruction 5)*

As a responsible person (see definition 4) of the trust or legal entity identified in Item 2 of this form, I am required to provide notification of the proposed making or acquisition and possession of the firearm described in item 4 of this form by providing a copy of the completed form to the chief law enforcement officer (CLEO) in the agency identified below:

Agency or Department Name

Name and Title of Official

Address (Street address or P.O. Box, City, State and Zip Code) to which sent (mailed or delivered)

Information for the Chief Law Enforcement Officer

This form provides notification of the maker or transferee's intent to make or acquire and possess a National Firearms Act (NFA) firearm. No action on your part is required. However, should you have information that may disqualify this person from making or possessing a firearm, please contact the NFA Branch at (304) 616-4500 or NFA@atf.gov. A "Yes" answer to items 6h or item 7b or 7c could disqualify a person from acquiring or possessing a firearm. Also, ATF may not approve an application if the transfer or possession of the firearm would be in violation of State or local law.

CLEO Copy

ATF E-Form 5320.23
Revised May 2016

6. Answer questions 6.a through 6.h. Answer questions 7 and 8 if applicable. For any "Yes" answer the transferee shall provide details on a separate sheet. *(See definitions 8-12)*

	Yes	No
a. Are you under indictment or information in any court for a felony, or any other crime, for which the judge could imprison you for more than one year? *(See definition 8)*		
b. Have you ever been convicted in any court for a felony, or any other crime, for which the judge could have imprisoned you for more than one year, even if you received a shorter sentence including probation? *(See definition 8)*		
c. Are you a fugitive from justice? *(See definition 13)*		
d. Are you an unlawful user of, or addicted to, marijuana or any depressant, stimulant, narcotic drug, or any other controlled substance? **Warning: The use or possession of marijuana remains unlawful under Federal law regardless of whether is has been legalized or decriminalized for medicinal or recreational purposes in the state where you reside.**		
e. Have you ever been adjudicated as a mental defective **OR** have you ever been committed to a mental institution? *(See definitions 9 and 10)*		
f. Have you been discharged from the Armed Forces under **dishonorable** conditions?		
g. Are you subject to a court order restraining you from harassing, stalking, or threatening your child or an intimate partner or child of such partner? *(See definition 11)*		
h. Have you ever been convicted in any court of a misdemeanor crime of domestic violence? *(See definition 14)*		

7a. Country of Citizenship: *(Check/List more than one, if applicable. Nationals of the United States may check U.S.A.) (See definition 12)*

☐ United States of America ☐ Other Country/Countries (specify): ____________________

	Yes	No
b. Have you ever renounced your United States citizenship?		
c. Are you an alien illegally or unlawfully in the United States?		
d.1. Are you an alien who has been admitted to the United States under a nonimmigrant visa?		
d.2. If "yes", do you fall within any of the exceptions stated in the instructions? Attach the documentation to the questionnaire ☐ N/A		

8. If you are an alien, record your U.S. -Issued Alien or Admission number (AR#, USCIS#, or 194#): ____________________

CERTIFICATION: Under penalties imposed by 18 U.S.C. § 924 and 26 U.S.C. § 5861, I certify that, upon submission of this form to ATF, a completed copy of this form will be directed to the chief law enforcement officer (CLEO) shown in item 5, that the statements contained in this certification, and any attached documents in support thereof, are true and correct to the best of my knowledge and belief.

____________________ Signature of Responsible Person

____________________ Date

Instructions

1. Completion: Each responsible person (see definition 4) of a trust or legal entity seeking to make or acquire a National Firearms Act *(NFA)* firearm shall complete this form in duplicate. (see instruction 9)
   a. Each responsible person must submit his/her fingerprints and photograph with this form *(see below)*.
   b. Please note that this form is not required when the applicant on Form 1, 4 or 5 is an individual.
2. Item 2- Enter the name, trade name *(if any)* and address of the trust or legal entity identified on the Form 1 (items 3a and b); Form 4 *(item 2a)*; or Form 5 *(item 2a)*
3. Item 3- Responsible Person information
   a. Provide the information for the responsible person in items 3a through 3e.
   b. Item 3e - Photograph: The responsible person shall attach, in item 3e on the ATF copy of the form only, a 2-inch by 2-inch frontal view photograph taken within one year prior to the date of the filing of the form. Item 3e is obscured on the CLEO copy.
4. Firearm information
   a. Type of NFA firearm: see definition 5 and as identified in item 4b of Form 1, 4, or 5
   b. Name of maker, manufacturer and/or importer: as identified in item 4a of Form 1, 4, or 5
   c. Firearm Model: identified in item 4d of Form 1, 4, or 5
   d. Caliber or Gauge: identified in item 4c of Form 1, 4 or 5
   e. Firearm Serial Number: identified in item 4g of Form 1, 4 or 5. Item 4e is obscured on the CLEO copy.
5. Item 5- Law Enforcement Notification: Each responsible person must provide a notification on this form of the proposed making or acquisition of an NFA firearm to his/her chief law enforcement officer having jurisdiction where the responsible person is located. The chief law enforcement officer is considered to be the Chief of Police; the Sheriff; the Head of the State Police; or a State or local district attorney or prosecutor.
6. Complete items 6 through 8
7. Fingerprints: The responsible person shall submit, in duplicate with the ATF copy of this form, his or her fingerprints on FBI Form FD-258 and the fingerprints must be clear for accurate classification and taken by someone properly equipped to take them. No fingerprints are required with the copy of the form sent to the chief law enforcement officer.
8. State or Local Permit: If the State in which the responsible person resides requires the responsible person to have a State or Local permit or licensee, a copy of the permit or license must be submitted with this form.
9. Disposition: The ATF copy of the form, with the fingerprints and photograph, shall be submitted with the ATF Form 1, 4 or 5. The other copy shall be directed to the responsible person's chief law enforcement officer identified in item 5 of this form.
10. Sign and date the form. The signature must be original.

CLEO Copy

ATF E-Form 5320.23
Revised May 2016

➢ ABOUT THE ≺

ATTORNEY AUTHOR

JAMES REEVES
AUTHOR

James Reeves is a partner with the New Orleans law firm of Melchiode Marks King in New Orleans, Louisiana, and a graduate of Tulane University law school. Mr. Reeves has also been a concealed weapons instructor since 2012, and holds instructor certifications from the National Rifle Association and the Louisiana State Police. He is a former federal firearms licensee, and has worked in the firearms industry since 2004. He has won several tournaments including the Glock Sport Shooting Federation indoor match, and he was named Maxim Magazine's "Maximum Warrior" in 2011 after winning the publication's annual shooting competition. Finally, Mr. Reeves has written for The Firearm Blog since 2013, and is the executive producer and co-host of the Blog's YouTube channel, TFBTV.

The U.S. LawShield® Legal Defense for Self Defense program is dedicated to preserving its members' fundamental and Constitutional right to self-defense through zealous legal representation by Independent Program Attorneys experienced in self-defense and gun laws. A cornerstone of the U.S. LawShield program is legal education.

U.S. LawShield boasts more than 380,000 members, including civilians, law enforcement and security officers, and military personnel. U.S. LawShield is honored to be affiliated with thousands of gun ranges, gun stores, FFL dealers, instructors, educators, and other firearms experts and professionals. U.S. LawShield is one of the largest civilian repositories of state-specific self-defense and gun law legal information available anywhere.

For more information about the U.S. LawShield Legal Defense for Self Defense program, visit www.uslawshield.com.

James Reeves is an Independent Program Attorney for U.S. LawShield with the law firm of Melchiode Marks King LLC. This publication does not represent an endorsement or solicitation for any product or service.